You Don't Have to Be Poor

John W. Ridley, Ph.D.

You Don't Have to Be Poor

Copyright © 2015 by Dr. John W. Ridley. All rights reserved.

No part of this publication may be reproduced, stored in a retrieval system or transmitted in any way by any means, electronic, mechanical, photocopy, recording or otherwise, without the prior permission of the author except as provided by USA copyright law.

The opinions expressed by the author are not necessarily those of Revival Waves of Glory Books & Publishing.

Published by Revival Waves of Glory Books & Publishing
PO Box 596| Litchfield, Illinois 62056 USA
www.revivalwavesofgloryministries.com

Revival Waves of Glory Books & Publishing is committed to excellence in the publishing industry.

Book design copyright © 2015 by Revival Waves of Glory Books & Publishing. All rights reserved.

Published in the United States of America

Paperback: 978-0692472514

Acknowledgments

The author of this work is thankful for the broad scope of information available in various versions of the Holy Bible and internet sites containing information from both public and published works. Where direct quotations are used, every attempt has been made to accurately present these quotes, and each of them are cited within the work. Large volumes of material have been excerpted from internet sites, and consolidated into the author's own words. Each internet site utilized is listed in the references section. Any material that appears to be presented verbatim or closely resembling that found in copyrighted materials is merely coincidental. Care has been taken to generally present the information from a large variety of sources with the author's interpretation and notations included. And finally, thanks to Bill Vincent of Revival Waves of Glory Books & Publishing for his help and encouragement.

Table of Contents

ACKNOWLEDGMENTS 3
INTRODUCTION 5
PURPOSE AND INTENT OF THIS BOOK 12
PART I: WHAT IS MEANT BY BEING 'POOR' OR LIVING IN 'POVERTY?' 14
PART II: INSTITUTIONAL CATEGORIZATION OF THE POOR AND THOSE IN POVERTY 23
PART III: BIBLICAL PERSPECTIVE OF BEING POOR 59
PART IV: WHAT DOES IT MEAN TO BE WEALTHY AND SUSTAIN THE ACCRUED WEALTH? 74
PART V: BUILDING PERSONAL WEALTH 98
PART VI: HOW TO AVOID BEING POOR OR LIVING IN POVERTY 114
PART VII: THE UNITED STATES AND THE GLOBAL ECONOMY 136
PART VIII: TALE OF THREE COUNTRIES 150
PART IX: WHAT CAN I DO TO AVOID BEING POOR OR TO ESCAPE POVERTY 180
PART X: HOW TO DOCUMENT INCOME AND EXPENSES 218
REFERENCES 230
CONTACT THE AUTHOR 234

Introduction

One thing this book is not is a manual of how to get rich quickly. It is a compendium of wisdom from the Bible and from practical experiences. It is intended as a learning tool, where economic facts are presented. In addition, you will be able to compare and contrast two countries with the United States as each is faced with economic issues as they compete on a global basis. Please note that I am not making a contract with the readers of this book purporting that they will possess all of the tools that will lead to great riches in short order. But it will help! Our world abounds with a wide variety of processes that lay claim to an ability to provide one with can't-fail activities designed to bestow wealth with little effort and almost overnight. But these strategies are almost if not always designed to benefit the architect of the scheme rather than the individual or family that adopts the prescribed program. Practically everybody is familiar with pyramid schemes and Ponzi schemes, but it should be noted (if you have not already done so) that only a few actually benefit from these types of activities. In most cases, these programs offered to enable quick riches are similar to or no better than these well-known scams and may even violate local, state or federal law. If one does his or her research, it will be learned that most of those (but not all) involving themselves in these schemes will result in the loss of significant amounts of money and the expenditure of a great deal of time, especially in those plans where direct sales are involved.

The money one has, or the lack thereof, has been an issue ever since the dawn of civilization, and either condition may result in difficulties. As you will see in this book, the drive to obtain money is inherent in almost everyone. However, there are certain cultures who seem to lack a set of genes dictating an acquisitive nature to the extent we see in others. For instance, the American Indians, at least in most of the tribes, had no concept of owning land. But they did pay obeisance for those that had items such as more horses, more buffalo hides, and better bows and arrows than other members of the tribe. And it was common for a brave to covet and sometimes steal the beautiful wife of another. So these tendencies are sometimes under the guise of Christians who have fleeced church members and even entire churches who invest in questionable investments. Often, those who are scammed by unscrupulous persons are already in desperate straits and do not need to be kicked while they are down. Instead, those of us who wish to be true servants of God should and are indeed commanded to love others and to do what is right for them. This includes various forms of help in enabling them to rise above any misery that they may be experiencing. Therefore, a little background is in order to help us to understand or to refresh our minds as to the Christian foundations of our country, the United States.

The United States was dominated by a Judeo-Christian view from its earliest beginnings and at least the majority of those early settlers came in order to worship as they were led by their Creator. Many of the official documents and governmental proceedings were seasoned by references to God, the Almighty, our Creator, and various references to a higher power not named as God or his Son. This belief system also has greatly influenced other countries of the Western World, though some have become more secularized as the centuries pass. Other dimensions of cultures from areas of the world other than the Western hemisphere have introduced other religions, some based on mysticism, animism, and deities other than our God. Although we must give respect to other belief systems, an understanding of western thought is an important element in the understanding of the history of the United States and should be at least acknowledged by religious groups other than Christians who live here.

An abbreviated outline of the economics related to the supply of money in the United States is provided to give the reader an understanding as to why only a limited amount of currency is placed into circulation. Few high schools teach economics to its students, and there is a woeful lack of understanding for most students regarding the creation of "money" and how it affects our everyday lives. This discussion is found in one of the sections of this book and is necessary before we can make decisions about the handling of our money and how we can best benefit our families by thoughtful and, it is hoped, prayerful decisions regarding how we will spend our money effectively. It should be understood that money is just a symbol of an asset of value, and has no inherent value in itself. It is a system of exchange that compensates those who work for their sustenance, and this compensation of money can then then be exchanged for the 'needs' and 'wants' that we and our families have.

In the traditional Judeo-Christian foundation and after humans were created, they inherited a garden of plenty, the Garden of Eden, in which all their needs could be satisfied with little effort. The first two humans were commanded to take care of and to tend the garden, and to enjoy the fruits thereof, except for the fruit of the forbidden tree (NIV, 1973, Genesis 2:15). These better than ideal working conditions were lost when sin entered the world due to disobedience to God's command not to eat of the forbidden fruit. As a result, humans were banished forever from the Garden. In Genesis 3:19, the human plight became quite serious. The first humans soon realized that there was a whole world filled with thoughts, attitudes and actions that fall outside the will of God, just as there is today when we do not follow God's plan for the lives of each of us.

The resultant life of sorrow and toil became the inheritance of humans for disobedience, as seen in the following verse. According to Genesis 3:19 (NIV, 1973), "By the sweat of your brow you will eat your food until you return to the ground, since from it you were taken; for dust you are and to dust you will return" . We know that physical labor is hard, and most cultures, including the Hebrew belief system, viewed work as a curse placed on humans by God. This disobedience was the original sin under which all humans must now labor. Numerous scriptures from the Old Testament in fact supported the act of work, and our forebears largely believed the Word and wrested a great nation by hard and untiring labor that was largely borne by all the members of each family.

Early in the history of our country, most families earned their living by farming, and the farming was not done at that time with large mechanical machines as is the case today. Farm labor is much easier today, and many of the younger generations do not realize the hard manual labor that was necessary just to place food on the table and to store enough for use when seasonal conditions were not conducive to raising crops. In our past history we were taught by our parents that there is joy in work resulting in a feeling of satisfaction from having supplied the needs of oneself and his family and can bring exceeding joy. In fact, it is believed that work is a palliative for depression, and those who find meaningful and enjoyable work often are blessed with good mental and physical health. For years the premise upon which work was based in this country was that it was necessary to prevent poverty and destitution as amplified in (NIV 1973; Proverbs 10:14, Proverbs 13:4, Proverbs 14:23, Proverbs 20:13, Ecclesiastes 9:10).

A number of cultures do consider or have considered work to be a curse, even those who didn't follow the edicts of the Christian Bible that we can follow today. Both the Hebrews and the Greeks seemed to regard work as a curse. The privileged classes of Greek and Hebrew societies considered manual labor as only being fit for slaves, and both of these cultures employed the use of slaves heavily. Of course, the Romans during the height of their power had enslaved members of a number of cultures as the Roman ruling class largely pursued war, large scale businesses and art. Architecture flourished in the Greek cities, and some of their works are still in evidence today, but again, most of the hard work after designs and plans were drawn was reserved for slaves.

The Greeks even disdained hard thinking, as mental labor was considered as a difficult exercise, particularly in the mechanical arts, since they required deep levels of thinking in order to solve difficulties when building machines and perhaps architecture. Although skilled crafts were recognized as being valuable to society for their pure aesthetic beauty, they were not considered as being worthy of the endeavors of the more privileged classes in Greek society. So hard work was avoided whenever possible, even when economic needs dictated such effort or was left to the direction of master artisans who were sometimes enslaved in order to utilize their creative abilities. Even Aristotle and Plato seemed to feel that work should be done only by those for whom it was required, namely the lower classes and slaves. This enabled those in the highest echelons of society to engage in pure exercises of the mind where truth was sought at any cost. Therefore, the higher levels of the Greek culture pursued games of the mind, such as politics, art, and philosophy We can see today how well these cultures fared when they did not change with the world about them, and were unable to adapt and compete with countries with a work culture. The same appears to be true today if we examine a world map.

Many versions of a phrase may be found stating that a democracy is in trouble when its citizens begin to believe that they can legislate themselves a living without working for it. A common statement heard today is, "The United States will only last until the time when the majority of voters believe that they can vote to obtain money out of the treasury for their personal use." If such a system would work, and it won't, what kind of system would we put into place in this country? There are a growing number of people in the United States today who are not working for various reasons, as almost half of the citizens receive one or more types of public assistance. This is chiefly due to the belief that they can't compete with others for desirable jobs, and in some cases this may be true due to physical or mental limitations. However, most ordinary citizens possess the ability to perform meaningful work, but many are unwilling to start on one of the lower rungs of the employment ladder that initially pays a minimum wage. It should be understood from a number of available reports that only roughly 3 percent of American workers are making the minimum wage, and that few workers stay at the minimum wage for protracted periods of time.

Others simply do not possess the will power or desire the feeling of achievement that comes with self-sufficiency and the work needed to make their own way in a free society. If one believes that the deck is stacked against him or her, due to the societal constraints in the free capitalist society, what should one believe should be done to remedy the situation? What system of government should we revert to in the United States? Is it an accident, some mysterious granting of a large measure of luck, or a beneficent Deity that the United States (for the moment) is the most powerful and most successful country in the world? Which of these beliefs is present in this country, when almost half the population relies on at least one form of public assistance in a country with great natural resources and the freedom to do what we wish with our lives, within certain constraints, of course? It is obvious that those in countries who are living under the yoke of a ruler such as found in a theocracy and one which is brutal and tyrannical, to see that those societies have not progressed sufficiently to enable the majority of its citizens to live free, productive lives. So it appears that there could be no better alternative where everyone has the opportunity to succeed (or fail) in a field chosen by each individual.

But many of the politicians who are in office in the twenty-first century in the United States and other countries, particularly those of Europe, have made efforts to take on the role of providing for the necessities of life and thereby creating a dependent society. We are in a global economy where we must compete with other governments for scarce resources, and for markets for the goods produced in each country. Countries which are not technologically up to date, and that have a well-trained and industrious society will be unable to compete with those countries who do have such a group of citizens. We do not have to abdicate our role as a leader in the world and to adopt the failed policies and sentiments of other countries so that we are on a par with them. This would place the United States in is book is not intended to predict that everyone who reads it will become either rich or wealthy.

Many choose not to develop their talents or are unwilling to make the effort to become educated in strategies necessary for the building of wealth. It is hoped that readers of this book will be able to avoid becoming poor or poverty stricken. And those who accumulate resources should share assist those already in economic niches of the poor to gradually and systematically escape the clutches of the lack of financial resources to provide themselves and their families with the necessities of life. It appears that the acquisition of money is the goal of perhaps everyone, and various means are adopted to obtain money. But money often become the god of those who gather much wealth and little is done to share with others. This is the crux of the problem in earning riches, where eventually the new-found wealth becomes all-consuming for the rich or wealthy person, and God is excluded. Verse 9 in Proverbs, Chapter 30, bears out the premise that many people who are blessed with prosperity keep their initial goals, purposes and values, while many who are poor continue to trust in the Lord to satisfy their needs and do not stray into wickedness.

In Proverbs 30:8-9 (NIV), God tells us in the following words:
> *8 Keep falsehood and lies far from me; give me neither poverty nor riches, but give me only my daily bread. 9 Otherwise, I may have too much and disown you and say, 'Who is the LORD?' Or I may become poor and steal, and so dishonor the name of my God.*

The King James Version substitutes vanity for falsehood in verse 8. I believe God is saying in these verses to beware as we prosper. Otherwise, we will place our trust in things of the world that are beyond our needs. We should provide for ourselves and our families the things that are suitable for our station in life and everything should be in moderation. By trusting in our riches and by crowning ourselves for our efforts, we will not be thankful for what we do have, thus abusing God's mercies. We ask to be delivered from vanity and lies in verse 8, and to be saved from poverty in verse 9, where we may feel a need to steal for our sustenance.

Purpose and Intent of This Book

Such a manuscript as I have provided here has been a burning desire in my life for many years, as I have been involved with counseling and teaching for my entire career, most often in the medical occupational areas. The task of teaching those who know little about the economy of their local area, that of the nation and of the world as a whole is daunting. However, the economic details that are covered in this book are at a beginning level, and is not intended to provide the reader with an education in finance, economics, or accounting. Treatment of the topics will be confined to the practical application of understanding the economics of the United States and how much money is in circulation relative to each citizen of the United States.

Stress kills, both physically and mentally. Financial problems are perhaps the greatest cause of stress leading to divorce, breakup of relationships. Money problems are at the root of many psychosomatic problems such as insomnia and a feeling of being permanently trapped in an undesirable environment and unable to escape the shackles of poverty or of just plain being poor. I am not an economist and have no financial training of an academic nature, but was forced to face the realities of the work necessary to become comfortable and to provide for a family. I have attempted to use layman's terms when addressing topics discussed in this book to facilitate the understanding of the average citizen. I do not approach individual and family economics or of the world economy from an academic viewpoint but from a Biblical and practical vantage point.

Some will wonder why I bother to discuss financial issues related to several countries but mostly the United States, rather than just tell the reader what to do. It is because each person's situation is different, and the economies of each country are different. We now have a global economy, and like it or not, our country, and by virtue of living in the country we do, are affected by the world economy. I hope to provide basic instruction as to why certain actions take place, why some economic decisions by our government are necessary, and even that some decisions seem shortsighted and even foolish. I have heard so many around me say, "Why doesn't the government do this?" Or "Why did the government or a big company do that?" I hope that each one who reads this book will have a better vision of why certain economic facts are reality. Some things I say will seem downright cold, and it is not my intent to be cold and judgmental. But in reality it is a hard and cruel world, and some may see it as the law of the jungle, where the strong prevail. So we must arm ourselves with knowledge from the time-tested Bible and from what we should do when we are constrained by economic realities.

Remember that for sustaining one's wealth, it is better to become wealthy slowly. Often those who obtain a large amount of money quickly do not handle it well. Remember, the Bible states in Luke 12:48 (NIV) that *"From everyone who has been given much, much will be demanded; and from the one who has been entrusted with much, much more will be asked."* This really relates to our knowing the Lord's will for our life and being obedient to Him in all things, particularly the acquiring and use of money. As you grow financially and in your walk with the Lord, you will find more opportunities to live a fulfilling life in taking care of your family and of serving others.

PART I:
What is Meant by Being 'Poor' or Living in 'Poverty?'

What is the Definition of Being Poor?

The most common condition to which most attribute a state is being poor is a lack of money. Being poor will mean different things to different people. It is often related to the geographic location in which one lives where the amount of money or property owned or earned may be relative to varying costs of living. However, most statistics do not take these factors into consideration, since calculating the differing costs of goods and services may deviate widely from the mean or median averages. The amount of money required to live in various parts of the world is relative since the costs of certain items and services vary widely from region to region. But we are speaking primarily of the United States with respect to this writing. A large amount of political fodder is gained during each political election campaign by catering to the poor and promising to take more money from the 'rich' and giving it to the poor.

All the political parties in the United States, particularly the two dominant ones, lay all the blame for individual and federal financial shortcomings on policies by the political party in power. When the election results in a change from one party to another, the cycle is repeated and when the newness wears off with regard to the new political party in office, the blame cycle starts again. It is frequently heard that the problems of individuals and families without sufficient income is the fault of the political party in power or the greedy owners and managers of businesses, who may be blamed for *allowing* workers to become poor or remain 'poor.' I hope to convince the readers that neither of these assertions is completely accurate.

How is Being Poor or Living in Poverty Defined?

So what is meant when the term "poor" is used? In 2012, figures were compiled by various offices in the federal government and by studies conducted by universities, study groups and charitable organizations. This variety of sets of data were then used to determine the parameters of being poor or in poverty. Later in this work the differences distinguishing the variations between being poor or in poverty will be made. So utilizing information from a variety of sources, the amount of an annual income of $23,050 was set in 2012 as the thresh-hold for determining those living in poverty. There may be a fine line between being poor or living in poverty, as some who are poor may also be constrained by the low level of income as reported here for those in poverty. But poverty is much more complex and presents a whole set of problem areas that is much more difficult to break than for those that are classified as being poor.

But the amount of income that is necessary to maintain the basics of life may be somewhat higher in some areas of the country than in other areas. The threshold amount will also depend upon the circumstances in which a family lives. The required amount is sometimes less than the figure provided in the previous paragraph, and a lower amount may be sufficient for providing an adequate diet and other costs of living such as shelter, clothing, and transportation, etc. Sometimes a support system will be in place for some families that will provide for the basic requirements for living without a large cash outlay by the individual or family that is in financial straits. And some families and individuals are better equipped to live a frugal existence and can live on less than others and, while not prospering, give the appearance of being somewhat comfortable and self-sufficient. More will be said later about this topic, where families analyze and budget their money in order to avoid shortfalls of cash when emergency situations arise.

Essentially, people who have a low income are described as being poor, although they may not outwardly appear to be financially challenged. Some are heavy borrowers and maintain a facade of doing well, but eventually the bills will come due and the result may be catastrophic. There are many causes of being poor and may result from the choice of a career and hard economic situations existing because of a number of factors beyond control of the individual or any number of circumstances. At least in some cases, the condition of being poor will be a temporary state since many people find themselves in this condition only due to an often sudden change or a combination of changes that affects their income levels. These families or in some cases, individuals, may be able to escape the condition rapidly through individual efforts, but will sometimes require external help in order to escape from the condition(s) that relegated them to the status of being poor.

However, they are as likely as those earning higher incomes to maintain aspirations and dreams that lead them to strive for the future and affords hope for many poor people. They may value education for the future benefits it affords rather than focusing merely on surviving from moment to moment or day to day. Some who are temporarily poor may have invested in a home or property where income will eventually be realized and will provide an opportunity toward improving their financial status for the long term.

The meaning of the term "poverty" is a condition which is sometimes mistakenly considered as essentially the same as being poor. There is a major difference in the two conditions, where the mental state of those in poverty allows little hope or chance of escaping the condition in which they find themselves. And those living in poverty most often have only a survivalist attitude. They possess the mindset that there is absolutely no hope or at least minimal hope that they can ever escape the shackles of poverty. Unlike the poor, they are unwilling or cannot even envision the possibility of sacrificing today for a better life tomorrow.

For instance, unlike the group labeled as simply "poor," those in poverty would not entertain the idea of even one member of the family attempting to achieve further education, even though avenues of help may be available for financing education. In some states, programs exist that are virtually free and may even provide a stipend for those in poverty who are seeking training or education, or a combination of both, to enable them to eventually live in better circumstances. People living in poverty may be extremely mobile out of necessity because they might have been forced into displacement for a number of reasons. This group of people will often move in with various relatives and friends who may soon tire of their crowded homes and scarce resources and will send these visitors away at a moment's notice, often resorting to a violent means of eviction.

Sometimes those who are fortunate enough to have enjoyed a rental house for a time may be able to move everything they own within 24 hours or less when they are unable or in some cases unwilling to pay their rent or utilities. And to exacerbate the condition, it may be difficult to impress upon children who are living in poverty of the value of continuing the educational route provided to them by the state and local government. The adults of these families cannot conceive of sacrificing today in order to gain an education for some uncertain day in the future.

Are the Conditions of Poverty and Being Poor the Same?

A portion of the conditions those who are poor and those who are suffering from poverty may be the same. But those who are poor find it easier to improve their financial lot than those living in poverty and have perhaps not beaten themselves down due to financial difficulties, which they may perceive as temporary. There are assuredly some individuals and families who are poor or living in poverty that are enduring less than ideal conditions as a result of conditions beyond their control such as bad luck, loss of a job, death of the primary provider for the family, regional economic conditions, or otherwise.

There may also be little hope for permanent solutions to poverty due to unchangeable factors such as age, mental and physical challenges that may restrict the individual's ability to find and maintain a steady job. These limiting factors when placed upon one already unable to work may also increase the burden for families who may be responsible for providing for other family members who are unable to care for themselves. Such boundaries may provide such an impossible burden that outside help is the only answer and as responsible citizens and perhaps Christians, we must step in and help.

A persistent problem that has increased in today's society is that of having children without any possibility of outside help for childcare, which is most often a considerable expense. In some of these cases it is cheaper to stay home with younger children than to find affordable child care while holding a job. This absolutely limits the economic choices for a growing segment of our population, especially for single women who are the head of a household. In addition, having large numbers of dependents, both children and older persons, will increase the costs of daily living even for those who have a steady job. These increased costs are frequently due to the need for a larger dwelling, more food and increased utility costs. There may be more need for transportation and medical needs, along with all the attendant miscellaneous items required by a household of larger groups of people.

As was previously stated, the basic condition ascribed to that of being classified as poor is based upon an income that is inadequate for maintaining the basic needs for sustaining life for oneself or one's family. So, the simple answer would be to increase the income by some means of the poor individual, but that is easier said than done. As a member of the poor segment of the population, the fact that an individual is poor is often related to choices made years before, and by extension would affect the individual's family as well. Choices or in some cases the lack of the choice of a career field has the greatest single impact on an individual's income.

Many "fall" into a job for convenience without making a conscious choice to gain a meaningful and financially rewarding career. This convenient acceptance of a position with low wages and lack of promotion potential leads to a dead-end job where one is likely to remain for an entire working career if no effort is made to improve upon what one currently has. These jobs are most often entry level positions requiring few skills, little or no training and a low level of responsibility. This combination offers a low salary and perhaps few if any expanded benefits beyond a paycheck, and almost assuredly no possibility of a promotion.

And in a frequent occurrence in today's society, divorce or separation often relegates the caretaker of any children resulting from the union to a lower lifestyle. In addition, many couples now cohabit without benefit of any religious or governmental seal of approval, and partners feel free to leave at any time. Those who leave suffer no financial burden and often little remorse for those adults or children left behind. The basic costs of living certainly are not diminished to any great extent for a single parent when compared with that required for a couple who have children.

So it is important to distinguish between being poor and being poverty stricken, as being poor is in a number of cases a *temporary* situation rather than a chronic condition. In many cases, those who are temporarily categorized as being poor know or have a reasonable expectation that they will escape the privation of being poor sometime in the future. However, poverty seldom allows for any realistic chance for escaping the bonds of poverty without a great deal of effort and sacrifice. And this lack of the basic necessities for life may result in the children born into poverty to be without the incentive to strive to exceed the accomplishments of their parent(s). Children that are born into poverty almost without fail also feel powerless to change their life's condition, and these offspring tend to repeat the mistakes of their parents. Children living in poverty are less likely to complete high school than those who are merely poor, and often the young women become pregnant at an early age, and the young men of these families enter a life of crime at an early age.

So we should consider poverty as much more challenging, and much more difficult to eradicate than enabling the poor to move up economically. Again, poverty includes a complex set of conditions which may have persisted for generations in some families. In 2012, it was estimated that the poverty level as reported by the US Census Bureau was 16 percent. Of this number, almost 20 percent were children and current trends seem to show an increasing number of adults and children who live in poverty. The emotional scars of being born into poverty, with little hope of bettering one's life, are difficult to heal, even with an infusion of governmental assistance.

Ironically the programs which provide financial support for people without including supportive means to remedy the situations which led to poverty are put in place will not achieve the desired effect. Financial help alone will in most cases only exacerbate the condition. Human nature tends to seek the path of the least resistance, and some receiving what is commonly known as welfare will become permanently dependent upon governmental aid as a way of life. Then this expectation for financial support without working may be passed on to the offspring as a reasonable alternative lifestyle. But it is difficult to stand by as children are not fed and do not have adequate housing, and have little or no healthcare, since they themselves are too young to take any steps to escape from these desperate conditions. From 2009, the unadjusted rates of poverty by state in the US, ranged from 5.6 – 20.7 percent (2012 Statistical Abstract, US Census Bureau)!

Stresses of Being Poor

The biggest single cause for marriage failure is that of poverty or at least being included in the ranks of the poor. An old saying is, "When poverty comes in the front door, love goes out the back door!" Being in the ranks of the poor is at an epidemic level today (2014). So it is appropriate to address the psychological and physical components of being poor or in poverty to make a long term change in the lives of the poor. Otherwise, they will always be in a state of wanting for food, shelter, transportation, clothing, and other essentials of life.

The physiological effects of being poor and undergoing the attendant stresses associated with the condition of being without the basic necessities of life are inestimable. These stresses are so significant that studies indicate that they can affect the brain development of those who don't have money for rent, utilities and don't know from where the next meal will come. The stress of being poor as researched by Professor Gary Evans of Cornell University shows that the more stress a child is under, the more the short term memory is adversely affected. Short term memory is extremely important in the classroom where concepts are built upon to form permanent learning. Laboratory testing of blood samples from children experiencing the effects of poverty showed significant changes in several stress hormones, the blood pressure, and an increase in body mass index (BMI) leading to serious levels of obesity that can cause lifelong diseases. And of course obesity is rampant among the poor today.

For many persons, it seems that having more money would be the answer to all of life's problems. But having more money is not the cure all for all the problems experienced in life. It certainly does not indicate that more money is a prescription for happiness. Subconsciously we may realize this, but it does not alleviate the stress we feel when we have insufficient monetary resources to obtain what we perceive that we need. According to widely published statistics, as much as 80 percent of the population of North America feel stress at least part of the time due to feeling that they need more money. I sometimes idly wonder if the super wealthy ever feels stress regarding money (perhaps stress related to keeping more of it). A common term we all hear is that a person feels he is robbing Peter to pay Paul on a regular basis.

But according to an expert from Money Magazine, it is not the lack of money that causes the stress associated with poverty, but the feeling of powerlessness to do anything to solve the problem of not having enough money. That is an important message I hope to stress in this book. The mindset needs to be reset, but will require that certain concrete steps be taken before achieving the uplift that will come when progress is achieved toward improving one's life.

Very few people are wealthy in the entire world and the rate of those deemed wealthy is estimated at about 1 percent. But we are all familiar with the 'soaps' where everyone, although many are not happy, are living on a high plane regardless of occupation. This is just an impossible scenario created by Hollywood. In the United States almost 49 percent of the population is included in the low-income level as estimated by the sociology department of the University of California.

It has been shown that the surest way to fight poverty is to achieve stronger economic growth regionally and nationally. During the Kennedy era this was true, throughout the years encompassing 1959-1973, when the economy grew at a rate of one hundred and 47 percent per capita (every man, woman and child) as reported by the New York Times, June 5, 2014.

President John F. Kennedy once used a catchy phrase in a speech, saying "As they say on my own Cape Cod, a rising tide lifts all the boats." Some say that he added, "particularly those stuck at the bottom." Can you imagine hearing a politician today saying this? Fortunately it is believed by some that enabling the improvement of our citizens by enacting policies that will emphasize economic growth will improve the lot of everyone. This growth in the previous generation has resulted in a decrease in those living as poor people from 26 percent to 11 percent. So the best cure for poverty was and is economic growth from outward appearances, and does not lie in providing more handouts from the federal and state governments which provide only a temporary Band-Aid.

So over the last generation in this country, growth has been fairly substantial, rising at a rate equivalent to that of the Kennedy era. But rather than showing a decline in poverty, the poverty rate has ranged from 12 to 15 percent, which is higher than it was in the early 1970s and regardless of governmental efforts to help by providing increasing levels of money for food, homes, and education. There is no apparent explanation for this phenomenon in the nation's fight against poverty except as a change in work ethics or in dependency attitudes. The official poverty measure published by the United States Census Bureau shows that in 2012, there were 46.5 million people living in poverty, a figure that has increased from 37.3 million in 2007. The 2012 poverty rate shows practically no decrease between 2010 and 2012 in the DeNavas-Walt findings for the years 2011 – 2013.

PART II:
Institutional Categorization of the Poor and Those in Poverty

How are Figures Defining Poverty Set?

Poverty is basically identified by an amount of money required to furnish the reasonable and socially acceptable amount of money and material possessions taken for granted and necessary to maintain a basic subsistence. The most important needs for families of a material nature are food, shelter, clothing and healthcare. The common measurement of poverty in this country is set by the federal government, and is called the "poverty threshold." Establishment of this threshold is performed by using the "consumer price index (CPI)."

What Exactly is the Consumer Price Index?

The Consumer Price Index (CPI) is adjusted periodically due to price changes based on a number of factors such as the cost of producing products, foods, and wages, and many other conditions the country faces. The CPI figures measure the average change over time in the prices paid by urban consumers for a market basket of consumer goods and services. A market basket is defined as "the basket of consumer goods" or things that are commonly used in practically all households. The list is compiled from an analysis of the average prices of a number of the most commonly bought food and household items.

The variations in the prices of the items on the list from month to month give an indication of the overall development of price trends and requires constant updating by consumer and research agencies. Sometimes the market basket prices are subdivided into several categories such as household items, personal goods, household services, housing and other categories. These categories may change substantially in certain regions and depend on the results of surveys of the entire country. Even non-essential items (which may be considered by some as essential) such as tobacco, leisure products, and alcoholic drinks may be included in the survey.

The CPI is the most widely accepted compilations by which economists measure the rates of inflation and may be affected greatly by the governmental economic policies. It is useful to note that inflation occurs chiefly due to the increase in the amount of money in *circulation* in the country's overall economy. Information about changes in prices in the national economy is used by government agencies and knowledgeable private citizens and are utilized to assist economists in making far-reaching economic decisions.

It should be remembered that rural dwellers will often have a completely different basis by which to measure the needs for a family's existence. For instance, a rural family may live on land that has been in the family for generations, so are not required to pay high prices for certain foodstuffs that are raised nearby or on the land on which the family or individual lives. Commonly, a portion of the required nutritional needs of a rural family may be satisfied, at least in part, by raising or having immediate access to at least a large share of the required foodstuffs, including grains, vegetables, fruits, milk and even in some cases a variety of meats.

So pinning down an exact amount that constitutes the level that measures whether a family is in poverty is similar to hitting a moving target, since changes occur regularly throughout the year and even depend upon the global economy. Some may wonder how the global economy would affect prices locally. In answer, if a shortage of a food item occurs due to drought or other natural occurrence in another country, exports to the country suffering shortages would increase. Local scarcity of the item would then result in a higher price.

Uses of the CPI

What population groups are included in the construction of the CPI? The two urban population groups that are represented are urban consumers, and urban wage earners and clerical workers. The all-urban consumer group represents about 87 percent of the total

U.S. population. It is based on the expenditures of almost all residents of urban or metropolitan areas, including professionals, the self-employed, the poor, the unemployed, and retired people, as well as urban wage earners and clerical workers. Not included in the CPI are the spending patterns of people living in rural non-metropolitan areas, farm families, people in the various divisions of the Armed Forces, and those in institutions such as prisons and mental hospitals. Two different measures are taken to differentiate between these two distinctly different groups in urban environments.

Consumer inflation for all urban consumers is measured by two indexes, namely, the Consumer Price Index for All Urban Consumers (CPI-U) and the Chained Consumer Price Index for All Urban Consumers (C-CPI-U). The Consumer Price Index for Urban Wage Earners and Clerical Workers (CPI-W) is based on the expenditures of households that are included in the C-CPI-U and is defined along with the meeting of two additional requirements. For calculating the CPI-U, more than one-half of the household's income must come from clerical or wage occupations, so in this case salaried persons such as executives who generally make more in wages are not included. In addition, at least one of the household's earners must have been employed for at least 37 weeks during the previous 12 months. So statistics for those who are unemployed or homeless are not included in the preparation of data leading to the CPI-U. The CPI-W population represents about 32 percent of the total U.S. population and is a subset, or part, of the CPI-U population and includes those who don't meet the employment criteria.

How Does the CPI Differ From a Cost-of-Living Index?

It is true that the CPI frequently is called a cost-of-living index, but it differs in important ways from a complete cost-of-living measure. The US Bureau of Labor and Statistics (BLS) constructs the CPI, and the data are widely used by both governmental and private entities for establishing wages and prices, and to gauge the level of inflation that has occurred monthly over the years. BLS collects information on goods and services to establish a realistic cost-of-living framework. A cost-of-living index is not an exact set of figures that is an alternative to the CPI. The cost-of-living index would measure changes over time as the amount that families would need to earn and subsequently spend to reach a desired standard of living.

But both the CPI and a cost-of-living index indicate changes in the prices of goods and services such as food, transportation, utilities and clothing. Additional entities other than the ones previously listed are valid considerations for the individual and families to achieve a satisfactory lifestyle. Other areas included in a cost-of-living index and beyond the control of a family are items such as environmental factors that affect the well-being of families and individuals. These items include safety, health care, transportation, water quality, and crime levels in certain regions of the country.

How Is the CPI Market Basket Established?

The so-called market basket is developed most often on a monthly basis from surveys of detailed expenditures for selected items from approximately 7,000 families and individuals based on what these persons actually bought. From a different group of individuals and families that are selected for each determination, the list of goods and services will vary at least slightly from both previous and subsequent calculations. As previously pointed out, prices for goods and services vary significantly from geographic location to location, and there are variations in what items are actually purchased from region to region. Since the CPI is based on the experience of an average household, comparisons of your particular expenditures may not correspond significantly with the national indices. CPI data are also collected and calculated for specific cities and regions. Remember that the cost of living varies significantly from one region of the United States to the other.

The U.S. Census Bureau's surveys are a valuable reservoir of data related to poverty. Information gleaned from these surveys include money held in securities, in bank accounts, and in real property in addition to the amount of earned income. Data from the 2012 report informs us on an annual basis that millions of Americans living in our wealthy nation continue to struggle at the economic margins of being poor or living in poverty and little or no signs of progress can be detected. The lack of a positive shift toward a lessening degree of poverty should be cautiously interpreted. This is because regardless of increasingly large monetary expenditures from the taxpayers, little has been realized as an accumulation of wealth indicated in investments by our working citizens. The official poverty rate released in 2012 was 15 percent, which represents 46.5 million people living at or below the poverty line. This marks the second consecutive year that neither the official poverty rate, wages, nor the number of people in poverty were statistically different from the previous year's estimates.

One of the major factors related to a reverse in financial fortune for both individuals and families is that of obtaining regular health care. Major health care expenditures, even when the disease is not considered of a catastrophic nature, will still cost tens of thousands per health crisis. Statistics from the US Census Bureau show that the percentage of people without health insurance coverage declined to 15.4 percent in 2012 — from 15.7 percent in 2011. However, the 48.0 million people without coverage in 2012 was not statistically different from the 48.6 million in 2011 since the population is growing through births and immigration.

The current federal government administration early in its second term gave an estimate that more than 42 million persons lacked health insurance. Then more than 6 million lost their insurance as many companies opted to get out of the health insurance business because of increased provisions and guidelines that would have to be accepted by a rewriting of the existing policies. This amounted to a total of between 49 and 50 million who were and are uninsured just before and after the Affordable Care Act (ACA) became law. Approximately 8 million have been reported to have initiated the process for obtaining insurance through the health care exchanges provided for by the federal government. But it is estimated that a moderate number of persons enrolling in the new health care plan have not paid their premiums in full.

So, since not all of these will complete the process by paying the first premium, there will still be large numbers of citizens and perhaps non-citizens who will remain uninsured. Major insurance companies estimate that more than 20 percent of those completing an application for insurance will actually not pay the initial premium. So if we subtract this revised figure of 80 percent that will ultimately become insured, we will still have perhaps 43 – 44 million who will continue to be uninsured. The numbers that are officially insured include those insured under governmental programs that provide Medicare for the elderly and Medicaid for those too young to be insured by Medicare.

There is a sizable group of persons also insured by Medicare that have been adjudged as being disabled. Under the ACA, the 'bronze plan' which is the least costly option, has a $7,300 deductible, and the plan does not pay 100 percent of the medical charges levied by physicians and medical facilities. How many persons can come up with this amount if the individual is already financially unable to afford a private insurance policy?

Do we often hear or read of these annual reports or other documents related to the poor? Apparently not since many people are not even aware of even estimates of these figures. It is likely that most persons no longer pay much attention to the facts previously presented, or feel hopeless to do anything to improve their lot in our social strata. Are these reports accurate, and do they take into account the monetary value of those who are somewhat self-sufficient and have adequate clothing and housing due to personal circumstances such as living on a farm but who still have a low income level? It is the hope of this author that this would be the case.

We all need to become informed about current meaningful trends as well as statistics of economic well-being, and the public schools as well as private schools could do a better job of keeping its students informed. The older readers of this material will remember the widespread teaching of Home Economics (Home EC) which taught the lady of the home to budget the income of the family and to buy for economy and reliability. Is it time to again teach these types of courses as well as basic economics in our high schools? Has the time come to teach a simple course in national and state economics as well as global economic policies so there are no misconceptions about what the government officials can do?

Stories abound as to those who were doing quite well for a period of time but fell into the category of being poor or poverty-stricken based on governmental figures. The focus in the 1970's was of families living in the Appalachian Mountains of West Virginia and rural Kentucky, where much of the income came from coal mining. As a university student with two children, I was working more than 40 hours per week, and was paying tuition as well as living expenses and was the sole wage earner in the family. Even though for much of this time this author only earned the current mandated minimum wage, I was unaware that I was extremely poor until I heard the salaries of these coal-mining families. They were categorized as working poor but their average annual income exceeded mine!

And later as a college instructor, an African student who had been reared in Europe and had lived in several European countries, was prone to engage in dialogue with his fellow students as well as with me. I decided to ask Derrick a leading question. I asked, "Who is at fault when citizens of a country are poor?" His immediate answer was that it was the fault of the government of that particular country. I then asked him what the country could do to assure that every one of its citizens was not bound by the shackles of poverty. He replied that the government in power could "give" everyone enough money to enable all citizens to be financially secure.

I asked him to consider what should be done for those who chose not to work and to live responsibly. His answer startled me and his fellow students. He insisted that even those who did not work by choice or who chose to live a carefree and hedonistic existence should be provided compensation equal to that of those who were more industrious and who would be working to support persons who chose not to seek employment.

On another occasion, when I was working in a medical laboratory that provided outpatient services, we were forced to stop accepting Medicaid clients as the reimbursement for most services did not even equal the raw costs of the testing materials for performing the procedures. A lady covered by Medicaid came for laboratory testing, and I told her we could not accept her method of payment. She asked why, and I explained that our reimbursement amount would cause us to lose money on each procedure performed and we would eventually be out of business. I was astonished at her creativity, when she stated, "The government should pay you what you ask for in return for performing the tests, regardless of the amount." She continued, "The government *prints* money, so all that is necessary is for more money to be printed so 'they' can pay you whatever you ask." She obviously needed a quick remedial lesson in economics, but it is doubtful that she possessed the ability to understand the basics of such a course.

I believe it would have been pointless for me to tell her that following World War II, Germany printed vast amounts of money to shore up the failing economy. After a period of time, a wheelbarrow of money was required to buy a week's worth of food. Imagine the scenario where the money was so worthless that a thief emptied the Deutschmarks from a wheelbarrow parked at the grocery store and stole the wheelbarrow, as it was worth much more than the money it contained! It is a foreign concept to some if not many, but is nevertheless a valid point to remember. The more money there is in circulation, the more the goods will cost when they are bought. In other words, every good and service will be evaluated as to the available money supply.

So, as salaries rise as the government raises the amount of money in circulation, the cost of the goods and services provided will rise to a commensurate amount, until the entire money supply is accounted for. Many who work in a job have experienced a situation such as I have where I received a small salary increase, but was then taxed at a higher level. In some cases payroll deductions for several taxes, health care, and perhaps retirement contributions will increase until take home pay will be less money than before a well-deserved "raise" is received.

Comparison of the US, Other Countries in Global Economy

H. Luke Shaefer of the University of Michigan and Kathryn Edin of Harvard University showed through their research that the number of people living on $2.00 or less per day per capita (per individual) has risen drastically. "Extreme poverty" is the term the World Bank has established for this category of individuals or families. In the United States, there are those who are expected to pay all of their living expenses with this small amount. The study reveals that an increase in the prevalence of extreme poverty among U.S. households with children between 1996 and 2011 has occurred. Assuming that there are six members of a family who receive $2.00 per day. This would be $12.00 per day or $360 per month, which will not even pay rent on smaller houses or apartments in any part of the country!

Assessment of the effectiveness of either or both state and federal government programs addressing the problem of poverty as means-tested transfer programs determine whether essential needs are being addressed. The term "means testing" refers to a determination indicating that either a one-person household or a family of more than one individual is capable of existing *without governmental subsidies.*

In the years spanning 1996 – 2008, a study conducted over more than a decade called Survey of Income and Program Participation (SIPP) was conducted by the United States Census Bureau. This study is used greatly by a number of institutions to obtain income and program participation in governmental programs. Data from this program determines changes that occur in the economic status of individuals and families, as well as education levels, physical and monetary assets on hand, the presence of health insurance, childcare conditions and dietary adequacy. Changes that include divorce rates and deaths are other areas of information included in the statistical data.

Using the SIPP data from above, it was estimated in 2011 that 1.65 million households or slightly more than 4 percent of households were living in **extreme poverty** based on monthly income. These data were derived from households that did not include an elderly member and that averaged roughly 2.1 children per household before tax credits, and that included subsidies for rent or home purchase, along with Supplemental Nutrition Assistance Program (SNAP) as additional benefits. In an attempt to improve the delivery of governmental aid, the Welfare Reform Act, officially known as the Personal Responsibility and Work Opportunity Reconciliation Act of 1996, fulfilled President William Jefferson Clinton's promise to ultimately change the welfare system as it existed when he was elected president.

This welfare reform act added significantly to those in poverty who were already receiving welfare benefits. The addition of food stamps (most commonly used phrase) or SNAP reduced the poverty level by more than 40 percent in 2011. With other benefits such as tax credits for children and work-incentive credits, the number of those in extreme poverty was reduced by almost 63 percent. Speaker of the House Newt Gingrich (R) of Georgia insisted on a personal responsibility component of the bill. This required the addressing of a number of issues such as low-skilled workers and the specific needs for a trained pool of employees for certain local industries and other enterprises. The program would provide a wide-ranging approach to the barriers to employment so many chronically unemployed persons could fairly compete in seeking employment. Programs were tailored and rightly so, to address meaningful training and was based on regional needs. Success in these areas would contribute to the overall economy of regions with large numbers of persons living in poverty.

In 1935 a federal effort to shake off the stranglehold effects of the Great Depression was begun by President Franklin Roosevelt and was entitled Aid to Families With Dependent Children (AFDC). This program was widely known as a welfare program, and was created to assist widows and families who were abandoned by fathers, but was later amended to include two-parent families. I must add here that sometimes families are abandoned by the women and this is apparently a growing phenomenon today. Ironically, since this program that was initiated for women with no husband, it has actually fostered a growth in one-parent families as some men (and women) failed to exercise their responsibilities to their families. Many of these men have grown to believe that it is the responsibility for the "government" to provide for their children.

Today it is not uncommon for one man to father children by two or more women with no fear of any legal action against him! It is inherent in God's plan for children to have two parents who address the issues involved with nurturing a child. But it must be pointed out that the "government" cannot provide the necessary moral support, even though hordes of social workers and other health care professionals employed by both state and federal governments may attempt to fulfill the surrogate role of a parent to these children.

In 1996, AFDC was changed to Temporary Assistance to Needy Families (TANF), and gained even more rules and conditions. But the program is anything but temporary in those families where a culture of poverty has evolved with little effort or hope by the recipients of "free" aid to better their circumstances. Federal regulations initially limited the time period a person could receive TANF benefits for five years, and new work requirements were put into place.

But these work regulations have been set aside in July of 2012 by the Obama Administration. So even this modest requirement of part-time work or volunteer work has not been in effect since administrative action in 2012. This requirement was designed to instill a work ethic in those who had never worked or who was not currently working. Childcare had also been made available for those with children to remove that barrier preventing or making it more difficult to perform at least a modicum of work.

In 1996, when Congressional welfare reform legislation was enacted, and TANF replaced the AFDC program which had been in effect since 1935, immediate effects of welfare reform were realized in significant ways. Since the 1935 legislation to 1996, the AFDC caseload had never experienced a substantial decrease, so from outward appearances it was not obtaining the desired objectives. However, with the advent of TANF's implementation, the caseload was cut in half over the next decade and a half. In addition, rates of employment and the earnings of single mothers greatly increased. Child poverty rates also declined along with the increased earnings of the mothers for obvious reasons.

There were approximately 3 million fewer children living in poverty in 2003 than in 1995, including 1.2 million fewer black children, marking the lowest level of black child poverty in the nation's history. In July 2012, after the current administration issued a bureaucratic edict proposing to overturn the work requirements that formed the core of the 1996 reform law, these undesirable rates of poverty among children are now on the rise again. The Heritage

Foundation has stated unequivocally that this action clearly violated the intent and the letter of the law.

The lack of financial stability among many black Americans place them in much more precarious financial situations than that generally found among white Americans. Their unemployment rate is significantly higher, leading to an increasing level of poverty within the black community. The rate of black individuals and families living in poverty in 2013 was more than 27 percent, while the rate was approximately one third of that rate for whites at 9.6 percent. A 2014 study by the Pew Research Center reveals that the gap between the earnings and wealth was at its highest since 1989 and is widening. It is a point of contention as to whether discrimination, cultural attitudes toward education and a host of other factors contribute to this disparity.

How Can the Poorest be Lifted From Realms of Poverty?

Why does the United States, arguably for now the wealthiest country in the world, have so many who are in dire need of the necessities of life, let alone the frills of a better life? And does it mean we are fighting the War on Poverty with a losing strategy? Citizens of the United States who are considered poor or living in poverty are diverse in the sources of income and disparities in their lifestyles. Thirteen percent of those occupying the poverty rungs are the elderly who depend perhaps entirely on Social Security and Supplemental Security Income, both of which are administered by the Social Security Administration. Roughly 10 percent of those receiving SSI benefits are those with disabilities and who are unable to work, and some children receive some sort of benefits from Social Security programs for various physical and mental conditions.

We sometimes hear the term "working poor" and slightly more than 60 percent of those occupying the ranks of the poor are found in working families. Most of the families that are included in this category are those called the "near poor," and are those primarily living in cities where the cost of living is high and in most cases wages are low because of large numbers of unskilled positions requiring no education in which these persons find themselves. Roughly one-fourth of the jobs in urban areas pay salaries that will place the family in jobs where wages relegate these workers to a poverty-level income. In some cases, more than one family member will work in a position paying low wages, and most of these families will have children. Therefore, perhaps 70 percent of children living below the poverty line are members of families of the working poor.

Let us dispel the myth that a significant portion of those who are without work choose not to work by choice. It is a popular sentiment that many people on the public dole do not want to work. But in reality work is often difficult to find, and many poor people do realize that they will never improve their financial lot by depending on governmental entitlement programs. But there are those who are somewhat content to live on government subsidies and to remain poor, but these might be in the minority. There are numerous reasons for such a sentiment that exists among some people. The chief one is that there may have been the absence of someone who is significant in the lives of children growing up who sets the example for wanting to do better socially, economically and educationally.

Major Expenses of a Household

Affordable healthcare and affordable housing are two of the major expenses of the family. The need for food, housing and medical care are the paramount expenses for life and it should be a priority for everyone to obtain and maintain these essentials. Usually when buying a house, the person seeking a mortgage loan must be able to provide 30 percent of the family's total income for housing expenses. For a family with an extremely low household income, 30 percent is devastating and will require that sacrifice be made in food needs, medical care and some non-essentials. In these cases, SNAP awards a certain level of sustenance for food, and in some cases help is available for utilities. But there are programs which help to finance home-buying for poor persons. However, it does take a courageous commitment for these families to take such a large step.

The experiment with public housing has now been recognized as an abject failure that does nothing to better the plight of the poor. Multiple examples exist where tenants form a hostile environment for families with drug deals, prostitution and property crimes being rampant in public housing. Expensive apartment buildings for disadvantaged families have been largely destroyed after only a few years of tenancy. A good example of this sad state of affairs is that of a housing project in St. Louis, Missouri, called Pruitt-Igoe, one that was once viewed as one of the best if not the best public housing projects in the nation.

But 16 years after it was completed and which during the interim had extensive and expensive renovations, the facility was finally demolished. Crime infested, home to gangs, and vandalism, including graffiti, use of the stairwells as restrooms, and general deterioration, the city's housing authority blew up three of the most vandalized buildings and demolished the remaining buildings within two years. So few if any new housing projects are planned for the future and these housing units are often called poverty traps. Few ever emerge from these developments to enter into the mainstream of employment.

Many public housing units are essentially being demolished gradually through neglect and are no longer habitable. Federal funding formerly collected from taxes and allocated to local housing agencies around the country has been declining steadily since the early 2000's. The majority of the nation's public housing inventory of units has reached an advanced age where repairs that extend into extensive rehabilitation has become necessary.

In part to fill the lack of public housing, programs such as Section 8 housing (called Housing Choice Vouchers by the federal government), have been instituted, where poorer families are being integrated into better neighborhoods and are leading to a lesser need for new units of public housing. In addition, government-sanctioned incentives to buy a home and to obtain historically low interest rates that require little or zero down payment has led to changes in the area of housing. But recent problems with the mortgage industry have emerged. Persons who could not afford a home or lacked the discipline to maintain and make payments on the homes has led to massive banking failures and were widely publicized in recent years.

Costs of Renting or Buying a Home

Buying a home is the single most expensive investment most individuals or families will ever experience, and a number of people are required to seek federal assistance for either buying or renting a home. But many family units or individuals are forced to rent a home in which to live due to cost constraints. Families that must pay more than 30 percent of their income for housing are considered disadvantaged, and this will cause problems in procuring clothing, food, transportation and other services that most take for granted. According to statistics compiled by the Housing and Urban Development (HUD) agency of the federal government, perhaps twelve million citizens of the United States are required to pay more than 50 percent of their income for rent or house payments. This is a

crippling amount to be paid by any family along with the requirements for utilities and food, as well as other expenses.

A divisional arm of HUD has been implemented to aid those who need affordable housing. Within the Office of Community Planning and Development, the Office of Affordable Housing Programs (OAHP) provides a number of grants and incentives dedicated toward providing a reservoir of housing affordable to low-income households. Categories of assistance are focused on renters, home buying, and homeowner assistance. Specific individuals such as homeless persons, youth, veterans, the chronically ill and victims of natural disasters and those who have had their homes foreclosed upon are addressed in some programs. HUD also has an office called the Office of Housing and Office of Public and Indian Housing which it administers to provide reconstruction of rental units for low income families and those below the poverty line.

The Home Investments Partnership Program commonly called HOME provides direct grants to both states and local governments for rehabilitating urban property to make it habitable, as well as building and buying units for rent or purchase. Large numbers of homes in failing cities such as Detroit, Michigan, and a number of others provide dwellings which can be obtained for only small amounts of money, in return for a promise to rehabilitate the property according to specifications mandated by local governments. It is the largest of the federal block grant programs used by state and local governments to provide affordable homes for the poor. Rental assistance is also available in certain instances for those who apply.

The Self-Help Home Ownership Opportunity Program (SHOP) provides funds to private non-profit organizations who purchase home sites for low income families and volunteer to help those who are willing to provide "sweat equity" such as the well-known Habitat for Humanity organization. This worthy program is of a private nature and is a program founded in Americus, Georgia. This program requires some "sweat equity" in return for having a home built for those who qualify. Most states have a chapter providing for the housing needs but unfortunately can only handle small numbers of individuals and families that qualify.

Those in consistent contact with the poor and those living in poverty, such as teachers, social workers, ministers and even volunteer groups realize the shortsightedness of those in poverty. Because of this so-called poverty mentality, a happy moment, however transient it may be, is sought rather than security and joy in the long term. Devices and material possessions that provide entertainment value are important, such as fancy cars, ostentatious clothing, hair styles and nail enhancements are used to help some forget their situation. It is incongruous, to say the least, when with easy credit, a poor family with few resources and a low income is free to purchase a 60-inch flat screen TV when it is a struggle to put food on the table. This mentality is the single most important barrier preventing an escape from poverty in existence.

Does the United States encourage poverty by providing aid to enable poor habits as just described? Do the manufacturers and the finance offices contribute to poverty and to poverty thinking by providing ready access to mainly entertainment materials and other indulgences such as the one just described? This idea of easy credit when there is little chance of the person in debt being able to pay for his or her obligations has contributed to the current credit mess. Has the federal government encouraged persons to buy houses who have insufficient income to make the mortgage payments? The bill for what is wanted and right now will come tomorrow, but in the meantime, I will enjoy my "toy" as long as I can.

A governmental law promulgated under the Carter administration called the Community Redevelopment Act was intended to encourage minority home-ownership. This law as an unintended consequence helped to create the market for sub-prime loans that are now considered by many liberals as "greedy and predatory" practices although they were passed under Democratic administrations. Clinton's obsession with multiculturalism led to guidelines where mortgage lenders could make somewhat risky loans and led to the difficulties if not the demise of a number of old Wall Street institutions.

Tough regulations forced lenders into high-risk areas with no choice but to lower their lending standards to make the loans that violated sound business practices. Failure of the loan institutions to follow this law has frequently resulted in stiff governmental penalties where violations are perceived. But real poverty is a lot more complicated than the availability of cheap money, and the question of what it is that serves to promote the attitude among those who remain poor or who sink into abject poverty needs to be assessed.

It really doesn't take long to sink into the ranks of the poor or even poverty. The following story, which is a true story, is of a successful specialized physician with a number of enterprises which he had created. Unfortunately he progressed from having a mere alcohol dependency to severe alcoholism. He went through a messy divorce and lost almost everything. He was reduced to driving a Mercedes with bald tires and was working part-time in another physician's pathology laboratory for only a small salary and was forced to live in a privately-run Christian charity home for alcoholics. A subsequent remarriage in which he was also victimized financially did nothing to return him to his former status as a wealthy professional. He told me it was a lot easier to sink downward than to climb upward against the current. When he passed away, nothing was left of his former wealth.

The 2013 poverty guidelines updated each year by the Census Bureau and reported as a Federal Register notice on January 24, 2013, are based on weighted average poverty thresholds since 1959 and are used statistically. The poverty guidelines are a version of the federal poverty measure and are issued annually by the Department of Health and Human Services. These guidelines are a simplification of the poverty threshold that is used for administrative purposes. This administrative version is used in determining eligibility for federal programs aimed at improving the financial lot of those who are poor or in poverty. As shown in the tables presented, there are significant differences between the 48 contiguous states and those in Alaska and Hawaii.

2013 POVERTY GUIDELINES FOR THE 48 CONTIGUOUS STATES, HAWAII, ALASKA AND THE DISTRICT OF COLUMBIA

Persons in household	*48 States	**Alaska	***Hawaii
1	15,510	$14,350	$13,230
2	19,530	19,380	17,850
3	23,550	24,410	22,470
4	27,570	29,440	27,090
5	31,590	34,470	31,710
6	35,610	39,500	36,330
7	39,630	44,530	40,950

*For families/households with more than 8 persons, add $4,020 for each additional person.

**For families/households with more than 8 persons, add $5,030 for each additional person.

***For families/households with more than 8 persons, add $4,620 for each additional person.

SOURCE: *Federal Register*, Vol. 78, No. 16, January 24, 2013, pp. 5182-5183

Changes in the Formula for Poverty Levels

The following table reflects the amount of money needed in 2008 to meet the threshold for being classified as in poverty and has changed significantly in the 48 contiguous states and for Alaska and

Hawaii. One can generally compare the needs for money in 2008 with the previous table for the year 2013. The increase of basic requirements from 2008 to 2013 is more than 10 percent for the 48 states, Alaska and Hawaii.

Federal Poverty Guidelines, 2008

Persons in household	*48 States	**Alaska	***Hawaii
1	$10,400.00	$13,000.00	$11,960.00
2	$14,000.00	$17,500.00	$16,100.00
3	$17,000.00	$22,000.00	$20,240.00
4	$21,200.00	$26,500.00	$24,380.00
5	$24,800.00	$31,000.00	$28,520.00
6	$28,400.00	$35,500.00	$32,660.00
7	$32,000.00	$40,000.00	$36,800.00
8	$35,600.00	$44,500.00	$40,940.00
Each additional	$3,600.00	$4,500.00	$4,140.00

SOURCE: *Federal Register*, Vol. 73, No. 15, January 23, 2008, pp. 3971–3972; National Center for Children in Poverty (www.nccp.org), Measuring Poverty in the United States

What is Meant by Being Wealthy

We have discussed the status of being deemed poor or in poverty and these terms in order to be relevant must be compared to another status to gain the true meaning of being poor or poverty stricken, and the opposite of this status would be the 'rich' or the wealthy. The federal government of the United States does not set parameters for such information, but apparently those that make more than $200,000 per year are considered wealthy. No differential can be determined from official and unofficial documents for those who are wealthy and those who are merely rich. So it is subjective and each person may draw his or her own conclusions. Since there is so much conjecture regarding the presence of wealth, I decided to conduct an informal class discussion. I might add that almost assuredly none of these students nor their parents or spouses had paid any income taxes based on their receiving financial aid in order to attend school, since eligibility for the financial aid they were receiving required a very low income level.

I was teaching a class required for entry into a program for a variety of health care professions such as for licensed practical nurses, medical assistants, certified nursing assistants as well as several other related programs. The class of forty or so was populated mainly by at-risk students such as single mothers and those who had been unemployed for considerable lengths of time. The purpose of this story is to point out the subjective nature of how much money is required to be wealthy. In addition, how much did the students expect to earn upon completion of a program and the completion of proper certification to practice the profession. Although this discussion was not listed in the syllabus or course outline, there were discussions on salary costs in health care, so I found it relevant to the course to take on such a discussion. I did so as I felt it might shed some light of reality among these students who had for the most part lived a life of scarcity up to this point.

I laid out the following scenario. I queried the students as to whether 'rich' people paid enough in taxes and if they should pay more. The consensus was that they should all pay more in taxes in order to 'give to the poor.' I then asked that each of the students write a note as to how much he or she expected to earn. The answers that were verbally called out ranged wildly from a few thousand per year to more than a hundred thousand (as a starting salary). I proceeded to tell the class that at least some of them would be earning as much as $40,000 to $50,000 per year, with experience, at which point the majority of the class grew extremely excited about their future prospects. I then asked them to list what they would do with the money. Almost all stated that they would buy a fine new and large house and a fine looking car.

I asked the students to then tell me in writing how much the payments on a good house would be per month, and the payments on a new vehicle. I asked them to assume that they would spend $500 per month on utilities. Then I asked them to divide a fifty thousand salary by twelve to estimate a monthly income, which came to approximately $4167.00. Their eyes popped, thinking that was an extremely large amount of money. But then we subtracted an income tax rate of 25 percent, car insurance of $100 per month, and utilities of $500, amounts that were assumed. The purchase of a modest home for $100,000 was assumed, but is problematic to find a 'fine' home for this price in many areas of the country. We assumed that property taxes and home insurance (T & I) of $200 per month (a lower rate than found in some markets) would be used, and a mortgage for 30 years at a fixed rate of interest of 4.5 percent.

Since most of the students had children, we used a figure of $500 for food and a miscellaneous category that included gas for the car, clothing, repairs, dental expenses and any other items not covered in the other categories. All of the figures in the following table are low to modest estimates. Then we performed the following *monthly* calculations:

Income	Taxes	Utilities	Vehicle	Car Ins	House	T & I	MED Ins	Food	Misc.	Balance
$4,167.	$1,042.	$500.	$400.	$100.	$507.	$200.	$350.	$500.	$500.	$68.00

So in the ensuing discussion, I told the students that they would have $68 to pay any unusual expenses, buy gifts, entertainment costs, education, vacations, or any variety of activities in which they would wish to participate. Their first question was, "Why are they (the government) charging us so much in taxes?" I told them that most of these costs were on the low end of normal expenses, and that the 'rich' people are asking the same questions that they are, since most 'rich' people have bigger and more expensive houses, more cars that cost more to operate and require higher taxes for houses and cars.

The silence that followed led me to think that perhaps they were beginning to realize that most middle class families are having increasing difficulties in the current economic status of the country in making their payments for essential living costs as well as other expenses that they incur. The rich people making $200,000 per year would perhaps pay $50,000 to $70,000 in federal, state income and property taxes. With an expensive home, the property taxes might range from $5,000 to $10,000 or more in some locations of the country.

I hope they got my point! But I sincerely hope they didn't decide it just wasn't worthwhile to work, but that they would be better off if they retained their dependence on governmental programs. I hope that those students and others will read this entire book and adopt sound economic principles and learn to live within their means by using prudence and good sense (with the help of the Lord). In the following section, it will be shown how costs vary from location to location, and the monetary figures used for major expenses will be based on data determined by surveys and studies.

Costs of Living Vary by Geographic Location

As indicated earlier in this writing, the U.S. government measures poverty by narrow income ranges that do not take into account certain aspects of economic status. The ranges are affected by such areas as material hardship (for example, living in substandard housing) or debt, but it does not consider financial assets that the individual controls, including savings and retirement accounts, or property. The official poverty measure is a specific dollar amount that varies by family size, but is the same across the continental U.S. According to the guidelines, the poverty level in 2013 is $27,570 a year for a family of four and $23,550 for a family of three. In reality, this is not a great deal of money and leaves little for other than basic needs.

The current federal minimum wage is $7.25 and some states have differing levels, but 38 of the states in 2014 were using this federal standard amount. However, raises to $15.00 per hour is under consideration in a number of states, and in a couple of states, the proposed wage hike exceeds $15.00 at an hourly rate. So the minimum wage amount for most states of $7.25 for 2080 work hours at 40 hours per week each year (2088 hours for a leap year that occurs every four years) would provide $15,080 per year.

So from the table for figures compiled for 2013, the wages earned can be compared and it is noted that for a family of five, the amount earned would need to be roughly double that earned by a single wage earner. In some families, there will be more than one wage earner, particularly in a family of five. This figure can also be put into context when it is shown that for 66 percent of US wage earners the average annual income for a working family in 2011, the last complete year of statistics at the time of this writing, is

$41,211.36. And seven other countries actually exceed the average income for those employed in the United States!

Why not Raise the Minimum Wage?

There are many reasons for not raising the minimum wage dramatically or at all. This sounds cruel, but is an economic necessity. Those making minimum wage are entry-level employees who are sometimes but not in all cases working at a low production level. I know of one business that was struggling and eventually failed, leaving 12 employees without a job when the minimum wage level increased by almost $2 per hour in 2007. None of the workers were making the minimum wage and in most instances were making $2 or more per hour above the minimum federal minimum wage. This increased the monthly requirements for salaries and the added social security taxes to be matched along with other required taxes by three to four thousand dollars per month, enough to destroy the business. All of the workers were young and lived at home except for a manager, a single mother, who was paid $35,000 per year. Some businesses allow young persons to work at minimum wage even if they're not essential to the operation of the business in order for them to gain skills so they can earn more as they gain in both experience and skills.

Just how many workers are making minimum wage as mandated by the federal government you may ask? The current U.S. population had just reached slightly over 319 million in 2014. In July 2014, there are 139 million people employed in the United States. This number is up by 209,000 employees since June and by 1.47 million from the beginning of 2014 but since 2009, there has been a decline of more than 5 million in those who are employed. In figures obtained from the Bureau of Labor Statistics, 1.6 million Americans earned the prevailing minimum wage of $7.25 per hour.

It should be noted here that a number of states require a higher hourly wage, and some have built-in incremental increases over the next several years. These figures show that only barely over 1.1 percent of workers earn the minimum wage. The Pew Research Center, citing references from the Bureau of Labor Statistics and the Bureau of Economic Analysis, reported that the following statistics:

People at or below the federal minimum (included in the working poor):

a. Disproportionately young: 50.4 percent are ages 16 to 24; 24 percent are teenagers (ages 16 to 19).

b. Mostly (77 percent) white and nearly half are white women

c. Largely part-time workers comprise roughly 64 percent of the total

Many products consumed by low income persons, if the minimum hourly rate increased, would affect the cost of almost all consumer goods resulting in increased prices. So even with an increase in earning power, the higher prices could actually erode the income for those on a subsistence level. In comparison to low income persons, those in the military invariably work more than the typical 40-hour work week. In addition, many of the perks or benefits they received in the past have eroded. In part, they must buy their own uniforms, pay for some health care and fulfill other requirements in order to remain employed. Most of them have families and are called away for protracted periods of time, during which their families must find ways to stay afloat financially. The deployed soldier, airman, or sailor must still take care of personal needs while away from home for extended periods. If each of the salaries of these lower ranking military personnel were raised by a couple of dollars per hour, the results would be a dramatic increase in the costs of salaries for the armed forces, where taxpayer money is involved.

The basic amount earned by an entry-level (E1) and lowest paid military person (soldier, sailor, airman) is $8.83 per hour. The work week is more than 40 hours per week in most instances even in peacetime periods, and there are mandatory duties extending beyond the normal working hours. Of course, those in combat arenas seldom have more than a few hours off per day. The second level, E2, may take six months or more to achieve, but with skills earned prior to enlistment, the starting pay grade for a small number is higher. Also, those above E5 pay grade often have advanced training that takes years to complete, and some even have associate degrees or higher. So, the question would be, should a soldier working extended hours and expending great effort make less than those earning minimum wage?

US Army Enlisted Pay Scale

Army Rank	Annual Salary**	Hourly Rate*
Private E1	18378	8.83
Private E2	20603	10.11
Private First Class E3	21665	10.62
Specialist or Corporal E4	23994	11.54
Staff Sergeant E5	26172	12.58

*Hourly rate is based on 2080 hours, as the typical work year; most military personnel work far beyond 2080 hours per year

**Some benefits are included, but many of these benefits, such as free uniforms, are being eroded on a regular basis

Note: Those of a rank above E-1 and E-2 have advanced training and experience and are not entry-level

Average and Median Income

The average when including all income levels is skewed by those making tens of millions per year. I have heard conversations regarding the fact that if all the CEO's would pay their *fair share* of taxes, which is an elusive number, that the country would be better off and the federal government would be flush with money. Actually, if the top 1 percent of income earners in the United States were taxed at 100 percent, the federal government would only be financed for a short period of time (less than a month by some calculations) with this money. But contrary to popular opinion, those in this income bracket are extremely few. Figures that are widely reported are approximately 0.23 percent of all taxpayers in the United States, or less than ¼ of one percent make the CEO-level salaries.

The United States median income has declined since 2007. It will be useful to remember that the median wage statistically means that half of the wage earners earn below a certain amount and half make above the target salary. Actual median family income in the United States peaked at $62,527 but today is $5,215 less, or 7.7

percent lower for the period between 2007 and 2014. It is thought that this trend might continue into the near future, as the recession beginning at the end of 2007 is stubbornly persisting in 2014, particularly in some sectors of our economy.

Another interesting fact regarding employment numbers in the United States is the fact that fewer persons are working today than in 2008. Figures show that 137,996,000 persons were employed for more than 35 hours per week in June of 2008. By June of 2014, only 119,470,000 persons were employed full-time, a difference of 18.5 million. A 13 million population increase, or 4.3 percent, coupled with the 18.5 million fewer working, indicates that 31 million more people are not working now. What do these figures suggest? They indicate that fewer people are in the workforce to pay taxes in order to fulfill the governmental obligations, so there are fewer people who must pay higher payroll taxes to cover the declining tax revenues!

The poverty guidelines are used to determine eligibility for public programs. A similar but more complex measure is used for calculating poverty rates. Costs for various categories of expenses, of course, vary by region and by city. It is difficult to determine the least expensive place to live due to the complexities of all the basic components of expenses.

Taxes tend to be higher in larger metropolitan areas which provide many more public benefits than those in rural areas where there is little or no availability of public parks, expensive thoroughfares, and other services such as consistent police presence enjoyed by the citizens of the city. But lower taxes in rural areas are offset by property insurance rates that are traditionally greater in rural areas due to long distances from fire stations. But in recent years, the existence of fire hydrants, even in rural areas that are often funded by the county government, might have ameliorated this difference in the cost of hazard insurance to an extent.

In the 1960's, federal guidelines assumed that families would spend one-third of their incomes on food. But with increased mechanization of farms, hybrid crops that produce more products per acre, and efficiency in transportation of the farm products in areas where needed have served to lower the cost of food. Coupled with chain supermarkets it is possible to buy large amounts of produce and other manufactured goods in bulk amounts at reduced prices. Therefore, food is generally more available and more economical for the poor in the past few decades in comparison to earlier years, particularly in the United States. Even though there are similarities between the poor and those in poverty, the availability of food at cheaper prices has made quite an impact on the lives of both the poor and those living in poverty. Of course calculations for determining poverty as compared with being poor is much more complex.

Another significant factor in estimating the cost of living relative to basic needs and the differences between urban and rural communities vary widely. Housing may cost significantly more in one area of the country, while transportation may be cheaper in another. Such is the case in New York City, where an abundance of cheap public transportation exists. The fact that many live in condensed populated areas which may be near their place of employment and to shopping may reduce costs of transportation.

The cost of medical care varies by a somewhat smaller amount than does housing. In more rural areas and in small towns, housing may be cheaper, but might require longer commutes to and from work and for shopping. Food costs are not exactly the same, but with chain supermarkets in areas where they are available to most residents, prices tend to be similar in urban and rural areas. Remember that those in rural areas may raise a substantial portion of their own food, but if they are forced to shop at rural community stores and non-chain supermarkets, their food costs may be greater than in cities with competitive stores nearby.

The information provided also assumes that the children are in child care centers while the parents work, with the older child remaining in an after-school program until the parents complete their work day. Except for New York City, where transportation is based on the public transportation system, the costs of private transportation are used in the calculations. The information is determined from the costs of four disparate geographic locations and perhaps slight differences will be the case in other parts of the country. These figures were compiled for the year 2008 and will differ today.

The following table shows the basic needs for living and the differences that should be taken into consideration when determining the amount of income that a family of four would require for just basic subsistence in the area in which they live. The tabular data is compiled for the needs of a family of four with one preschool-age child and one school-aged child and is taken from the National Center for Child Poverty (NCCP's) Basic Needs Budget Calculator. Figures can be accessed at www.nccp.org/tools/budget.

BASIC NEEDS BUDGET FOR FAMILY OF FOUR MEMBERS IN FOUR SELECTED RURAL AND URBAN LOCATIONS

Location	Urban, New York, NY	Urban, Houston, TX	Suburban, Aurora, IL	Rural, Decatur County, IA
Rent and Utilities	$15,816.00	$10,224.00	$11,328.00	$6,324.00
Food	$7,878.00	$7,878.00	$7,878.00	$7,878.00
Child care	$20,684.00	$15,422.00	$18,793.00	$11,682.00
Health insurance plans	$2,609.00	$2,834.00	$2,265.00	$2,436.00
Medical costs, not covered by insurance	$732.00	$732.00	$732.00	$732.00
Transportation	$1,824.00	$4,808.00	$4,808.00	$6,288.00
Miscellaneous expenses	$6,397.00	$4,887.00	$5,185.00	$3,270.00
Payroll taxes	$5,113.00	$3,873.00	$4,437.00	$6,324.00
*Income taxes (includes credits)	$5,787.00	-$34.00	$2,572.00	$304.00
TOTAL	$66,840.00	$50,624.00	$57,998.00	$42,748.00
Percent of federal poverty level	315.0 percent	239.00 percent	274.00 percent	202.0 percent

Some costs of living have increased, while others have unbelievably gone down. In the website provided previously, one may calculate the basic needs for any state and some major metropolitan areas by adding the characteristics of the family, such as number of children, if single-parent or two-parent family, and if both are employed. The number of children and their ages may also be entered for an accurate estimate of the costs associated with caring for a family. Note that the food costs are relatively stable, since residents of most areas have access to food market chains. Health insurance costs could potentially be adjusted either up or down, based on the passage of the Affordable Care Act (Obamacare). *Not all credits and grants are included in these figures in some instances. Certain income, such as Social Security disability payments for children will not be reported as income.

It is variously estimated by a number of agencies that 46-47 percent of the wage earners in the US pay no income tax at all. Typically, a family of four with an income of less than $48,000 will normally pay no income taxes at all, and may receive a cash payout based on the family size and the level of earning income. In addition, the Earned Income Credit, or EIC, is a federal tax credit given to individuals or families whose income falls below published guidelines. The families who qualify for the earned income credit will not owe any federal income taxes and would potentially receive a refund after filing a tax return for any taxes withheld along with an additional disbursement from the Internal Revenue Service. Depending on the income level and number of individuals in the family, this could amount to potentially several thousand dollars a year.

Why Changes Should be Initiated to Measure Poverty

The current poverty measures are inadequate in two major areas. As seen earlier, food expenditures have dropped by one third of a typical family's living costs to one seventh of the family's income during the past few years. However, a number of costs necessary for maintaining a family have risen somewhat sharply. Transportation, health care, housing (rental and purchase price) and child care necessary for the single parent family and those where both parents are employed have increased. It should be mentioned that during the past few years, housing had dropped precipitously, at least as far as the purchase of a house, with rent being affected only slightly, but prices had again begun to rise by 2014.

This bears out the need for adjusting the cost of living on a regular basis, and gives the reader an idea of the complexities of the merging of all the costs required to maintain a family, even as they change, in determining the wealth status of a family and the level of need where the income is supplemented. Therefore the poverty level will not reflect the accurate cost of supporting a family. In reality the current poverty measure is a national standard that is not continually adjusted for the sometimes significant variation in the cost of living from state to state and the differences between urban and rural areas. More accurate estimates of typical family expenses, and adjustments for local costs would produce substantially higher dollar outlays. And since governmental budgets are established for a future period of at least a year, the money budgeted for providing these supplements to income would be rapidly exhausted, and require midstream adjustments by legislative action in the budgets and the development of new revenue streams.

As it can be seen, it is difficult if not impossible to develop an accurate method to determine whether a family is indeed poor, and current calculations do not take into consideration certain family resources. For instance, the family might have inherited land or a dwelling, which might not be a factor included in the calculation of funds administered by state and federal governments for assistance. Sometimes more than one family may live in the same house or apartment, with more than one person working for wages, but the financial need is based on only one income. Sometimes changes in fortune occur but are never reported to the agency administering the aid to the family.

In the process of determining if a family is poor or living in poverty, income from sources included in the calculation of the needs data include certain income. Not included are interest payments, stock and bond dividends, cash assistance from various sources, and particularly Social Security benefits, but should be. Income is tabulated before payroll, income, and other taxes, overstating income for some families. One other substantial source of income for the poor is that of the previously mentioned federal Earned Income Tax Credit that isn't counted as income causing an underestimation of income for some families with at least one working member.

Also, in-kind government benefits that serve to aid low-income families, including "food stamps" which are not stamps at all today, but are in the form of EBT (electronic benefit transfer) cards, Medicaid, housing and child care assistance are not taken into account. A word about EBT cards – these cards are sometimes fraudulently obtained and are sold at premium prices, or the cards are used for items other than food for which they were intended. This means that official poverty statistics cannot be used to analyze the effectiveness of these programs. The dollar cost of EBT card fraud is impossible to accurately gauge, but one man in Georgia was prosecuted for having performed fraudulent activities based on EBT cards to the tune of more than four million dollars over a period of time.

Alternative Developments to Measure Poverty

In the early 1990's, Congress asked the National Academy of Sciences (NAS) to study and propose alternative ways to more effectively assess poverty at least as far as income is involved. A panel of experts at the direction of the NAS reported in 1995 that certain factors should be included in the determination of poverty and the level of need based on meaningful scales relative to variable factors due to specific characteristics of each family. The panel's recommendations included the following:

1. Create new poverty thresholds that more accurately reflect the cost of food, clothing, and shelter.

2. Adjust thresholds by region to account for variation in the cost of living.

3. Use families' post-tax income;

4. Include earned income tax credits and the value of near-cash benefits (such as food stamps and housing assistance); and

5. When counting families' resources to determine whether they fall below the poverty line:

6. Subtract the cost of work-related expenses (such as child care and transportation) and medical care.

Adoptions of the above recommendations would take into account regional differences for certain work-related expenses. It would also take into account income areas not previously included in the computation of income. It was estimated that if the NAS recommendations were adopted, millions more people would be considered officially poor, increasing the funding needed for the increase in the pool of recipients eligible for receiving government aid. But even these recommendations underestimate the cost of family expenses and thus produce poverty thresholds well below what it takes to make ends meet. The result would be that for a family of four, the poverty level increase would only be about $3,000 annually.

What if All the Money in the US Were Divided Equally?

We have all heard others, and perhaps each of us have said that if all the money were divided equally, then everyone would have an equitable share. Please consider the reality of this statement. In the United States, it is estimated by the Federal Reserve that there is a pool of approximately 1.27 trillion dollars in the M0 (circulating money) in the money stream (source is Federal Reserve Bank of New York). That is an incredible amount of money, is it not? Wouldn't it be wonderful if this were possible? No, because in this case everyone would be poor!

This includes the bills and coins in people's pockets and mattresses, and the money on hand in bank vaults to include all the deposits those banks have at reserve banks (Hamilton) and holdings that can readily be converted to cash. According to the Federal Reserve, there was $1.2 trillion in the *M0* supply stream as of July 2013, as published by the Federal Reserve Bank of New York. That sounds like an incredible amount, but think about it this way: According to the CIA, there were 316,668,567 Americans alive that month according to Central Intelligence Agency (CIA) sources.

If all the figures were derived of cash in circulation and the total population of the United States and divided it up equally, each person should have about $3,800 in cash for his or her use. Depending on the data sources, these figures will vary by a few hundred dollars. In 1990, this amount was only about $2000 each. Some would no doubt stuff the money under the mattress or some other creative place to avoid having his or her hard-earned money divided with others who do not choose to be a wage earner for whatever reason(s). There are other calculations that include other moneys that are not in general circulation, so it is interesting to examine these figures that may be surprisingly low.

In addition, one-half to one-third of the total amount in circulation in this country is owned by United States institutions and may be found currently in foreign accounts where multinational businesses operate in other countries. Why don't they bring it back to the United States? The answer is that our country has an incredibly high tax rate for money brought into (repatriated) in this country. The companies would then perhaps lose more than one-third of the amount received when placed in circulation in this country. Depending upon one's view, that would make the companies show greed by not giving away the money they had earned or by showing good business prudence by investing the money in the country in which they earned the money. If the leaders of our country would realize that if this money were brought back, even tax-free, and invested in this country's economy, the result would be the creation of more jobs and more businesses expanded or created in the United States that could be taxed.

Creation of Jobs to Combat Poverty

Companies are regularly leaving the United States for countries with lower corporate tax rates than those found in the United States. There are few persons who realize this, and that it does dampen the zeal of many companies to start businesses but who might instead just sit on their money. The United States has the highest or next to the highest corporate tax rate in the world, at least among the developed countries. Of course in some third-world countries, graft and corruption may exact higher "taxes" by the governing class, but that cannot be documented in many cases where outright bribes are required in order to perform business functions.

But with a need for creating more jobs so our unemployed persons can return to work, we are losing ground in trying to maintain the jobs we already have. Some call the companies greedy because they are so uncaring as to expect to make a profit. From the net profit these companies pay dividends to stockholders who hold an interest in the company in which they have invested their own cash. In some cases the money invested was earned from working in an extremely difficult job. Perish the thought of wanting a profit is the response of some! But the opposite side of this coin would be to have only state-owned industries, which some communist nations have tried for decades, only to abandon or at least in part abandon the plan, which destroys any initiative workers have to perform well in their jobs.

It is alleged that a decade or so ago a large United States company wanted to sell one of its plants in France and to expand the company here in the United States. There were several hundred million dollars that this company received when it sold its foreign interests. Upon learning that the tax burden would take a large portion of this money, the company decided to expand its business in the European country where the tax bite was not so great. So our country missed out on an investment where at least hundreds, if not thousands of jobs would have been created.

Measuring Poverty in the United States

The National Center for Children in Poverty (NCCP) is based in the Mailman School of Public Health, Department of Health Policy and Management at Columbia University. The administrators of this facility are aware that the federal poverty scales grossly underestimate how much is required to support a family of four. To this end, this agency has compiled a basic needs budget for a family of four in selected urban, suburban and rural areas of the United States. Recent NCCP reports show that about one half of children in the United States live in low-income families and one-fifth live in poverty. NCCP fact sheets show facts relating to the poor and low-income children and their struggles. An on-line tool allows one to obtain information for each of the states, where differences in costs of living have been provided.

Given that the federal poverty level grossly understates how much it takes to support a family, researchers have developed budgets that realistically quantify basic living costs in specific localities. Building on earlier efforts, NCCP has developed Basic Needs Budgets that include only the most basic daily living expenses and are based on modest assumptions about costs. For example, the budgets in the figures for the most basic of living costs assume that family members have employer-sponsored health coverage, even though the majority of low-wage workers do not have employer coverage. Basic Needs Budgets by NCCP do not include actual necessities such as life and disability insurance and an emergency fund to help with unexpected expenses such as repairs and medical emergencies that are common in the lives of each individual or family.

Of course, loss of a job, catastrophic medical expenses and major repairs, as well as the occasional natural disaster can set a family back for years, and some families are not resilient enough to ever emerge from these crises. In addition, they do not allow for investments in a family's future financial success to insure a secure retirement, or savings to buy a home or for a child's education. As in a portion of the other calculations we have examined, there are certain aspects of the budgets that are not addressed in order to determine a true amount that is necessary for a family to cover their most basic living expenses. There may be enough just to subsist, but there is not enough to even envision getting ahead.

Across the United States, families will need an income close to twice the official poverty level ($42,400 for a family of four) to meet basic needs. In high-cost cities such as New York, it may take an income of over three times the poverty level to make ends meet, whereas in some rural areas, the figure may be less than double the poverty level. To restate the salaries earned at minimum wage levels, almost three salaries would be necessary to achieve an income that is close to twice the posted poverty level income in the United States.

In short, even if the official poverty measure is revised along the lines suggested by the NAS, it would remain a measure of deprivation and would create severe hardship and be insufficient for providing a meaningful life economically. In contrast, Basic Needs Budgets provide a way to think about the goods and services families need to maintain a minimally decent standard of living. An understanding of certain factors, and the answering of pertinent questions should aid an individual or family in understanding why certain products cost as much as they do and why some persons make a higher income than others.

Conclusions

Based on the figures provided by the federal government and some educational and social programs, the following definitions and explanations may be derived from those dry figures mainly found in tabular format.

Costs of Goods and Services - The costs passed on to the consumer is based on total money in circulation in the United States and is related to inflation rates

Salary Parameters - If everyone was paid a high salary, everyone would be poor due to an increase in the amount of circulating money. Should everyone make the same wages? Why or why not? What contributes to a disparity in wages? Individuals should evaluate their beliefs as to what causes and will cause income disparities.

Handling Money - What does it mean to 'plant dollars?' Utilizing the best family budgeting tools available will help one make the most of his or her earnings. Being able to set aside some of one's earnings for the future (planting) may seem to be impossible. Here's a little secret: budgeting doesn't have to be difficult. Many formal budgeting systems are available on the internet and perhaps often through programs offered by churches to aid individuals and families in establishing a reasonable budget.

Wealthy and Being Rich the Same? - What is the difference between being rich or being wealthy? Is there a difference and if so can we separate the two similar concepts?

PART III:
Biblical Perspective of Being Poor

The handling of money from a Biblical standpoint is that it is a spiritual matter, and the handling of money should be approached with that in mind. Proverbs 3:13-18 informs us that a person who knows right from wrong and has good judgment and common sense will be happier as a result than a person who is immensely wealthy. One could conclude that the person who has merely been bestowed with great financial resources, and does not possess the character trait of knowing right from wrong, and practicing it, will not be happy even though wealthy. So, wealth does not necessarily bring happiness. In addition, possessing a measure of good judgment and exercising common sense would come from practice and perhaps continuous meditation as to how to handle one's business affairs as well as conducting the ordinary decisions made in daily life. In Proverbs 2:10, Solomon tells the believer that wisdom and truth will enter the very center of one's life, filling the believer with joy. In other words, the use of wisdom and truth in all transactions in life will bring happiness.

Spiritual Health in Finances

As we read this material and examine the four Biblical principles repeated over and over in the book of Proverbs, and particularly in the third chapter of this book, our correlation of spiritual health and the handling of our personal finances will become clear.

1. **Money as a Spiritual Matter**

Money is mostly a spiritual matter and includes much more than just financial knowledge gained from a business education. A good example of this is demonstrated by David Green, the founder of Hobby Lobby. He and his family practice Biblical principles in their personal lives and in the running of the ultra-successful business built in the living room of Green's home with a $600 investment. Many will recognize Green's name as standing against the federal government in his refusal to include certain contraceptive drugs in his health care plan that is considered by some as destruction of the beginnings of life for a human embryo. Some neglect to acknowledge that he does provide coverage for a number of contraceptive devices and drugs through his employees' health care plans. It would not be truthful to state that he has not been financially successful even while strictly adhering to his Biblical principles.

2.   Struggle With Money

People struggle with money and its use because of personal struggles with sin of various types. The most notorious and visible examples of committing sin by the use of money would be revealed in the wanton lifestyles practiced by some entertainers, athletes, ultra-wealthy business owners or executives, and members of the movie industry. There are no-holds-barred in the actions of some who are widely exposed and even praised by the media who spend much time following these individuals that practice a completely hedonistic existence. And at least as much to blame for these excesses in ownership and activities are those who follow and enjoy the antics and the corrupt lives exemplified by these self-indulgent characters.

3.   How to Avoid Money Struggles

But why do we have so many struggles with money? The answer lies in the mathematical functions that will serve both individuals, families, businesses and even federal and state budgets. What is required to construct a budget? Addition and subtraction in most cases and no higher math is needed other than the basics learned in the second grade, or at least they were included in elementary school in the past. It is simply a matter of adding income and subtracting expenses. What does it take to balance a check book? There are 2 types of people in the world (some consider that it is divided into "haves" and "have nots" or conservatives, liberals, and different degrees of liberals and conservatives. But principally from a financial perspective, there are those who live on less than they make; and those who live on more than they make. I know that many have difficulties in earning a living income, but with effort and planning, accompanied by the practice of Christian principles, this should not be the case for a lifetime. It is often a gradual transition from being financially strapped and being comfortable by paying for goods and services on time. All it takes is a basic set of character skills, with which we may be born and inherited from our forebears. These skills include basically some discipline, the ability not to put off things that can be remedied before they reach a crisis state, and the choice to be content with what one has for the moment. This does not mean you should not make efforts to achieve skills and attitudes that will enable you to take advantage of well-paying jobs and financial opportunities to improve one's lifestyle.

4. **Every financial decision should be approached as a spiritual decision.**

Many of the readers of this book will have lived through the "bull market" of the late nineties, and then perhaps suffered defeats at the crash of the stock market in 2000 to 2002 (the dot.com burst). Some of these victims find it hard to again begin to invest money in today's market. There are general guides in the Bible that will lead you to make wise investments that don't compromise your principles. But the Bible does not list specific investments that will be successful. We are given guidelines, but not a playbook to follow. Several questions many are asking themselves today are:

a. Should I diversify my portfolio by selling a portion of the poorly performing stocks?

b. Should I modify my retirement plan by putting my money into "safe" instruments such as bonds and money markets, although they typically don't produce growth or income to the extent that stocks do?

c. Should I sell a losing investment that had great promise to buy something else that might be no better?

Sound Financial Decisions are Based Upon Biblical Truths

If it sounds too good to be true, it probably is! We have all heard this statement and yet people are figuratively burned when making financial decisions, in romantic situations, and in the purchase of automobiles, homes, and other big and small ticket entities. Consider the following verses, again from the Book of Proverbs:

Be open to the counsel of Godly friends. *This practice can be found in the Bible!* Proverbs 15:22 (NKJV) states, "Without counsel, plans go awry, but in the multitude of counselors they are established."

Consider all the needs to finish the job. This is also found in the Bible, in Luke 14:28-32, NKJV. "For which of you, intending to build a tower, does not sit down first and count the cost, whether he has enough to finish it, lest after he has laid the foundation, and is not able to finish, all who see it begin to mock him, saying, 'This man began to build and was not able to finish'? Or what king, going to make war against another king, does not sit down first and consider whether he is able with ten thousand to meet him who comes against him with twenty thousand? Or else, while the other is still a great way off, he sends a delegation and asks conditions of peace." It is infinitely more complex to build a life and to teach your family the ways of the Lord!

Focus in the Bible Regarding Wealth

Why does the Bible focus so much upon the status of one's wealth or lack of wealth? The Bible does so because this is often the root cause of most human discord, where one individual, company, or country has more than another. It even extends to countries who go to war because of feeling wronged in perhaps access to precious resources (land, oil, metals, ocean harbors etc.) and sometimes even in religious differences as we see so often in the Middle Eastern countries for the past several decades. Since history began, and as stated before, everyone on occasion struggles with money issues. It is no more a problem now than it was 3,000 years ago, but only in the amounts of money and possessions and their assigned values that have greatly escalated.

One of the most confusing issues to some regards the possession of wealth from a Bibliographic perspective. Since so much is said in the Bible about wealth, perhaps the most controversial statement of all is that of Jesus' admonition about wealth in Mark 10:25 (KJV). In this verse of Scripture, Jesus says: "It is easier for a camel to go through the eye of a needle than for a rich man to enter the Kingdom of God." A significant portion of people take these words literally and believe that since it is impossible to pass a camel, even a young one, through the eye of a needle and regardless of the size of the needle, that rich person shall not inherit the Kingdom of God.

Some Christian denominations teach that the words found in Mark 10:25 (KJV) indicate that since the description of the passage by a camel through a small opening is an impossibility, then Christians are advised to remain poor. They should strive to remain poor or at least not enrich themselves (becoming "rich"). Identifying someone as rich or wealthy indicates that there is a specific amount of possessions of wealth that accords that person as being rich.

But the term 'rich' is an entirely subjective term and in some areas those who have just enough to survive at a comfortable level would be wealthy while the same amount in other areas of the world would be only a trifling amount. There are those who believe that any accumulation of money or instruments of money, perhaps as the holding of stocks, and possessions beyond their basic needs, is sinful. But most persons who possess great wealth will not describe themselves as being rich or wealthy, as most seekers of wealth will never consider any sum as "being enough."

Some interpretations by Biblical scholars say that the description of the camel's route of passage refers to the small, narrow back gate of a city's walls, where camels may pass through in the evening after the main gates are closed for the night. When these city gates were used, camels may have had to have their burdens removed before they were able to pass through the narrow opening, and even then the passage would be extremely difficult to negotiate. It is important to focus on the entirety of the words of the Bible that relate to wealth and how it is observed or used. There are numerous words relating to those who are wealthy, but they were not condemned to eternal damnation through the words found in the Bible. As a contrast, remember Solomon in all of his glory and wealth, asked God for an abundance of wisdom rather than great riches. And because his heart was right toward God, he gained both wisdom and wealth. Abraham, as the Father of Judaism and Christianity and even revered by the Muslim faithful, was certainly wealthy even by today's standards.

In Matthew 26:11, New American Standard Bible, Jesus says "For you always have the poor with you; but you do not always have Me." There are several other verses from both the Old Testament and the New Testament which mirror these words almost exactly, regardless of the particular version being used. In Mark 14:7 (KJV), Jesus was quoted as saying, "For ye have the poor with you always, and whensoever ye will ye may do them good: but me ye have not always." Perhaps Jesus made these statements on more than one occasion, with slight variations on His words, or the two disciples heard differently, which is quite possible. At any rate, Jesus intimated that we are to help the poor. Unfortunately, some persons want to say that it is inevitable that some will be poor, as though it were a character trait of certain individuals and in a psychological sense this might be the case in some due to undesirable personality quirks.

But most people wish for more wealth and some achieve it without cheating others for the sake of gaining wealth. The Bible also speaks of this issue. In Matthew 8:27-29, the parable of the unforgiving servant is provided. In essence the lord of a slave who owed him much money felt compassion for his slave and forgave him the debt. The forgiven slave then went to one of his fellow slaves who owed him 100 denarii, a relatively small amount. He proceeded to choke the one owing the debt and to demand payment immediately.

The fellow slave was unable to pay the debt, but the slave who was owed the money did not in turn forgive his fellow slave, even though the debts were quite unequal. Does this sound familiar? In the Lord's Prayer, we ask to be forgiven our debts even as we forgive our debtors. In plain words, we should have a forgiving and understanding heart instead of demanding better treatment while we are unwilling to bestow the same regard to others. So, have compassion on the poor regardless of the circumstances that led to the poverty of either an individual or family.

Many read in Matthew 18:22 where Jesus tells the rich young ruler that he lacks one thing in order to gain eternal life and take it literally. He must sell all he has and give to the poor, then take up the cross and follow Jesus. The rich young man exhibits a sorrowful countenance, as he had kept everything from his youth forward and is quite wealthy. His attitude toward his wealth is obvious to Jesus so He tests him in this manner.

In today's world, we would not survive if we gave away every material possession that we have. But our attitude should be that it is all the Lord's anyway, and we would be willing to part with our possessions for His sake. We would have little to give to the poor if we lost our income, and the word *gives* indicates a continuation of giving rather than to hand it all out at one time and have nothing left to survive upon. If we are to give everything away, and everyone did so, the world would cease to exist as we know it today.

There are many conditions leading to being poor. Some may be avoidable while others may be attributed to 'bad luck.' Some notable and common reasons lie in conditions of poor physical or mental health or business reverses that wipe out the monetary resources accumulated perhaps over a lengthy span of time, or a multitude of other issues that may afflict humans. The latter reasons for poverty are becoming more common today, but may be due to overextending oneself in borrowing money without the means to repay it. Could you imagine the representative of a bank or other financial institution saying, "Your debt is forgiven?" That representative would no longer have a job!

Scriptural Perspective on Tithing

Since Jesus stated that the poor would be with us always, it appears to some that He has relegated certain persons to the eternal realm of the poor. This would indicate that certain persons can do nothing about their respective stations in life where they are without significant resources. But this belief would appear to be dispelled by other verses of Scripture that appear throughout the Holy Bible. The most oft-quoted Scripture comes from Malachi 2:10 which states, "Bring ye all of the tithes into the storehouse, that there may be meat in mine house, and prove me now herewith, saith the Lord of Hosts, if I will not open [to] you the windows of heaven, and pour you out a blessing, that there shall not be room enough to receive it (KJV)."

Note that the words of God state "mine house" and not "thine house." The purpose of tithes as food in God's House is to finance the ministry of the local church and this use of money and tithed by the believer extends into local and foreign missions. God said to bring the tithes to the local place of worship so there could be meat in His house. Those who receive teaching and preaching from dedicated ministers and their support staffs should support these servants of God financially. Giving to charitable organizations is certainly laudable, but should not be a substitute for tithing in order to get to the prescribed 10 percent tithe for all income.

We are admonished by God in Galatians 6:6 with the words "Let him who is taught the Word share in all good things with him who teaches." Some denominations require that the pastor and other workers within the church carry on with a full-time paid job, and to perform the work of the Church as a part-time position. This does not seem to be in accordance with the previous scripture or the words in Acts 6:4, "but we will give ourselves continually to prayer and to the ministry of the word." However, I do not condemn churches who have certain beliefs or do not have the resources to pay a full time salary and the pastor finds it necessary to work.

Financial support from members of the local church serves to allow the pastor to engage in full-time ministry of the Word along with unceasing prayer. In I Thessalonian 5:17, the words "Pray without ceasing" are found. Although we can pray sporadically throughout the day while on the job, it is difficult to properly meditate while fulfilling the performance requirements of most jobs. In addition, it should be remembered that we are to care for the poor and a substantial portion of the tithes of many churches go for mission efforts, including programs to aid the poor of the local community and around the world.

Tithing is not a get-rich-quick scheme. We should not give in order to receive a reward. We should tithe of our own free will because it is the right thing to do for supporting God's work. Sometimes the rewards of being a "good steward" of one's possessions, including money, will not come until after sometimes years of practicing regular giving according to God's plan. Some begin to tithe with good intentions, but quickly abandon the practice when visible results do not occur within a short time.

In one example, a man explains his decision to quit tithing due to the circumstances for what seemed to be a better option. He stated simply that tithing was not working for him. He was supporting his family with funds from an insurance settlement coupled with his wife's Social Security disability payments which were awarded as a result of chronic pain resulting from an automobile accident. These funds were insufficient for meeting their basic needs, where the needs exceeded the amount of income he and his wife were receiving for the money required for house payments, food and utilities. So rather than allowing God to work in their lives, they accepted additional governmental funds for food, subsidized housing, and medical insurance paid by the taxpayers.

One person reports that he and his wife have tithed by giving offerings even when they only had $30 with which to support their family of five for one week (I cannot begin to understand how this was accomplished). In miraculous ways God has provided for food and the other basic needs for their family in ways that they could not fathom. Over the years, He faithfully honors His promises, even though it was never easy to pay a tithe.

Our lives were fraught with doubts and daily wondering as to the wisdom of offering these very small amounts during our times of great need. We have been greatly blessed in the past over these early years of poverty. A number of people may even give offerings as a test for the Lord to meet their needs. However, this attitude is not what God wants and we are doomed to failure when we hope to profit through a businesslike investment where we expect an immediate return on our investment. We should not gamble with God's money and we should not give "seed offerings" that some "ministers" promise will increase at least a thousand times and we will be wealthy beyond our wildest dreams and expectations.

Seed Money

Not all televangelists and traveling ministers are sinfully

crooked and are trying to separate you from your money in return for a great deal of money or perhaps even improved health. Perhaps only a handful of these charlatans are those that promise a hundredfold or a thousandfold return if you will only plant "seed money" in their ministry and will be rewarded for your faithfulness. Some offer prayer blankets or other items that have been anointed by teams of dedicated and righteous people that are "praying without ceasing." The planting of "seed money" is not mentioned in the Bible.

Not all televangelists that ask for seed money are dishonest, but some charlatans have used the term "giving seed money" with the promise that the donor will earn large amounts, perhaps multiple amounts of increased wealth (or health) based on the amount of sacrificial gifts. Sometimes the instructions themselves that are to be followed by the donor of an offering are downright suspect. But God doesn't play games with us. For instance, a picture of Jesus may be sent that has to be returned within a certain length of time along with a donation in order for the seed money to grow. You may be told that Satan may place barriers in your way through admonishments by other persons, or may sow seeds of doubt in your mind to prevent you from receiving a substantial "blessing."

It is a duty of Christians to tithe and not to do so for the sole purpose of obtaining a large reward. Those who tithe have generally found success over an extended time period by being blessed both spiritually and materially because their hearts are right toward the Lord. It is important to first honor God by giving from the "first gifts." The meaning of the term, first gifts, relates to the offerings to God in which the youngest and best of crops and livestock are offered to God, and these gifts should be without blemish.

In Biblical times, earnings and rewards for working were not always compensated by receiving money. Much of the subsistence for a family came from growing crops and from raising livestock. So the giving of one-tenth of one's wealth to the temple priests was different at that time. So today's requirements for giving are generally described as one-tenth of the money one earns, and to tithe as a first gift above all other needs on which our money will be spent. Over the ages since man was wealthy or poor due to the amount of crops or livestock he had or didn't have in the past, most people now work for wages if they work at all. So a tithe is generally accepted as a monetary gift.

Abraham was one tremendous success story from both a material and spiritual perspective. By placing his faith in God and by giving one-tenth of his earnings or increase in wealth to God for his use in furthering the Kingdom, he did not think to himself that he would regret doing so if a drought or natural calamity occurred. We are urged to give sacrificially, but a significant amount for one person to give may not be a significant sacrifice for another person.

The widow's mite, found in Mark 12:41-44, was apparently all she had, and represented a real sacrifice, while those that were rich gave much more, but giving by them was often no sacrifice. Apparently those able to contribute more to the synagogue castigated the widow for giving so little, but Jesus came to her defense. The widow had given out of her need rather than from her plenty, as her detractors did.

A modern-day example of sacrificial giving is that of R. G. LeTourneau, who initiated an industry that produced heavy earth-moving equipment and even some specialized vehicles used in World War II. Many of the pieces of equipment used in creating our freeway and interstate highways were built using equipment from the Westinghouse plants that LeTourneau built.

As a young man, LeTourneau thoughtfully and prayerfully considered going into the mission field, fostered by his seriousness about his faith. But he was led to go into business and to provide the means for missionaries to minister to others. A missionary friend was the one who realized that LeTourneau could best serve God by using his talents to organize businesses and to make vast sums of money for use in furthering the dissemination of the Word. He followed a "reverse tithing" principle of giving 90 percent to the Lord and living on 10 percent. Of course, few people with family commitments make enough money to follow this principle.

Mitt Romney, a recent presidential candidate, makes a practice of giving 30 percent of his earnings to charity, which includes tithing to the Church of Latter Day Saints. As seen from scripture, we as Christians do have a mandate to serve our fellow man, and teach those who have little in the way of the basic needs of life to provide for themselves. It is ironic that those who describe themselves as politically liberal statistically give much less to charity than do those who describe themselves as being politically and socially conservative.

Those described as liberals believe that government should be all-encompassing in providing programs to serve the poor. It may be noted that for income tax purposes, charitable donations include offerings to churches. This mindset would actually violate the admonitions of Jesus to give to the poor. When money is filtered through official offices, usually only a portion of the money goes to benefit the needy while charitable and Christian entities often give direct aid that is often equal to 100 percent of the donations.

It is our willingness to sacrifice for Him that means more to God than the actual amount. The financial situation will vary widely based on the amount earned, the amount of wealth accumulated, and the differences in earning power based on geographic location, and family size. No less of a factor is the level of indebtedness that optimally would have been achieved prior to learning of Biblical management of money. Sometimes unexpected and drastic expenses occur that make it impossible or virtually impossible to give at all, but this should be considered a temporary condition and efforts to "catch up" should occur as soon as finances stabilize. So the greater the blessing to the giver, the greater the gift should be because of considerable assets above living expenses.

Due to these many limiting factors or variables, it would be impossible and non-scriptural to set a monetary amount for what constitutes significant giving for each individual or family. God sets a different standard based on our willingness to give, and not out of habit or out of a desire for obtaining a reward. In 2 Cor.8:12, it is the presence of a willing mind that leads us to give and not the monetary amount that God desires.

God, the Creator of all things, does not have to depend on his followers to further his Kingdom, but it is our duty and desire to give offerings that fosters the practice of tithing. Paul used the willing Macedonians as a model, and instead of starting with a request for money, in the manner of many who seek tithes, he gives an example of sacrificial giving. It is important that we realize that we may give significantly no matter how little we may have or how much we may have when all personal factors are taken into account as the gifts are relative to our possessions.

Possessions of Great Riches Are Not Always a Blessing

Money is not always a blessing, at least for perhaps most people. We have all heard stories of sudden great wealth, which was not advantageous to some persons. Many who win the lottery are in dire straits just a few years after this sudden infusion of money into their lives, with the money spent foolishly and for items which are not healthful. If we follow the scriptures, we must admit that God may bless us in many more ways than just with money. In fact, money is a curse if God is not placed ahead of money, possessions and everything else we "own."

Of course, God owns everything and he allows us to manage his possessions. Some lasting blessings may be in the form of financial security, but real security lies in peace and joy that comes from following and obeying God. The blessings of giving to God far outweigh any financial rewards that we receive in our lives. God has blessed many families for tithing by bestowing health, security and the things we need for a secure life. He has taken refrigerators that are empty and vacant freezers from empty to overflowing in inexplicable ways. But even if we have material needs, everyone should still tithe and give offerings, which may be above and beyond the requisite tithe.

Compiling a Portfolio 'Religiously'

Many investment schemes put together by the holder of the stocks, bonds, etc., was done on a random basis, and does not mesh with future goals. Sometimes the purchases of investment instruments were made upon the advice of the person selling them, and he may be the only one who profits in the long run. A right investment decision is one that is consistent with a specific and Biblically sound long-term strategy you've adopted that is the correct one and not one that is a "good deal" or so you were told. The purchaser should be the one who decides on which instruments to purchase and should not do so at the behest of a seller who probably does not have your best interests at heart.

You as the investor should be the **initiator** or the one planning for the development of an individual investment strategy tailored to your goals. One should not react to an advertisement or phone call as a **responder.** Those who react to sales calls and make investment decisions individually for each stock being analyzed are actually aiding the person selling the instruments and not oneself. The appropriate investments can be more rationally made when the investor educates himself as to his goals and his strategies and then perhaps by seeking expert advice.

The right investment step is the one where you as the investor seeks out and knows how your investment strategy will fit with the overall plan to match your goals. How do you know when you are making the right decision in choosing investment strategies? Be assured that the correct investment decision is one where you've taken time to pray and to seek counsel from trusted, experienced professionals. Remember that your decisions have a long-term impact and you should take adequate time without hurrying to become informed about the steps you are anticipating.

Of course, hindsight is 20-20, and we cannot predict the future. Even when we prayerfully consider an investment strategy or opportunity, we may still lose on some of our investments because we are all human, even Christian advisers who are capable and caring. You will suffer from buyer's remorse at times, and may frequently lament your failure to buy certain investment instruments that prove to rapidly rise in value. This happens to everyone and for each loss you should have a win in the long run.

Remember the majority of stocks will rise in value over time, but not as a steady gain, but will have gains and losses over a long period of time. Those who sell stocks, annuities, bonds, etc., may practically promise a great yield, but you cannot hold them to their promises. We do not know the future with any degree of certainty, so it is obvious that no investment portfolio can ever be perfectly in a position for us to profit from future events. So the correct portfolio is one where the investor realistically faces where he or she is at the current time and looks years ahead to the place wished for.

PART IV:
What Does It Mean To Be Wealthy and Sustain the Accrued Wealth?

What is the Difference in Being Rich or Being Wealthy?

Either one of these conditions is good unless you are one of the rare persons who does not enjoy financial security. In both categories, one would be able to provide for the daily needs of him or her and a family. In addition, there would be an accumulation of money, goods and property that could be used for improving the lifestyle of the person so blessed. Unless one's dreams have faded, or the barriers seem too great to overcome, this is the station of life for which most people would search. So, what are the basic difference or differences between being rich or being wealthy? Perhaps you have never considered this question before.

Being Rich!

Being rich is a current state of being that can happen overnight. They have quite a bit of money, but only have that money that may come from only one source. Becoming rich can happen in an instant, but at the same time it can disappear in an instant. Many categorized as being rich depend upon a salaried job in order to maintain benefits such as health and life insurance and consistent income to pay the major costs of living. It is what they do with what is left that differentiates them from the average worker who spends all he makes. There are many who are rich but who never earned an extremely high salary and stories of these types of people abound.

Examples of those who earn quick money or who enjoy high salaries are lottery winners, new found celebrities and even high paid professionals such as physicians, dentists, corporate executives, lawyers, politicians and famous authors, to name a few. Now let us not leave out ministers of the Gospel. I am not kidding and there are perhaps only a few ministers with a broadcast system that goes into millions of homes who actually belong in the category of the rich. But at least some of these give most of their money to the ministry and to some charities. One example of this is Pastor Rick Warren of Saddleback Mountain Church in California, who authored the book, "The Purpose Driven Life" which sold over 30 million copies.

Here is an interesting thought! You might already be rich and not know it! Some people never calculate their net worth and when they eventually do, they find that they are worth more than a million dollars, which would put them into the "rich club." Most people who are millionaires do not exhibit any outward signs or symptoms of suffering from the malady of being rich. There was a book entitled "The Millionaire Next Door" by Thomas J. Stanley, Ph.D. (Nov 30, 2010). It is estimated in 2014 that there are perhaps 6 million millionaires in the United States! There are approximately 112 million family units in the United States, according to the last census bureau figures. So about 5.4 percent of the families in the United States are classified as being a member of a millionaire household.

I know a family well that consisted of 5 children and the mother and father. The parents had a tremendous work ethic and apparently instilled that trait into their offspring. The mother had grown up on a farm and the father had worked for his father at an early age and neither inherited large estates to aid them in reaching their financial goals. When the two married following college, they worked almost night and day in a variety of business enterprises, from a mobile home park where they rented the units and did their own cleaning and teaching in a local college. Other businesses followed and the children and the parents were driven to work almost incessantly. At the death of the father, one of the children delivering a eulogy drew laughs from the mourners when he said that they thought they were poor until he was 14 years old. Someone from outside the family apparently informed them that they were rich. And by the way this family was and is faithful in their service to the Lord and conducted their multifaceted businesses in a Christian manner.

Being Wealthy!

Wealth involves being rich, but being rich through ownership of vast assets, including money, items and other possessions of value and in particular real estate. Wealthy people do not rely on a salaried job as the source for maintaining their wealth. Their wealth may have been initiated by a regular job, but the accumulation of wealth often starts modestly with a job where certain skills are obtained. To gain wealth, a portion of the salary is saved in order to fund the start-up costs of a new business or businesses. Even natural talents are not used on a continuous basis by the wealthy, since business interests are often handled by hiring experts practicing in their particular field and providing valuable management and advice to their employers.

Wealthy people own assets and even those who work in the traditional sense of punching a clock would still be wealthy after losing the job. However, the loss of an income stream which is many cases is often widely varied, is possible with losses occurring in all sectors of the wealthy one's investments and businesses. The complete loss or almost complete loss of this income stream upon which a wealthy person depends would result in a rapid loss of wealth.

We've all heard of "get rich quick schemes" but never do we see an advertisement for a "get wealthy quick schemes" (actually to be grammatically correct, the phrase should employ an adverb and the correct phrase would be "get rich quickly." That is because wealth is gradually built over a given period in time. As an example, a large building is framed by girders and a strong foundation, before the bricks or other materials with which the building is constructed is carefully and deliberately tied to or affixed. So wealth cannot be built overnight.

Is the Possession of Wealth and Possession of Great Riches the Same Thing?

What's the difference between being rich versus being wealthy? Is there a difference and if so how can we separate the two similar concepts? Many people apparently equate the two, and give little thought as to being rich. This point is made by a famous comedian and actor Chris Rock. He discusses the differences with a down to earth soliloquy which unfortunately is laced with profanity, but does get the point across in a somewhat accurate fashion. You will find this presentation on YouTube, but since the video is full of racial humor and graphic cursing, it is not recommended for those who are easily offended and for those who are very young.

Many ascribe the fact that some are wealthy and others are not rich is based on the fact that some are *less fortunate* than others. Nothing could be farther from the truth as everyone is provided certain God-given abilities and how they are used is the most important factor in the wealth obtained by some. Remember that only 4 percent of those who are rich were born rich. There are schemes aplenty on the internet, by mail, and as presented in "opportunities" by professional spokespersons to entice those willing to spend some of their cash where large amounts of money are available for the taking. But wealth or even becoming "rich" which is a relative term are not gained unless sound principles are built, almost always through sacrifice and hard work.

Do you want to be rich, or perhaps wealthy? The answer by most will be a resounding "yes!" Just as it takes preparation to achieve riches (being wealthy or rich), it takes effort to maintain and manage one's money. To do otherwise would actually be sinful, and great responsibility resides in those who become rich or wealthy. Remember the talents of the Holy Bible? Even Daniel Webster as well as average citizens did not seem to have a firm grasp of the distinctions between wealth and being rich. For instance, "The Lexicon Webster Dictionary" defines "rich" as having abundant material possessions; well supplied; abounding; producing abundantly; productive; wealthy. This dictionary also defines wealth as: having wealth; affluent; opulent; ample; material possessions in all their varieties; "a collective term for riches."

The differences lie in the perspectives of the person being so adjudged. Very few people will admit to being rich, although they may have an abundance of possessions in money and materials of value. Those who are rich continually seek to gain more acquisitions and seldom stop to say, "I have enough, so I'll take my foot off the production accelerator." Those who are wealthy may also be hesitant to expound upon their wealth. But the very wealthy usually show their wealth by a profligate lifestyle, and in some cases seek to become more wealthy than their wealthy friends and acquaintances.

But fortunately, those with wealth tend to make large donations to worthwhile charities for the sake of accolades from others. These charitable organizations would otherwise be unable to perform good works to the extent that they do. And in today's world, at least a portion of the wealthy appear to contribute vast amounts of money to their favorite political candidates, which for some is unquestionably done in order to be in the spotlight in the presence of powerful politicians. It is also possible that some of these political donors do so in order to encourage decisions by the government that will result in favorable treatment for their business interests.

Sustaining riches is sometimes difficult, and is often lost in succeeding generations, but the ability to maintain one's money and possessions makes the person wealthy sometimes after a relatively short period of time. Some who become rich quickly lose their money just as rapidly and are no longer even rich. Remember, being poor is a temporary situation for some and for those who are rich, the same is true of being rich. Before you become rich or wealthy, you should define what it means to you to be rich or wealthy. What are the first things that come to mind for you? Most people who seek to win the lottery do so to somehow quickly gain riches and dream of a life without a job, without cares related to debt, a bigger and more luxurious house, a boat, expensive cars, and exotic vacations.

Ironically, when one achieves wealth quickly, and seeks to buy more and bigger and better toys, happiness does not follow. This is particularly true if no plans are made as to how to maintain the newly obtained fortune, and none of the money is dedicated to helping others whether individually or through charitable institutions. When no plans are made as to how the money will be managed over the remainder of the recipient's lifetime, often depression and feelings of unease will pervade the person's mind.

I knew a woman, now deceased, who was given a large amount of money in a trust fund. A cousin received a commensurate amount from the same benefactor at the same time. This woman seemed to feel that the money would last forever, and she made several unwise real estate investments, spending large amounts of money on improving the real estate, and then selling at a loss. Several trips to Europe consumed a large amount as well as a number of other somewhat foolish expenditures, and at her death, nothing was left. The cousin carefully husbanded her wealth, and lived modestly, but comfortably. She to this day still has a sizable amount of wealth to keep her comfortable as she ages, as well as to perhaps leave an inheritance to her children.

Your Concept of Being Wealthy or Being Rich

The personal concept of being rich or being wealthy varies greatly from person to person. For instance, as stated before, some people never 'feel' rich or wealthy. For some there is never enough and these people constantly seek ways to make more money and to pile up possessions. This urge in some is so strong, even up to the last years of a person's life, that it must be genetically enhanced. I watched an interview of a man who was approaching 100 years of age and who possessed great wealth. He stated that his first waking thought was how to make another million dollars, and that this made him extremely happy.

Some persons may be extremely fortunate and become wealthy overnight, typically from an inheritance or from winning that elusive lottery. You have heard of someone with the Midas Touch, where everything the individual touches turns to gold. This is an atypical personality for most, but we all know of those who began with only a few dollars and spent countless hours pursuing riches and/or fame, and becomes an icon of success. It is not unusual for anyone, perhaps everyone, to dream of obtaining great wealth quickly, and this author is no exception. To understand your attitude toward wealth, it is important to take an inventory of your feelings about wealth, if you hope to become rich or even wealthy.

Did you upgrade your list of material things by playing over in your mind a set of possessions you would like to obtain? Instead of merely thinking about a new car that is reasonably priced and utilitarian, did you envision owning a Lexus, Mercedes Benz, Ferrari, Bentley or even a Lamborghini? Did you crave a bigger house that is a mansion and the exotic vacations on your bucket list, even those you would take on your own yacht? Did you think of a varied schedule of luxurious meals, or entertainment through large and well-attended parties? How you answered the previous questions is important in determining if you will be merely rich or will become wealthy. But the ultimate question that cements one's attitude toward wealth is the one that really distinguishes the rich from the wealthy and is discussed in the following paragraphs.

Are the riches that were just realized sustainable? Do you still see yourself as maintaining an adequate lifestyle in your "golden" years? Wealth is sustainable and can endure for generations, depending upon the successors of the one who became wealthy. Wealthy people, through prudent decisions regarding their ability to maintain their money plan forward and make decisions where their money works for them. It is important to contract with the appropriate professionals early in the newly found wealth status in order to achieve and maintain a desirable lifestyle.

Being rich can be a very good thing when it is approached in the right manner, but by the same token can be bad for some, as it brings out the worst attributes such as greed. Many who acquire wealth by whatever means, but particularly those who acquire sudden wealth, will be in worse financial shape in the future than before. When one stops working for money, the supply will eventually run out unless research and study of the "science" of making money work occurs for those who possess a sufficient supply for daily living as well as a surplus for investing. With the right investments your money can work for you on a continuous basis year after year. When a person determines a way to make his or her money work harder, one is on the route to success and wealth. Wealth of knowledge promotes wealth building education rather than an education in building riches, which is what is often advertised on TV and the internet.

Of course riches can be fleeting if the wrong decisions, or in some cases, no decisions at appropriate times, are made with regard to maintaining the wealth one possesses. Many persons dream of winning the lottery, an extremely difficult feat to accomplish, as the chances of being struck by lightning twice in a lifetime may be greater than winning a large lottery prize. For example, it is broadly reported that 70 percent of the lottery winners of the larger pots are bankrupt only a few short years following a win. Remember that all of them were "rich" initially but 70 percent didn't know how and didn't take the trouble to learn to stay that way by turning their riches into wealth. They didn't understand or perhaps even care to learn the differences between being rich and becoming wealthy by turning their quickly won riches into long term wealth.

Let us imagine that on the day before you became "rich" that you were one of the average American households that had been earning a salary of around $45,000 or slightly more annually. More than likely you will immediately think of yourself as rich, and you actually are, although a million dollars is not what it has been in the past. But almost assuredly most winners would feel rich after winning a $1,000,000 lottery jackpot. Would it be wise to abandon a job, even if the person does not find much if any enjoyment in his tasks? The answer is a resounding "no" for the following reasons. For one, a job keeps a person focused and helps him to maintain structure by adhering to a schedule. Secondly, in order to maintain some wealth without exhausting the supply in only a few years, the initial surge of spending stimulated by the euphoria of winning should be dampened. The bolus of cash should be used to maintain any kind of budget in place at the time of winning. The winner should keep a portion of the constraints on excessive spending that were previously necessary.

A woman with whom I am acquainted was involved in an automobile accident where a teenage driver crossed the center line and hit the car head on which my friend was driving. This was the second time the driver of the car that entered the opposite lane had done so, causing an accident, in the past two months. A very small settlement was awarded to my friend, but the occupants of the other car which was hit head on suffered a broken leg and lacerations and bruises. A settlement of $200,000 was given jointly to the members of the family who were injured in the accident.

The members of this family immediately bought three new cars of a rather expensive variety. These purchases practically exhausted the cash given them, but in a little more than one year the members of this family were unable to even pay the increased taxes and insurance on these expensive cars and they had to be sold. Imagine the results if the family had purchased a comfortable home in a good neighborhood and allowed a couple of older second hand vehicles to suffice for their transportation needs. They might have been well on the way to a life of comfort without the attendant monthly house payment. In the area of the country where this family lived, the amount they received would have been enough to purchase an extremely nice home at the time they received the money.

Another true story that comes to mind is that of a friend of my secretary in a position I held in the early 1980's. An acquaintance of the secretary was injured in an accident involving a train where the crossing was not clearly marked. He received several million dollars and immediately began to spend the money with no plan for how the money would be spent and for future needs. He purchased a mobile home and bought motorcycles for all of his friends. His friends enjoyed the money as much or more than he did, and in 4 years he had none of the money left and was again relegated to the ranks of the poor, where he had been unarguably rich just a few short years before.

In the unlikely event that you picked the correct set of numbers and won a lottery of several million dollars after taxes, it will take careful planning and adjustments in order to maintain this wealth for a number of years and to pass the remainder to one's heirs. A several million dollar jackpot would be depleted in a few years if no attempt was made to place at least a portion of the money in an instrument that would pay dividends or gain in value. Simple savings accounts at banks will in most years not keep up with the pace of inflation so it would be prudent to maintain an income from working even while enjoying at least a fraction of the fruits of the newly found wealth. If your income were around $45,000 per year from your current job and you received benefits such as health insurance and a retirement plan, it would be wise to hold on to the position at least for a few years.

Remember that the majority of lottery winners are sometimes destitute within a few years following winning, and you should not want to be in that situation. Assuming you did not change your lifestyle by more than a modest increase in spending, without some income from work and/or investment of the winnings, the money might not last more than a few years. If you assume that you would spend the money over a period of perhaps twenty years, if you hit the jackpot in your early twenties, you'll be out of money before the age of 50. Are you still thinking of quitting your job? It is not a good idea until you determine how much you will be earning from your winnings and how much your new lifestyle will consume annually.

Some who are *merely* rich will eventually reach the status of being wealthy, but most won't achieve the trappings of wealth because of critical mistakes made soon after obtaining the riches. Remember that if you become rich you should first strive to reach sustainability before any significant spending of the money occurs, and perhaps this milestone will eventually lead to your becoming wealthy. If you quit your job, you realize that you can only play so much golf or fish and vacation just so much per year. If you are like most persons who like to feel productive, you will quickly tire of a life of ease.

Many who get a bolus of money, especially those who are wise, will begin a business by investing at least a portion of the money in a start-up enterprise. Again, the difference between being rich and wealthy is sustainability and your riches will eventually deplete to nothing. Just ask a few of the people I will outline in this story who come from fabulously wealthy families but who are no longer wealthy. One of the unspoken rules of finance is that without sustaining your income, those who are rich but not wealthy will almost assuredly sink to a low level of existence over time.

Even if you won't win the lottery or be fortunate enough to inherit a large sum of money, you can still amass wealth starting with what you currently have on hand and what you earn in the future. It requires a plan and goals of small steps to eventually get to a point where you will have money that you can safely use in a variety of ways to make even more money. Becoming wealthy requires the knowledge to use that money to make even more. Having the knowledge, however does not automatically assure that the rich person will use the wealth wisely and will increase his or her holdings in order to strive for sustainability.

Just as is the rule that a baby had to crawl before he or she was able to walk, the same is true with investing in your own business. Those who intend at least to become financially comfortable if not rich will need to embark on a path of education regarding the basics of making investments in products or stocks that will work for the family or individual. Keep in mind the proverb: "Give a man a fish and he will eat for a day. But teach the man to fish and he will eat for a lifetime."

Nowhere does this contain more truth than with building wealth. Even those who are not in a high income tax bracket (euphemism for being paid high wages) can become rich over time by assiduously implementing a set of strategies that produce high returns. However, you must choose a reasonable strategy and stick with it, and must never employ one of the "get rich quick" strategies that you will pay for and that are advertised on TV and the internet as a "no-fail" and "no brainer" decision. Most of these "programs" will not bring success to you, and will take what little hard-earned cash you may have to "get started today." And if you learn to manage your business to make it work for you, you will be on your way to becoming wealthy.

But being rich, by earning a high income, is a function of how much you earn. Don't confuse being rich with earning a high income while at the same time drowning in debt, but by showing a large accumulation of money, property and other possessions. Becoming rich requires the knowledge to make money, but again knowledge is but a tool for obtaining wealth and is not the only tool needed. And after becoming rich, one must have the ability if not the knowledge to build true, sustainable wealth. Riches are unencumbered excesses above what a family needs for day to day living costs. So one should never spend more than one earns, and please relay this message to the federal government and to a number of state governments who are basically bankrupt!

Now I will offer a straightforward example of "rich" versus "wealthy" that leaves no doubt as to the major difference. There is many a professional athlete who is rich, but it is someone else who collects the revenues from the sports venture and distributes a portion of the money to the individual athlete. The latter representative is the one who is wealthy and not the athlete who collects only a portion of the revenues earned.

Many are rich at one time or another, but relatively few become wealthy, and this is in part because many do not have the vision to do the things required to become wealthy. History is filled with professional athletes who are paupers before they die. Joe Louis, the heavyweight champion who boxed from 1937 to 1949, was perhaps unarguably the best boxer of all times. But bad business decisions, graft by his handlers, and his charity toward his family members left him seriously in debt at his death.

While the owner may be truly wealthy, all of his money may be at risk. That is, unless he shelters a portion of it. I hasten to add that both the team owner or the athlete himself or herself can easily become less than rich or less wealthy in short order with one of more bad moves financially. Where a high debt level has accumulated, or the athlete suffers a career-ending injury and eventually becomes too old to participate anymore, the wealth status cannot be maintained past this point in life. The wealthy owner may suffer some social setbacks such as an expensive divorce or lawsuit and lose his wealth because he does not get the business endorsements or his team loses its competitive edge and no longer has a fan base to support the team.

It may appear that I am lauding the wealthy and that everyone should strive to become wealthy. Even if I did, there are many who would never get past the starting point. I am merely saying that if one has the vision, the energy and the knowledge to gain great wealth, the person will have the burden of sustaining the wealth. And most of all, the wealthy one has the utmost responsibility to handle the wealth in a Christian manner, where the money is used for the glory of God and the advancement of His kingdom. In addition, if everyone became wealthy and maintained that wealth, there would be no workers to perform the duties of the business enterprise, and everything would be priced at an ever-increasing level. But we should not prevent the pursuit of wealth by governmental edicts since little progress would be made in our nation's economic growth, which is required for the country to prosper and be able to provide the functions of government (preferably Constitutionally mandated functions only, of course).

Historical Loss of Wealth

I had often wondered who coined the phrase, "A fool and his money are soon parted" but had never seriously looked for the originator of the phrase. This statement until recently was attributed to the circus owner, P. T. Barnum. But it has now been discovered that the first apparent use of the phrase was by Thomas Tusser, a Sixteenth Century British farmer, horticulturalist, chorister, musician and writer, who first penned the words, "A fool and his money are soon parted." Thomas Tusser's most famous book, published in 1557, was titled *One Hundredth Good Pointes of Husbandrie*. (This work was amplified and republished in 1573 as *Five Hundredth Pointes of Good Husbandrie*.) It appears that it takes more intellect to retain wealth than to make it, although the opposite would seem to be the case. Apparently the traits necessary to accumulate wealth is unfortunately not passed on to the families of the wealthy one, as an inheritance, as shown in the next few paragraphs.

Inherited Wealth

History is replete with families possessing exceedingly great wealth and then leaving it to heirs who proceed to lose the entire fortune with little or almost no effort. The last phrase "without effort" is key here. And don't forget the famous actors and athletes who die almost penniless along with industrialists and business owners. Most families in the United States can relate tales of relatives who held vast wealth, or nearly gained great wealth but did not act in time when an opportunity arose. Some of the most famous family names in the history of our country are included in those who lost vast fortunes. In the 1800's, Cornelius Vanderbilt, a name many of us attach to great wealth, amassed through railroads and other enterprises more than one hundred billion dollars when adjusted to today's dollars. In 1973, a family reunion of the descendants of the elder Vanderbilt did not even have a single millionaire among those gathered!

Barbara Woolworth Hutton, daughter of the founder of the E. F. Hutton Company, to which everyone listens, and heiress to the Woolworth five-and-dime fortune was said to be worth as much as 900 million when adjusted for inflation. She died with a net worth of only $3,500! Why are those who inherit great riches unable to hold on to at least a portion of the money and perhaps property? The Wall Street Journal reports that an average of 70 percent of wealth held by one generation of a family is lost by the hands of the succeeding generation. And during the second generation following the gift of wealth, on average 90 percent is lost by this generation. The Family Business Institute states that only 3 percent of family businesses are still in the hands of a family member after three succeeding generations.

Invisible Millionaires

Millionaires lived in 5,100,000 households in the United States in 2012. The number of households in the United States stands at 114,235,996 so 4.46 percent of these households included a millionaire. Therefore the odds are that an individual lives in a millionaire household 4.46 percent of the time, indicating that one out of every twenty-five homes houses a millionaire! Current figures in 2014 showed the percentage of millionaire households at 5.4 percent. The differences are not due to a rise in wealth but to a rise in stock prices due to increased amounts of money in circulation, and is not real wealth increases.

In The Millionaire Next Door, by Thomas J. Stanley, the author points out how it is not so unusual to find a number of millionaires nearby except in the poorest of neighborhoods. And in some of these poor neighborhoods, it is surprising to find that illicit drug trade brings in unbelievable amounts of money, upon which no income taxes are paid. This is evidenced by the occasional publicized raid upon dealers' homes or other places of business with the confiscation of several hundred thousand dollars in some instances.

And of course, a million dollars today is not as much wealth as in the past and does not carry the clout that it did just a few decades ago. Today many houses in portions of the Unites States cost at or near a million dollars even in the average middle-class home. Most often, the elusive and unheralded millionaire does not have the appearance of wealth, and is frequently wearing average off-the-rack clothing and drives a car at least several years old. A modest home coupled with the purchase of goods from chain retail stores are the norm for many of these, since they obtained their wealth through frugality and common sense.

King Solomon issued a warning in Proverbs 20:21 that states "An inheritance quickly gained at the beginning will not be blessed at the end." As was true during King Solomon's reign, those who inherit wealth will most likely tend to spend the money on possessions, pleasures, or other purposes that are of transient value. The money is almost never invested to insure the future generations of equal access to wealth. There are numerous accounts of lottery winners and beneficiaries of other sources of great wealth who "blow" their windfall in short order, leaving them in worse straits than before the "intrusion" of wealth into their lives. This ready source of wealth tends to undermine the pursuit of accomplishments with a higher purpose. The 19th-century steel magnate Andrew Carnegie reportedly stated, "The parent who leaves his son enormous wealth generally deadens the talents and energies of the son, and tempts him to lead a less worthy life." Many of us have observed this phenomenon personally, perhaps not in our family but in others.

When heirs receive money without prior coaching on the purpose for earning and maintaining money, they will seldom take the time to understand the values that helped accumulate the value of the inheritance. Inheritors do not understand the blood, sweat and tears invested in accumulating the wealth. Nor do heirs with money have much motivation to develop a bias toward being diligent, experiencing delayed gratification, thrift, and other values needed to maintain healthy relationships with people who contribute to wealth accumulation.

In a modern-day example of wealth, Mitt Romney, Presidential candidate for the 2008 election, was widely reported to have received a great deal of money from his father, George Romney, at the elder's death. This turns out to be true, as it was reported by a number of publications and newscasts. Mitt Romney chose to give away that money to charity, and included Brigham Young University. During the presidential campaign, Republican chairperson Reince Priebus says that the younger Romney "gave away his father's inheritance" and this has proven to be true. The younger Romney stated that he had sufficient money earned at Bain Capital and did not need the inheritance. Most of Mitt Romney's current wealth has been earned most recently through his business interests in the well-known Staples office supply business. Therefore, in this case, the person receiving the large inheritance chose to earn his wealth the old fashioned way, and perhaps he will be more successful that some others in passing these character traits to the future generations of his family.

Most often there is a complete lack of purpose that would socially and/or personally benefit those who inherit the wealth from predecessors. Jesse O'Neil is the author of *The Golden Ghetto: The Psychology of Affluence*, and he demonstrates how money that is transferred to heirs who have no meaningful purpose in life is squandered. This "free" acquisition of wealth most often fosters a condition he coined and called "affluenza." Heirs often do not possess or appear to lack the drive necessary for a purposeful pursuit of a goal that results in an elevated self-esteem and self-worth. A heightened sense of self-esteem and self-worth leads in the cultivation of motivation, self-confidence, and a personal identity based on what one has accomplished or intends to accomplish.

O'Neil postulates that a vacuum is left by the absence of a healthy purpose in life that may lead to undesirable character qualities. The inheritor of wealth has often been unable to resist instant gratification, and the beneficiary often succumbs to the desire to own more and better cars, houses and other expensive baubles. The traits of that acquisitiveness accompany this impulsiveness and leads to an unwillingness to tolerate frustration, to feelings of failure and a sense of entitlement. Unfortunately, some of these same traits are found in those who seek governmental funds that they receive without making an effort to work for them.

Inherited Money Versus Government Funds

In either situation where inherited wealth and the "free" supplements from the coffers of governmental agencies are concerned, the progress toward worsening problems is the same. Some of these may be the avoidance of personal accountability and the more severe social disorders that lead to the commission of crimes and the abuse of drugs in an attempt to assuage feelings of personal and family failures. The presence of money sometimes serves as a catalyst to personality disorders and frequently the abuse of drugs and alcohol. Accompanying disorders often limit the ability to form vital relationships except superficial ones where those wanting to obtain something such as money from the one with wealth to spare become "hangers on." These "friends" tend to leave victims (the one who holds the wealth) unable to find a comforting sense of goal-setting and the wealth may be quickly lost in an attempt to buy friendships.

Parents may think that they can minimize the risk of affluenza by having an estate or financial plan with a clear purpose. Unfortunately, the purposes of an estate and financial plan (e.g., "transfer the business to my sons or daughters" or to "generate an after-tax retirement income of $xxx,000") are quite often too narrow to inspire and motivate heirs. Even if a plan is technically perfect, experienced advisers know that plans quite frequently are never implemented because heirs and advisers do not have agreement on purpose. When the plans are implemented, they are too likely to transfer money to heirs who quit their jobs and then live purposeless retirements without goals and plans for maintaining the wealth.

Dr. Gerald D. Bell of the University of North Carolina's Kenan-Flagler Business School details how heirs tend to drift into roles in which they play rather than work toward increasing their wealth or maintaining what they already have. Many of these pretend to be golf pros, skiers, artists, or writers, but lack the motivation to maintain the wealth by growing, preserving, or planning for the effective transfers of wealth.

Since there is a prevalence of heirs of wealth who have no goals, plans, or purpose in life, it is not astonishing that three-fourths of parents tend to worry that the lives of their heirs will be adversely affected by the inheritance bequeathed upon them. Estate planners who have watched inheritors over the decades will almost always agree that these fears are well-founded. Almost all cultures have evolved sayings that exemplify the loss of wealth earned by the parents or grandparents within a short order of time after inheriting the wealth. This loss of wealth within a few short generations is a verity and is not exclusive to any particular country or culture.

Perhaps in most cases there is at least a modicum of prosperity between the generation that actively achieved the wealth that initially extends into the generation that squanders the riches. In America, it is often heard in the words, "Shirt sleeves (working clothing) to shirt sleeves (back to laborers) in three generations." In Asia, where rice is a staple of the diet, families speaks of going from rice paddy to rice paddy in three generations (no gain in prosperity that can be measured). Europeans relate tales of the entrepreneur who achieved enough success that he no longer needs to wear clogs and then watching the grandchildren (third generation) as they squander the wealth that required so much toil by their forebears, with the phrase "Clogs to clogs in three generations." And in Italy, families who inherit wealth are said to go "from a barn stall (manure cleaner) back to barn stall" in three generations." A saying originated in China over two thousand years ago in the most succinct and venerable words "wealth never survives three generations."

What is the Midas Curse?

The most famous King Midas was at one time studied in Greek mythology in our nation's public schools, but in all probability is not taught to any great extent in the twenty-first century. The king had the ability to turn everything he touched with his hand into gold. Eventually he became quite unhappy as even his food turned to gold! This so-called curse came to be called the *Golden touch*, or the *Midas touch*. Today, you will hear the statement with some variations, "Everything he (or she) touches seems to turn to gold." This does seem to be the case with some people, but upon deep scrutiny, one will see that a great deal of thought and preparation preceded the fortuitous business transaction that brought in a great deal of money.

In a previous paragraph, one can see that the person acquiring the wealth would have to have the drive and the goal of living better than his parents. The generation that spends the least effort, if any at all apparently loses any goal or drive to better what he or she had had before. Frequently the loss of wealth does not even take three generations, but perhaps just a few years. Rod Zeeb and Perry Cochell, in *Beating the Midas Curse*, tell of a family that squandered wealth accumulated over five decades in only twenty-four months.

Only 1 out of 10 families successfully pass their unity and prosperity from one generation to the next. For as long as historical records have been kept, the three-generation cycle of boom to bust has been the painful reality for nine out of ten families. A century ago in Brazil it was 'from the stables to the stars to the stables' in three generations. Even when many diverse cultures are examined, there is only one tragic pattern of loss and failure that is common from location to location.

When watching your family's financial assets fade away, it is saddening enough, but it is worse when watching the emotional and perhaps physical damage done to individual family members. Individual achievement and family cohesiveness suffers in large part due to the failure of addressing the Midas Curse in traditional inheritance planning. Cochell and Zeeb determined that a significant number of families were failing to engage in meaningful planning for future generations. They instead entrusted the inheritors of wealth to protect the family fortune throughout the generations, but this seldom happened.

But in *Beating the Midas Curse*, the more important question centered on the 10 percent of families who continued to thrive and to prosper beyond the normal third generation. What were they doing differently that was effective? The book about the Midas Curse and how to combat the inevitable failure by the majority of families to turn the tide is the product of decades of research and practical experience with hundreds of families. These families included numbers of families that inherited various amounts earned at all income levels, from average income earners to billionaires. It details the practical, proven methods identified by Cochell and Zeeb that have been used for centuries by the 'successful 10 percent' to beat the Midas Curse. Start with the information in this book, and then begin your family's own multigenerational journey to greater unity, strength and prosperity – right now!

There are studies conducted in America that provide contemporary evidence showing that families still lose their wealth following the time-tested pattern regardless of the broad sources of information that could be utilized to prevent the loss. This trend is still present even though business conditions have changed dramatically since the example was given by the Chinese saying from two thousand years ago, 'wealth never survives three generations.' For emphasis, it bears repeating that almost two-thirds of families with substantial financial resources waste away their wealth by the end of the *second* generation. And by the end of the third generation, 90 percent of families have little or nothing left of the money received from grandparents. Eventually, 95 percent of *all* traditional inheritance plans result in failure of the families who inherit wealth to maintain it.

Historical Business Failure

Statistics collected from businesses started by family provide equally sobering results. Less than one-third of businesses survive at a significant level into the second generation following establishment of a business. In addition, only about 3 percent of these family-built businesses is generating a profit during the third generation. The entire world, including Australia, which has no estate tax to blame for the loss of family fortune, is also subject to the dismal lack of success found in family businesses. It appears that the two generations succeeding the generation where the wealth was earned do not learn any sort of lessons from historical data. In fact, more than nine-tenths of estate value will have been lost, and this third generation can relate very little in general as to how the wealth was earned. Nor can it demonstrate or extol the values that were instrumental in the initial success of the business during the first generation.

Does all of this mean that family businesses, which usually range from just a few employees up to five hundred, will always suffer the same fate? Absolutely not! Remember the 10 percent that continues to succeed? What did they do right? And, according to Automatic Data Processing (ADP), which uses payroll data to track U.S. employment, most of those employed in the United States are working for a small company of less than 500 employees, although most people consider that only large corporations hire most of the workers in the United States. ADP's data show that the share of employees in United States businesses with fewer than 500 and often much fewer employees is approximately 83 percent of U.S. employment. So this country can ill afford to lose these businesses, and the expenses of start ups for these companies are vital to our continued financial health as a country.

Even if financial wealth is not completely lost in the third generation, the vision is frequently lost and the progress of the business may be arrested. Family members without an effective plan to process the transfer of wealth to the next generation may have heirs working at cross purposes. Disruptive changes of leadership are frequent and may be merely power struggles through seeds of discord sown years before and that have progressively festered. It has been shown that wealth may be transferred, but personal values and traits possessed by the founders of the business are impossible to transfer to the next generation.

Conflicts that arise during the succession planning may cause a business to fail sooner than later. Planners that conduct meetings with regard to wealth planning invariably face arguments that often end with irretrievably broken relationships that adversely affect advancement of the company. Many businesses commonly begin to dissolve within months after the founder dies, and often there are no winners that arise from the struggles.

Loss of Drive to Succeed in Heirs

If as often occurs, the founder of a family business neglects to develop the next generation of leaders and to instill in the heirs the importance of maintaining the business and the element of trust within those standing to inherit the business deteriorates. Relationships among the heirs that fail to include those of the founder's core values, and fail to maintain the vision and goals of the founder will most assuredly lead to business failure. The surviving heirs often engage in a struggle to assume power and the loss of the leadership of the founder leaves a vacuum to fill, perhaps by one who is at odds with the original vision of the founder when sudden death occurs. Legal wrangling may go on for years and result in the loss of much of the value of the estate, where day to day business transactions virtually cease and the business enterprise never recovers.

As mentioned earlier in this work, 10 percent of the heirs of a family business will defy the odds and will maintain the original goals, values and a sense of purpose enabling the accumulation of significant wealth. But the heirs must be aware of greater future challenges to the continued success of the business. This is chiefly the danger of holding on to the fortune after it is earned and invested. The danger of business failure is elevated even if the next succeeding generation manages to maintain the vitality of the company. The odds of failure in the next generation of heirs does not diminish because the first succeeding generation maintained the company's progress.

As Ralph Waldo Emerson, Unites States poet and essayist from 1803-1882, instructs us, "It requires a great deal of *boldness* and a great deal of *caution* to make a great fortune, and when you have got it, it requires ten times as much wit to keep it." And it only takes a little research, sometimes including those who have been successful in business, as experience teaches us that it is difficult and time-consuming to accumulate wealth. But it is even more difficult to maintain it, and hardest to give it away prudently. But we are commanded by the Holy Scriptures to give our money wisely to those who most need it. But currently the transfer of wealth through the world is perhaps accomplished with little or no planning or forethought.

Therefore the traditional transfer process of wealth is most often ineffective, and the resulting problems could not have been anticipated and for sure would not be appreciated by the donor of the wealth. A family's estate plan should be established with help from a skillful and knowledgeable estate planner to guard against a repeat of the patterns just outlined. Family members that will be heirs to a business or other types of wealth should be able to provide a clear understanding regarding how the benefactor bequeathing the wealth would like it handled initially and for the long term.

The founder, often out of love and devotion toward his family, passed on his (or her) fortune with the hope that the heirs would be adequately cared for and could enjoy happiness and success from the founder's efforts. Perhaps unanimously the ones who pass the wealth to family members would wish them to establish and maintain healthy relationships rather than continually bickering until the wealth is wiped away.

All the family members along with unrelated business associates and legal and financial advisers should be in agreement as to who should receive ownership, management, and control rights for the wealth that was bequeathed to your family. Most persons will struggle to provide meaningful and well-thought plans regarding the future of the business and use of accumulated wealth. It is most helpful to clear up any misunderstandings particularly with regard to control of the company as quickly as possible, even before or at the latest, quickly following the passing of the wealth from one generation to another.

An appointment with a trained wealth counselor would be wise and often an unrelated person can clear up matters without the attendant emotions that may arise between family members. It would be prudent to work out the relationships before the wealth is distributed. This is necessary in order to help the heirs develop their relational values before they inherit their portion of the wealth. One should heed the wisdom of Solomon by transferring not only financial resources but by being instrumental in bequeathing a relational inheritance along with the financial inheritance. This should be accomplished over time in a manner that establishes a foundation for blessing many future generations.

How Can Success be Realized?

It is important to realize that success may be different things to various persons. Being successful does not always entail the possession of wealth, although many use the two terms synonymously. One can be successful in many things, and even happy, without possessing great riches! While financial success due to the accumulation of money and possessions that exceeds the amount needed for basic subsistence for a family is the most prominent measure of success, this is not the only element important in achieving "success." Peace of mind due to beloved family members and the relationships with the extended family causes some to feel successful. Complete debt-free ownership of the proverbial rose-covered cabin with a picket fence may cause some to feel successful, regardless of the real value of the cabin and its contents. Having time and talents to pursue their life's dreams will cause some to feel successful, based on what they desire in life.

However, a certain amount of money or at least a sufficient ability to otherwise obtain or continue to obtain, perhaps through work, the basic needs of life is necessary. A little more (or perhaps a significant amount more) in savings or in negotiable stocks and bonds for tapping into during emergencies such as illness or loss of job is becoming more of a necessity than ever before. Years ago in the United States and also in other countries, most families were self-sufficient and required little income from outside sources to maintain a comfortable existence. You will remember that this is still a factor when considering the amount of money needed in various parts of the United States and in other countries due to geographical differences. The costs of goods and services may differ greatly based on location and a family may be able to provide some goods and services for itself without monetary cost.

My earthly father, with whom I did not have a relationship until the latter years of his life, since he vacated the premises when I was just over a year old, never worked any job for a significant length of time. But his idea of success was quite modest to say the least. He would work when he had to and often lived in mobile homes or small houses owned by relatives. But he felt good about having a car, and the fact that he maintained insurance on the car was a status symbol to him. But he only had money for gas and simple meals such as hot dogs when he wanted them. But as far as I know, he appeared to have a good self-image of himself, although he never accomplished much monetarily nor did he ever expect to, but he seemed at least to be content.

PART V:
Building Personal Wealth

How Can a Family or individual Take Steps to Create Personal Wealth?

The first question that each should resolve is whether to pursue wealth. First of all the individuals or even the entire family must determine how he, she or they feel about those who are wealthy and of personally becoming wealthy. As strange as it seems, there are some who feel unworthy of doing better and that it is wrong to deviate from their family's historical path by changing the economic status of the family. As mentioned earlier, some feel that it is impossible to be wealthy as a Christian, and this can be a big barrier to confront and then cross to insure one that seeking to improve the financial position is not in itself a sin.

There are many who point out the following scripture from Matthew as well as the parable about a camel being able to traverse the eye of a needle more easily than for a rich man to enter the Kingdom of Heaven. "Do not lay up for yourselves treasures on earth, where moth and rust destroy and where thieves break in and steal, but lay up for yourselves treasures in heaven, where neither moth nor rust destroys and where thieves do not break in and steal. For where your treasure is, there your heart will be also (Matthew 6:19-24, ESV)." In this sense, it appears that the treasure must refer to gold and silver, precious and rare spices, jewels and other objects of beauty.

But we sometimes use the term 'treasure' as a verb where we say that we treasure our relationship with someone. And it is somewhat silly to think that we could lay up treasures of gold, silver, and jewels in heaven while we are earthly humans as it would be impossible. So what does the Bible actually mean? Apparently it means to store up good deeds and works such as kindness to those in distress, as we are commanded to do through numerous scriptures, as a guarantee if you will of our reward in heaven. But good works alone will not guarantee a one-way ticket to heaven!

If you define and discuss the American Dream, it seems that everyone is consumed with earthly treasure, as something that is tangible or is at least on paper and can be turned into cash or other material items. During Jesus' time on earth, those to whom Christ was speaking, and this was mostly to Jews, were very familiar with the phrases "heavenly treasure" and "earthly treasure." But today we seldom refer to deeds of kindness and consideration for others who need expressions of sympathy and material help as "treasure." In Luke 12:33-34 (ESV) and in Matthew 6:19-24, Jesus is apparently referring to the idea of treasure in heaven by saying "Sell your possessions, and give to the needy. Provide yourselves with moneybags that do not grow old, with a treasure in the heavens that does not fail, where no thief approaches and no moth destroys. For where your treasure is, there will your heart be also."

Faith is normally used as a noun, and expresses a condition such as in having faith or being faithful. But in order to build faith, action on our parts is required. In each situation we must trust in, or rely on something intangible (cannot be touched physically) to produce something that is tangible. When we begin with or persist in relying only on ourselves to accomplish certain deeds and to obtain results within the scope of our knowledge and skills, we have faith in ourselves. When we have this faith in ourselves as an instrument to accomplish what we would like to do, this belief is something with which to team up. We then have faith in our human intellect, drive and spirit with which we can become a team member. What we wish to do may be either good deeds or sinful deeds, and we have this choice as to which path we will take by teaming with God.

Biblical faith gives all of us the opportunity to accomplish wonderful things in ways we could not imagine and to an extent that we alone could not achieve. This section is written to inform the reader of the fact that there are situations at play that should be discussed before the "how to" of avoiding being poor or poverty stricken. First of all, being poor or poverty-stricken is a state of mind. This mindset is at best difficult to break, just as it is difficult to break a long-standing habit. But with God and a heart that is right, we can accomplish manifold deeds and be blessed accordingly. At first, there are those who will dispute this assertion that the most important aspect of being poor involves the mindset. But the feeling that nothing will ever change unless there is a miraculous gift from some long-lost uncle or that you win the large lottery you have dreamed of is common among those who possess little in the way of earthly treasure. But one word of caution. In the holy Bible, Provers 13:11, (The Living Bible) says: "Wealth from gambling quickly disappears; wealth from hard work grows." This verse exemplifies the message that is intended for this book to portray.

But being extremely poor, especially when it involves those without physical and mental handicaps, requires that one avoid thinking about escaping the trap of poverty through a sudden finding of wealth and dreaming of such occurrences, which is an extremely rare event. Rather, efforts should be taken in miniscule steps to gradually change one's approach to life and how it is lived. These can be very simple but must be based on a rational plan rather than merely dreaming of achieving effortless wealth. The hopelessness of being mired in poverty, sometimes for generations, is incorporated into the mind of the poverty-stricken individual or family. Without thinking, efforts to move into a more productive mindset take courage and hard work. This feeling of having no control is all-powerful, and is the biggest barrier to improving one's financial condition and in turn becoming successful.

In addition, one must avoid the common misconceptions surrounding poverty. I have heard many with whom I have had conversations state that wealthy or "rich" persons are just plain 'lucky.' I will admit that some are born wealthy and actual statistics indicate that only about 4 percent of wealthy people inherited their riches. And perhaps that is sometimes the luck of the draw, but it takes work and thoughtful approaches to life's circumstances and opportunities that avail them to maintain their riches. Previously, I wrote of the Vanderbilt family and others who lost their wealth more quickly than it was gained. More than one person I know has gone from wealth to a state of having almost nothing following a rancorous divorce or some other calamity. Each of these assert that it was a lot easier to go down the path to poverty than climbing to wealth.

Is Becoming Rich Just Being Lucky?

As a college instructor, I became acquainted with a number of young people in my class who believed that the government can solve all of the problems of the poor and those in poverty. I had informal conversations initiated by some of them who asserted that the obtaining of wealth was all a matter of luck. If these students were asked "Whose fault is it that some families and individuals continue to be poor or living in poverty" invariably the answers from most would be at least in part the fault of the government. Almost never did I hear an answer that considered the lack of personal responsibility as the primary cause for being poor.

As I should, I tried to encourage all of the students in their studies, and told them that they could be quite successful without any attendant luck or any heroic efforts by the "government" to lift them up financially. Often time and to emphasize my point, I would provide some disturbing news for my students. The message was that no one will ever rise above the category of being poor if he or she depends upon the federal, state and even local government agencies to meet the needs of a family or individual!

I could make the prediction that if the students in my program completed their course of study in an allied health field and became licensed the following would transpire. They should all be earning fifty to sixty thousand dollars per year if they applied themselves and gained some valuable experience. Many of them would still be in their twenties after a few years of working in the field. Some could not believe my predictions of success, but to my knowledge most of those from whom I occasionally hear have accomplished the goal of earning a significant salary.

As a sort of pep talk, I would relate stories of success from students I had known. I related one story about a chronically unemployed young man (a true story) who completed a heating and air conditioning program at a technical college and became quite successful. This was during the 1980's, so one must make adjustments in his or her concept of the value of a given amount of money in that time period as opposed to the current date.

This young man had a vision. After completing his program, he did not settle for merely going to work for small company in the local area. He traveled in his old truck to chains of grocery stores where his services might be needed on a wide basis since the groceries had multiple cooling and freezing units in each store. He persisted and after six months of effort he landed a contract to provide services to a large grocery chain. He was forced to hire other helpers to handle the unexpectedly high volume of work. He netted almost eighty thousand dollars during the first year of work. Can you imagine my astonishment at the response of one of the young men whom I was teaching? He replied, "He was just lucky because he was given such a rewarding contract!" This was notwithstanding his six-month efforts without income and often with little to eat and difficulty paying for gas before he reached his dream.

A common misconception of the poor is that those with some modicum of wealth was fortunate in obtaining a good-paying job, and accumulated wealth in that way. Most often this is far from the truth. Most persons who become wealthy worked more than 40 hours per week and did not fail to take the advantage to earn extra money, including holding more than one job. It has been said a number of times that the average person who becomes wealthy by whatever means worked close to 70 hours per week at least early in the quest for financial success. There is nothing 'lucky' about having less sleep, fewer weekends for leisure, and having less time for the family.

Thomas Jefferson once said, "I find that the harder I work, the more luck I seem to have." Hard work is almost always rewarded with more hard work and then the money may begin to flow. Those that have that sentiment often are like the cat who always lands on its feet after a short fall. There are many persons who have suffered a significant number of setbacks before reaching a goal by being persistent.

One prime example of this intestinal fortitude is that of Rowland H. Macy, Sr. an American businessman in the mid-eighteen hundreds. He founded four retail dry goods stores, including the original Macy's department store in Massachusetts to serve the textile industry employees there. These stores all failed, but undeterred, Macy moved to New York City in 1858 where he established his new store, R. H. Macy Dry Goods. On his first day of business he sold a grand total of goods worth $11.08, which is equivalent to $301.47 in today's currency. Note that this small volume of sales did not deter him. For he continued to reach toward his goals, and there were many people, including his employees who benefited from his perseverance.

Victim Mentality of the Poor

Most of the beliefs that are associated with the categorization of being poverty-stricken are espoused by those who have a *victim mentality*. What is meant by a victim mentality? The first time I heard this term was during a college sociology class, where those who are poor and on welfare showed a victim mentality when interviewed to determine eligibility. They had the idea that fate and even other people were against them from the start. But most of these people have the ability with the correct coaching to become self-sufficient.

Of course I am speaking of the average person who does not have lifelong handicaps of either or both mental and physical difficulties that would make it virtually impossible to improve his or her lifestyle and outlook on life. But there are programs for those with limited abilities, and many of these are privately run, who help handicapped persons to maintain their dignity and usefulness by engaging in some pursuit for which they are capable. And before we relegate everyone with limited capacities that began at birth to a state of poverty, the following true tale is offered.

A woman with syphilis and who has eight children becomes pregnant. Her husband has tuberculosis, a highly contagious disease that is easily transmitted to those who live in close proximity to or comes into contact with the person infected. Of the eight children, three are deaf, two are blind, and one is mentally retarded. When this scenario was presented in an ethics class, a professor questioned his class as to what would be the best course of action for the mother to take. After much heated and emotional discussion, the class arrived at a unanimous consensus that the prospective mother should seek an abortion. The professor then informed the class that if an abortion had been selected, the world would have been without the music contributed by Beethoven. And incidentally, Ludwig van Beethoven began to grow progressively deaf from the age of thirty, but still composed musical works for the remainder of his life.

What is Income Inequality and Who is Responsible?

Although this work is not intended as a political commentary, some current elected members of the federal government are becoming increasingly vitriolic about a topic called "income inequality" and those running for office in high positions of the government. Of course, there is income inequality, but what can reasonably be done about it? Should everyone make the same salary regardless of the preparatory requirements of training and years of experience? If this action were ever attempted, as some seem to believe it should, there would be no incentive to seek higher education and training, or to strive to succeed in the workplace. Then our country would not maintain a place of leadership in the world.

This has been tried on a limited basis and eventually was seen to be an unworkable plan. Some jobs are intended to be entry-level jobs for teenagers and those just entering the workplace, and should be viewed as just a 'foot in the door' to gain a more profitable position. This has long been a practice in the civilized world, as apprenticeships, some non-paying, were prevalent in Europe and the United States for a considerable time period before the well-trained person entered the workforce and earned a commensurate salary based on his skills.

Some well-known politicians, news persons and others in high profile positions have attempted to make the issue of so-called income inequality a sexist issue. A popular talk show host on a morning network TV station continuously stated on at least two occasions over a couple of days that it was disgraceful that the women made only seventy-six cents for every dollar that men made. He failed to complete the entire story along with the pertinent factors.

First of all, he rounded the figure down instead of up to seventy-seven cents for every dollar men made. In order to understand how half-truths arise, the figures were quoted separately for the *median* wages for male workers and for female workers in the United States. Since women typically are employed in retail sales, childcare, restaurant work and other typically low-paying jobs, the figure was undeniably lower than that for the median wage of men. However, men are most often employed in jobs with technical emphasis such as plumbing, electrical work, information technology, heavy equipment operators, etc. But there are some women who also choose these service jobs and do quite well with them and in that situation, they are paid equally with men, given equal experience and training. Therefore, the salaries proclaimed by this "newscaster" were skewed.

On a practical basis, those employed in retail sales and childcare are valuable in the economy and are an important piece of the economic apparatus in this country. But if these categories of workers received significantly higher wages, sales would be slowed, perhaps causing the closing of at least some retail businesses. And women who work would be unable to pay for more expensive private childcare which would consume a larger portion of their salaries than it now does.

Such a change in pay would almost certainly result in a decision for the women in particular and men to a lesser but increasing extent, to decide if being employed is actually worthwhile. Where women and men are employed in positions requiring equivalent training, experience, and education, both sexes receive commensurate compensation. This author has frequently been in positions where females actually made more than men because of in some cases, but not all, superior qualifications and more job responsibilities.

And to avoid belaboring this argument, but to respond to the misconceptions of some, the Hay Group was tasked to answer the gender complaints about equal pay for equal work at a major Southern University in the 1980's. The Hay Group is a well-known business which evaluates and compares salaries for a wide variety of positions of employment and is used by a variety of industries. The group was tasked to examine the differences in salaries for men and women based on complaints ostensibly lodged by female employees. In answer to those who say this story is not useful because of the time since it was conducted, I would say this. Along with record transparency and access to computerized data on salaries that is more accessible today than at the time of the study cited here, we would obtain similar results even today.

In the study, areas used for classifying employees chiefly included level of education and training, years of experience in the position or related position, number of employees reporting to each position, the number of tasks requiring planning, etc., and physical requirements, as well as other characteristics identified by the employer. Lengthy checklists were completed by each employee and data presented by the employees were verified. To the surprise of many, it appeared that females made slightly more than males for similar levels of education and responsibility of the positions being evaluated, so the data were considered flawed and was disregarded!

The benefits of the economic boom resulting in increased wages in the last decade, but which has abated during the past seven years, have been divided among all segments of the business community. But the boom has occurred in an extremely uneven pattern. According to a survey conducted by the Federal Reserve at the end of 2001 in the midst of the economic recession, economic inequality grew markedly even as incomes increased at practically all of the various levels. There have been numerous studies with reference to income inequality among several different racial groups over the past several years. These studies have attempted to explain how various socioeconomic factors or conditions affect income distribution.

Until the dawn of the 21st century, it was evident that there has been an apparent gap between Caucasians, Blacks, Asian-Pacific Islanders, and Hispanics in the United States and up until a few decades ago, there was certainly some bias. But the gaps now are chiefly due to differences in educational levels and experience levels. To a significant degree the differences are also present because of the work ethic which causes some persons to be driven to work more hours than others and enjoying less leisure time. The crucial question is whether the difference is statistically significant. The causes of the gap are not based on a systematic use of a pay scale that benefits one group over another. But the perceived benefits, rightly or wrongly, that one employee provides his employer rather than a racist mentality justifies the differences for some salary ranges.

Laws are in place to protect everyone and it is quite simple to initiate an investigation by appropriate governmental agencies that enforce these laws. And as an educator for students entering the health care professions as I was, it is necessary to avoid criminal activities or associating with those who are on the fringes of criminal activity that might result in an adverse record. Most licensing and certification agencies perform a criminal background check prior to licensing or certifying potential entrants into a healthcare profession, and will deny accreditation for those without a 'clean' record. As an instructor, a few of my students who did not divulge previous criminal convictions prior to entering into the program were denied certification or licensure after years of endeavor.

Governmental Contribution to Lack of Wealth

Some of you will wonder what the following information has to do with individuals and families that are poor or living in poverty. I understand why you would ask the question. I again want to reemphasize why it would be impossible to pay everyone or every family a large amount of money. Remember, it has been said that a democratic form of government will fail if the voters realize that they can legislate themselves a salary without working. It is a fact that almost half of the citizens of the United States receive some sort of government funding for their existence. And I would be remiss if I didn't add that some of these funds are entirely necessary for a number of reasons. But please remember that you will never, and I repeat, never going to gain wealth by depending upon the largesse of the federal and state governments for your livelihood.

The United States was formed with a belief by at least a portion of the founding fathers that the less government the better. There are two Americas today. These are divided into the 'have-nots' and the 'haves,' but some argue they should be divided into the 'do's and the don'ts. 'The voting public represented by their respective political figures is divided into the liberals and the conservatives. The liberal citizenry believes at least in part that it is a responsibility of the federal government to provide cradle-to-grave support for everyone, while most conservatives believe that each person should be personally responsible for his or her success in society. And I would be remiss if I didn't say that neither of these two groups has been always right 100 percent of the time.

Increasing Size of Federal Government

Bigger government means greater costs for administration of the government, and someone has to pay, as nothing is free. Differences between the philosophies of the liberals and conservatives have virtually shut down the federal government on several occasions during the past few decades. In many instances there is no right or wrong answer to a particular problem faced by the country.

But the size and scope of the federal government and even state governments have continued to grow in size and scope of power. As a side note, many do not understand that the misnamed United States Civil War that is known variously by other names, was not merely about slavery and its spread to newly forming states. It was a more intrinsic issue based on the increasing power and far reaching arm of the federal government, which encroached on state sovereignty, a belief which was alive and well at the time of the signing of the Constitution of the United States. And there are many, in increasing numbers today who are content to allow the federal government to control every aspect of the lives of its citizens, rather than to depend upon their own initiative to improve their lives. These people prefer the security by the government over the loss of privacy.

There has been a trend toward ever-increasing size of federal government since early in our history, shortly after the nation was born. President Franklin D. Roosevelt and his New Deal was only a small part of the bloating of the federal bureaucracy, but probably had little effect on the size of the federal government under which we labor today. Size increases under Herbert Hoover's four years in office actually exceeded that of Roosevelt's seven years under the New Deal.

Before the ratification of the Sixteenth Amendment which initiated a federal income tax, there was relatively little growth in the size of the federal government from 1785 to 1913. And at the time the Sixteenth Amendment passed, federal spending was only 2.5 percent of the Gross National Product (now known as the Gross Domestic Product). For the past 48 years the country has averaged around 19% of the GDP in federal spending. But since 2009, spending by the federal government spending has averaged almost 23% of GDP and the percentage is growing. A huge surge in the GDP occurred in 2009 and has not lessened since. In addition, deficit spending has increased since from an average 17.5 percent rate, but since 2009, the deficit spending is more than 52 percent, or 57 cents of every dollar spent by the federal government is deficit spending.

And before 1913 there was growth in power, but not in the amount of money available for spending. When the original thirteen colonies came together, the newly formed country was seen as a defender of the liberty for its citizens. This meant protection of each individual person and his or her personal belongings. At the founding of the country, most individuals saw the federal government as the biggest threat to personal rights and freedom, hence the right to bear arms by its citizens. But by 1913, the goal of the federal government appeared to focus chiefly on the nation's economic well-being.

Today the federal government is viewed by many if not most as an entity designed to guarantee the economic welfare of its citizens. The federal income tax led to continuous expansion of the size, scope and power extending throughout the twentieth century. But the initiation of an income tax is not the sole reason for the growth in the federal bureaucracy. It merely provided the means to increase the tax level and provided the means for financing an increasing array of 'services' at an expense ostensibly provided by all citizens, but this sharing of costs is not a reality. But as alluded to previously, the growth of the federal government based on legal and regulatory power began shortly after the formation of the United States. Constitutional amendments must have at least some popular support to gain the approval of two-thirds of both houses of Congress. So it would lead to the conclusion that Americans wanted an income tax because they wanted more government. And they wanted more government because they believed it would enhance their economic well-being.

According to the conservative view, the federal government should perform only those duties required by the Constitution, such as a common defense of the sovereign states. Included would be a protective system of tariffs to insulate the industries from undue foreign practices by selling products at levels less than the cost of producing them domestically. A common monetary system and a common language (although this premise is under assault) are generally understood as the major duties of the federal government. In the Constitution, the term 'general welfare' meant something different than the welfare system which goes by many monikers and is in place by both the federal and state governments.

It is a common belief that the federal government is in charge of the state governments and supersedes them in all things related to government. The opposite is actually true as the federal government serves at the pleasure of the states, and the states have reserved all the powers not specifically assigned to the federal government including those just mentioned. The federal government may be compared to the very large dinosaurs that roamed the earth many years ago. The larger ones grew bigger and bigger, much as the federal government does. They consumed more and more of the scarce resources that fed the smaller dinosaurs and animals to sustain their gargantuan size. When climactic changes occurred, as is supposed, the food sources were wiped out. The smallest dinosaurs were first starved out and then the larger ones could no longer live on what remained as food.

Just as was food for the dinosaurs, the federal government is sustained by a large bureaucracy and an increasing influx of tax revenues. It is possible that when the size of the government becomes too unwieldy and political winds change, that smaller businesses will be eliminated due to overwhelming administrative requirements. The taxes formerly paid by these small businesses who hire the majority of workers in the United States will no longer be in existence to sustain the government. And the government will no longer be able to survive due to a scarcity of revenue to feed the federal programs without squeezing more and more taxes from the workers of the country.

In a complex process initiated by the federal government in 2008, 2009 and 2012, a number of financial institutions and several automakers were 'bailed out' using taxpayer money. The term bandied about was that they were 'too big to fail' meaning complete failure would place the government in financial jeopardy with lost wages and tax revenue. There were some singular successes, but the only automaker who didn't accept these funds was the Ford Motor Company, and it survived the financial crunch of the Great Recession in rather good shape. The government is closing the accounts for many of these bailouts, but the taxpayers are still owed more than $200 billion from some of the most highly publicized bailouts.

In the European Union, which is a consortium of almost all the European countries, even entire countries required massive infusions of cash to prevent complete financial collapse. This is in spite of the fact that citizens of Europe are in general taxed at greater rates than those in the United States. In part, the higher tax rate is used to provide socialized services such as medical care. Even churches in some countries are supported by governmental aid and the churches are known as social organizations rather than religious ones.

One economic fact that surprised this author when I first heard it as a college freshman has stayed with me since. If the government (federal or state) requires more money, should taxes be raised or lowered to accomplish this? The answer should be a resounding "no" but many disagree with this assertion, particularly the liberal brand of citizen. And it has been proven that higher taxes do a great deal to decrease the productivity of industries.

Also there is a rule called the economic multiplier effect. Many factors affect this phenomenon, including where the money is spent, where the raw materials for a manufactured good are obtained (even foreign sources), and if the money remains within the community. One should be aware that money paid in taxes to the federal or state governments often takes at least several months before the money is returned to the economy. But money spent locally is most often used for purchasing goods and paying salaries, both of which stimulate the economy where the money is spent.

A number of factors dictate how much time elapses before the money is spent ("turned over" or spent for a second time) over a year's period of time. But for argument's sake, the answer is the general term of "several times," regardless of where the money was spent. Each time the money is spent for salaries or products, it is taxed a number of times through sales taxes, excise taxes, property taxes, insurance taxes (yes, there is a tax on insurance) and utilities (have you ever checked your telephone bill and other utility bills for the number of taxes included in the bills you pay?) So in real estate parlance, the money is "churned" and is taxed each time it changes hands.

Increasingly Common Use of the Term 'Trillion Dollars'

Just how much is a trillion dollars? We have become inured to the enormity of this numerical amount. The use of the term has been bandied about by the federal government, at least for several years, and some state governments even have budgets of hundreds of billions annually. A trillion is accurately described as one million million dollars in our economy. It is such an enormous amount that it would take one million days at $1 million a day to spend a trillion. To put it in context, one million days is about 2737.85 years, or more time than has elapsed since Christ's birth!

Another way of measuring the magnitude of a trillion dollars would be to place dollar bills end to end around the earth at the equator. The earth is more than 26,000 miles at the equator, and is slightly larger than the circumference at the North and South poles, due to gravitational distortion as the earth turns. It would take 256,964,529 dollar bills to accomplish this feat, so a trillion dollars could encircle the earth almost four times. During the years encompassing the 9/11 attack on the United States by Islamic extremists, Donald Rumsfeld, Secretary of Defense, on 9/10 announced that 2.3 trillion dollars was currently unaccounted for. That figure would count for roughly $8,000 for every man, woman and child in the United States! When the Pentagon was attacked and a wing was destroyed, records of transactions related to this money were wiped out, so no accounting will ever perhaps be available for the missing money.

Let's consider how many dollar bills it would take to reach the moon, a trip that was accomplished by NASA on several occasions. The moon is approximately 238,900 miles from Earth. A new dollar bill that would most easily be a true thickness if it had never been handled and soiled, would be roughly 0.0043 inches thick. If dollar bills were stacked to reach the moon, if it were possible, it would require roughly 3.5 trillion dollars! So with the money lost by the Pentagon, we could go two-thirds of the way to the moon if only we could recover it! The last updated and outstanding United States debt is in early June of 2014 was $17,544,581,789,209.83. At this historical point, it would only take 20 percent of the national debt to stack dollar bills to a height reaching the moon!

What if one wanted to theoretically line up dollar bills end-to-end to a distance that would reach the moon? How many dollar bills stacked end-to-end would be required to reach the moon? Only 2,513,280 bills would accomplish a one way journey when laying the bills end-to-end all the way to the moon. And to compare this amount of the current national debt, the result is astronomical. The length of dollar bills from end-to-end would reach the moon thousands of times. And to add another perspective, the *interest* paid on the national debt in 2013 amounted to $415,688,781,248.40. No individual or family could operate with a budget such as that of the United States government. Two years of debt service would amount to almost a trillion dollars or approximately enough to reach a third of the way to the moon!

So now the reader should understand why we can't print enough money to make everyone rise above the poverty level. There isn't enough money in the treasury to prevent everyone from being being poor. Remember that the more money that is in circulation, the more everything will cost. Some of you will remember the joke about the astronaut who was lost in space for many years, but finally returned to earth. He immediately found a telephone (a cell phone perhaps) and contacted his stock brokerage firm to find out the status of his investments. He was told that he was worth several billion dollars and in his excitement he ran about yelling, "I'm rich! I'm rich!" He decided to purchase a cup of coffee, a luxury he had greatly missed in outer space. Everything was automated now and upon making his selection of coffee, a metallic voice intoned, "Please deposit 2 thousand dollars."

PART VI:
How to Avoid Being Poor or Living in Poverty

Achieving wealth, even a small amount of it, is the most proven way to avoid remaining in the ranks of the poor or it could mean joining them if the wrong steps are taken in the quest for achievement of financial security. To insure a comfortable life, an individual and perhaps the family requires planning and careful use of the money available, regardless of whether it is little or much. A disorganized life in which one goes 'with the flow' and does not seize the reins and place any direction in an individual's life will lead to financial insecurity and almost certain poverty sooner if not later. So it is important early in life to formulate a plan to achieve success. This will help to avoid the missteps that may lead to financial ruin and a life lived on the edge of uncertainty. Many persons who were born into a family living in poverty have determined early in life to do what is required to avoid suffering the same fate as the families of origin in adulthood and have succeeded.

Unfortunately, there is not as much desire in this day to take the necessary steps and to practice delayed gratification for future success as there was earlier in the history of this country. Most people in this country were living on small farms up until a few decades ago, where work was long and hard and ease of life was absent. The entire family was conscripted by family members or 'evil' landowners who took advantage of those who lived on their land and were forced to work hard in order to eat and to buy clothing.

Today, we indeed live in a land of plenty where even the poor have more trappings than those who live in other parts of the world. Even the poor today expect certain benefits to be provided to offer a life where at least the fundamental needs for survival are provided even without working. But such an arrangement was not always the case when almost everyone suffered from a lack of even food and clothing at times, and housing that was basic and often crowded due to a large family would be determined as uninhabitable today.

And there are several unwavering truths discussed earlier that must be repeated for emphasis as well as several conditions that must be remembered and should be repeated in the succeeding sections of this book. It is true that not everyone will become wealthy even if one is employed in a meaningful job. But practically everyone can become more secure with the ability to obtain the necessities of life that exists when observing certain facts of life.

Another truth that has been evidenced over and over is that there is no one and I repeat, NO ONE, who will become increasingly successful and secure for the long term by depending on the federal and/or state government to provide the means for all of the necessary living expenses. Those persons who obtain governmental aid must use this help as a temporary solution to a long term journey and must seek ways to remedy the situation on an individual basis.

Governmental aid may provide a modest level of comfort, but the recipients of this aid for long periods of time will never advance past the lowest rungs of the ladder that leads to success. The governmental assistance programs may provide for food, medical care, housing stipends, and other services to enable one's life to be more comfortable, but that is the extent of this largesse. And it bears repeating that there are certain inescapable conditions over which the recipient of government assistance has no control. These may be chronic conditions of physical and mental health that cannot be improved upon. Those who are unable to improve their lifestyles due to disabling conditions must and should be able to depend on governmental help due to certain physical illnesses or emotional and mental disorders. But it would be better if social and religious groups provided this help.

In addition, as stressed before, those who have reached an advanced age and have few resources may be required to care for others unable to care for themselves. In these cases there will be restricted opportunities for work, education and training which would lead to a better financial future. However, it is true that many persons who have debilitating medical conditions over a substantial length of time became disabled due to lifestyle. But it is not the time to cast blame as the damage has already occurred. So it is incumbent upon us as a society to provide meaningful education to reduce the incidence of debilitating conditions.

It is quite common to see those who are simply too heavy to walk and who lack the energy to work due to their physical sizes because of too much food and/or the wrong kinds of food. Others have abused alcohol, cigarettes, food and drugs (both prescription and illicit) and have deteriorated to the point that rehabilitation would be very difficult or virtually impossible. But we must help these as our Christian duty even though they are responsible at least in part through ignorance and lack of initiative for their debilitated conditions. Everyone should be aware that foods of the wrong kinds and in large quantities lead to significant health problems, perhaps more than any other single factor. Some diseases related to the misuse of food are diabetes, cancer and a plethora of other health-related diseases.

So we are not discussing persons suffering from these medical and cognitive disorders when we discuss taking the proper steps and avoiding certain activities that almost surely will lead eventually to an inability to function normally in the workplace. And as a first step toward success, a person should do his or her best to avoid a lifestyle that will contribute to poor health usually at a later point in life. Remember, life is a journey, and the future must be erected much as a strong building would. A strong foundation and framework is then built out to complete a strong and safe edifice. Another thing to remember while we are building this testament to the Lord is that our body is a holy temple created by God and that it should not be abused.

Also, there are a few benevolent people in the world and particularly in the United States who may give some of their riches to deserving but poor people. In one instance with which I am familiar, a man who owned two paint supply businesses and had no children, left both stores to a faithful employee who had worked tirelessly for him for more than 30 years. However, this is quite an unusual occurrence so don't place your faith in such a windfall. Depending on this to happen would be less likely than winning a large lottery, it would appear.

However, it takes work to maintain this infusion of money and to make it grow. So usually it is a requirement that one must work with what he or she has received to take advantage of the hand up (not a handout). So one who is not thrifty with the money gained from a donor could end up again living in poverty or in a state of being poor in short order. This would be a situation similar to the third generation of those who inherit wealth and rather quickly lose their financial status due to poor planning and use of their money.

What Governmental Programs Can't and Should Not Do

It is important to realize that when the government attempts to help the poor and those living in poverty, the people of the country should also be involved in helping. There is a vast array of "programs" to help them, but providing handouts is the wrong thing to do if people need to be helped to become independent rather than dependent upon the productive members of our society. For instance, a boy and girl I knew were raised by their grandparents who were poor but proud. They felt that it was an affront to their dignity to accept "free' school lunches that would show that they did not take care of their own. The two children certainly did not take a balanced meal to school with them from home, but what they did eat sufficed to get them through the day. I recently saw someone carrying a poster and appeared to be a person who had it right. His poster stated, "Government, please stop 'helping' me!"

Sadly, these sentiments of self-reliance are not exhibited very often in our society today. The Digest of Educational Statistics, for the years 2001 through 2009, reports for each state the number of students receiving free or reduced meals which may even include breakfast and is rising. By rough estimates extracted from this report, one-third to one-half of the public school students receive free or reduced meals and the percentages are increasing in all the states with the exceptions of Arizona, Utah and Wyoming, which showed modest declines during 2001-2009. Reports from various school districts around the country, even those which had previously been upper middle to upper class in income have shown dramatic increases in the numbers of children eligible for free or reduced lunches since 2009. Part of this has occurred undoubtedly by the economic downturn and larger numbers of unemployed persons.

It is vital to point out that much of the increase in percentages requiring aid in getting school lunches lies in the declining economy where massive layoffs have occurred. And only those with the coldest of hearts would not believe that children should be fed. Several internet sites report that approximately 70 percent of students in the school year 2012-2013 receive free or reduced lunches. In some schools in a number of regions of the country free lunches and perhaps breakfasts are provided for *everyone* regardless of ability to pay. Now that would seem to remove the obligation of parents to care responsibly for their children. Unfortunately, when a program is initiated where no one is required to pay, the clock will never be turned back even when economic fortunes reverse. This is definitely something the government should not do and that is to take the responsibility away from the families to care for their own, amplifying the effects of moving completely into a *nanny* state.

Avoid Counter-productive Spending Behaviors

Everyone can cut spending by a certain amount, albeit for many this may be a miniscule amount. Assuming responsibility for ending poverty entails cutting habits out of your life that contribute to poverty. Unnecessary spending should be avoided, as many purchases are done as what is called impulse buying. Catchy ads and displays are scientifically engineered to get the most visibility and to entice further buying where other items in the same category may be placed on a display stand. In that way, there is a 'gotcha' at least two times. Food items, for instance are placed where they may be easily reached by children, and in areas where staple food items are found, so no one can miss the visual stimulus of a tasty treat. Don't spend money on things that are not needed. For instance, men will buy tools which they could borrow or find in a yard sale, and which may be seldom used if ever.

Always avoid paying the full price for an item that can be bought more cheaply. Wait for sales or when coupons are available for items you must have. Buying items at a discount store, and there are many chains of these businesses, makes a great deal of sense. Pawn shops and thrift stores may have just what you need, and items may be practically new. Yard sales and consignment shops are also good sources of bargain shopping. Internet purchases are generally much cheaper than those found in brick and mortar stores and shopping centers. As an example, I once needed a power cord for a laptop computer, and was told that the cord was $100 dollars in a computer store as well as a big box department store. I went to a store selling used computers and parts, and was also told the cord would be $100 even though it was used. I logged on to the internet and quickly found a new cord for $24 and some change, and it was the brand name item for the computer!

Buying Chances to Win (Gambling With the Lottery)

Betting on the slim chance of 'winning' such as for the state-run lotteries can be addictive. I have heard the phrase, "It only takes one time with luck" and "someone is going to win so it might as well be me." And it bears repeating that the chance of winning the big lottery is less than being struck twice in a lifetime by lightning. It is much preferable to plan for the future as your 'chances' are much greater when reason is employed rather than blind luck. Studies show that the poor spend nearly twice as much on lottery tickets than the affluent and it is sometimes called a volunteer tax on the ignorant. So in statistical terms, the purchase of lottery tickets rarely pays off and frequently contributes to poverty. When some states without the lottery were studying whether to get into the lottery game in the 1970's and 1980's, it came to light that the poorer classes of citizens in one northern state were spending an average of more than $1800 per year on lottery tickets. Sadly, only a few winning tickets for the big games were sold in a year.

There is another unintended consequence based on the adoption of a state run lottery that many are not aware of. The sale of lottery tickets actually cuts down on the amount of money spent on other items such as snack food and drinks. Since a sales tax is not charged for the lottery tickets, state revenues may be diminished and the attendant sales decrease for the businesses which distribute the tickets may result in the loss of a modest number of jobs. And there is one other consequence resulting from the sale of lottery tickets that I am sure will raise the ire of some who think they are benefiting from the sale of chances to win the lottery. This situation deserves a complete paragraph of its own, as follows.

The local committees were sometimes formed to study the effects of adopting a lottery, from which most of the earnings would be funneled into education. When speaking with citizens employed in educational facilities in other states, the messages relayed in no uncertain terms were that there would be less money for education than before once the lottery was adopted. More than likely you are thinking, "How could this be?" Please don't castigate me me for this as there are many proponents of the lottery, but having worked in higher education for many years, I will quickly tell you that many are seeking degrees and certificates who should not even have attempted higher education. There are more buildings built for the influx of students, along with staff increases, utilities and a myriad of other expenses. Many, if not most, jobs do not require college studies, but may require some level of technical training. Since many schools are operated as a for-profit business (online college programs, particularly) a decrease in the numbers of 'colleges' and training programs will not likely occur in the near future. Many of these programs provide questionable quality as to the knowledge and wisdom gained from paying for a degree for many of these schools.

Public schools buy equipment and supplies that in some cases are not needed because they are awarded the money with strings attached that it must be used for certain categories of expenses. This practice may sacrifice the old tried and true curriculum based on rigor and practice. But I will say that some dedicated teachers use their own money for certain items the school will not fund. Principals and college administrators constantly seek funding for better and bigger physical facilities and more staff, a practice that for some appears to be a status symbol for being the biggest and prettiest. How did this happen that we spend more on education that we ever did, with questionable quality of results even when monetary value is adjusted for inflation? I don't know the answer to this question and I doubt anyone else has the answer either.

Tried and True Methods to Avoid Being Poor or in Poverty

In the presidential election campaign of 2012, Senator Rick Santorum was asked the following question by a reporter. He was asked, "Given the crisis situation among a group of historically disadvantaged Americans, do you feel the time has come (for the government) to take special steps to deal with poverty afflicting one race?" I find fault with the question, but not the answer. This should not be a question of what is happening in one of the primary racial groups in America. First and foremost, the rate of poverty and worsening financial plights of Americans is not confined to one race, although the rates may be disproportional.

The rate of poverty has grown greatly in recent years after a brief decline during President Clinton's tenure through welfare reform led by Speaker of the House Newt Gingrich, in a somewhat rare display of bipartisan agreement. In November of 2012, the United States Census Bureau stated that more than 16 percent of the population of the country lived in poverty (not just poor) but living on less than $23,850 annually. One of the wealthiest states in the country, that of California, had the highest poverty rate at the time of 23.5 percent!

Rick Santorum presented his opinions as to how poverty could be prevented and perhaps alleviated using a 2009 study. His tenets which I have placed in an order that would occur naturally in the normal course of events in life. I have freely added to or otherwise modified his list of preferred steps in life. Only 2 percent of those living in poverty as adults complied with the following steps to aid in succeeding in life! So 98 percent of those living in poverty skipped at least one of these steps, and some skipped all of them. They are:

1. **Education**

Completion of high school as a minimum level of education should be the first and foremost goal of all young people. The United States has an appalling record for dropout rates, and of course public school and sometimes transportation to school is free, and even the providing of lunches (and sometimes breakfast) to those who cannot pay. This is through no fault of their own, since they are usually too young to work and surely had no choice in the matter of being born. In addition, being accepted in a job requires at least a high school diploma. In addition, ongoing and continuous training and pertinent experience is required in order to retain the job and to advance in the position, which should be a paramount goal of everyone in order to escape being poor.

2. Engaging in Sex Prior to Marriage

Becoming sexually active is not a simple biological function and is not an activity to be taken lightly, regardless of the appeal of casual sex that is represented in the media. It is a complex emotional and physical act with extreme consequences, including incurable venereal diseases and the beginning of a new life that requires 24-hour per day care for the first few years of life. And the job responsibilities of rearing a child does not stop automatically when the child reaches a certain age. The practice of abstinence and entering into a stable marriage is the first and foremost step to be taken. Sexual practice often occurs even in the early teen years and babies are often brought into the world to these children who are now mothers and fathers. It should also be stressed that those fathers, some of whom are older than their sexual partners, are never forced to provide for any of the responsibilities of the upbringing of these children.

Not everyone plans to or wants to be married, but if future plans include children, marriage should precede the conception of and birth of children. The added benefits of being married would be that a potentially two-income source of revenue before children are born to aid in accumulating a savings and perhaps a down payment for a home. So marry prior to having children in order to have two parents who are committed to raising a responsible child. Of course, having both parents at home does not always cause a child to grow up as a good representative for his or her community, but the odds are infinitely better.

3. Get a job!

Although I have been rebuked a number of times by significant numbers of people when I have stated that a poor job is better than none at all, I will continue this mantra. There is something to be said about learning a work ethic and gaining the experience to move on to other positions within or outside of the present job location. And I had heard over the years and then came to the realization that it is easier to get a job when one already has a job. When a person is unemployed for a period of years, a condition called *hard core unemployment* occurs, and it is difficult to reenter the job market since some of these job applicants may be perceived as damaged goods. In the early 1970's I began a job that paid only the minimum wage, which at that time was $1.40 per hour. But I spent time studying and seeking to make myself more valuable by becoming more skilled and by learning new skills associated with the job. Five years later I was making almost three times that salary because I worked hard and did a creditable job for my employer. I have heard that of those who start at minimum wage, only a very few are still earning the mandated minimum wage six months later.

Methods to be Used in Improving One's Financial Lot

It takes work to find the resources one may use in order to gain a better position in life. The applicant for financial aid must maintain an attitude of dignity and demonstrate a desire to do better when seeking help. This approach is in order to gain the most advantage from programs designed to give a hand up to those who are experiencing financial difficulties as well as help for other extenuating circumstances that prevent the full enjoyment of life. The following steps are ways in which to improve one's financial status.

1. The Advantage of Government Assistance Programs

These programs should ALWAYS be considered as a ***temporary*** contribution and may be necessary at some stages of life for many. They should be used as a stepping stone for overcoming poverty, if the funding provided by the program is used to pay for necessary expenses of living. During this time when assistance is accepted, individuals and families should seek ways to improve their financial situation even while receiving assistance. Remember that nothing is free, and those *evil* working people who pay taxes and businesses which are heavily taxed are forced to pay for this assistance by both the state and federal governments. Applications may be made to a number of governmental agencies with local, state and national government agencies for things such as food, healthcare, education loans and grants, rent and utility assistance. In addition, there are numerous private agencies who help with rehabilitation, food, medical care, child care and many services needed to gain a productive position that pays a salary.

Many churches and consortia of churches and other ecumenical groups provide food pantries, clothing pantries, and Christmas items for children as part of their ministry where they are commanded to aid the poor and the widows.

2. **Seek an Increase in Income After Providing Valuable Service to Your Employer**

This can seem a daunting task, but sometimes one is rewarded for taking the initiative to seek a wage increase. Some employers like for their employees to be somewhat assertive but not demanding when seeking more pay or benefits. Effectively improving your financial standing will require that you have a steady stream of income to do more than just cover the financial obligations that arise on a monthly basis. An increase in salary should be seen as an opportunity that in addition to covering living expenses it also allows a saving plan as an investment in a future that does not include poverty. You might employ only one of these methods to increase your income, but it would be best to seek and try several avenues to attain the objective of an income increase. After a period of satisfactory performance in your job, you should ask for additional duties or responsibilities. This exhibiting of maturity in your job may lead to a job advancement. If you ask for a raise in your current position, be prepared to justify the reasons for which you feel that a raise is deserved. Also, be aware of retirements and open positions leaving a job vacancy within your company or institution, and apply for a higher-paying position within your organization of employment when a position becomes available.

3. **Take a Second Job if Necessary**

The addition of a part-time job other than the primary position is an excellent way to earn extra cash for perhaps saving or investing part of one's income. This second job could be a component of a plan with the temporary purpose of overcoming poverty while providing for the future while you work toward a more permanent and full employment position.

Look for side work where there are small and quick jobs that can be performed for a fair sum of money. If you have a marketable talent or skill, then you can use it to generate extra income for overcoming poverty. For example, you can babysit, cook meals, clean houses, mow lawns, do handyman repairs or paint houses or apartments to earn extra money.

4.   **Alternatives to Occupational Income**

Yard sales are a source of additional income as almost all families have unneeded items that can be sold. Items sold in a yard sale are tax-exempt, as they are termed *casual sales*. For larger items, an auction of items on dedicated auction websites is easy by use of the internet. Smaller amounts may be obtained by donating blood and blood products such as platelets and plasma. It may be possible to participate in medical research studies as an example of miscellaneous ways one can increase his or her income outside of work. And saving is the same as earning, as Ben Franklin said, "A penny saved is a penny earned." Almost everyone has the opportunity to raise vegetables even if living in an apartment. There are vegetables that can be grown in planting containers. Large numbers of tomatoes are possible to obtain by planting a garden when land is available or in containers where land for planting is unavailable. If a small amount of land is available, it is possible to grow in season a large variety of vegetables in an area that is only 20 feet by 20 feet!

5.   **Find Instruction on Money Management**

When one is on a restricted budget, it is important that the small amount of resources be handled carefully by taking measures to organize and allocate any income funds available. ALWAYS remember to pay the obligations necessary to live before doing any discretionary spending. First of all, the house payment or rent must be paid. Secondly, food is necessary to maintain life, and is even more important if a family is involved. It is difficult to explain to children why there is no food. But remember that there are volunteer organizations that are willing to provide basic food products free of charge. Thirdly, certain utility payments must be made to avoid disruption of services. In particular, electricity and water are mandatory for basic existence. If you think electricity is not essential in today's world, try experiencing a power failure and decide again!

Meet with a professional in a financial institution to discuss balancing a checking account, creating a savings plan and using credit accounts. The internet is loaded with schemes to take your money. It is the time for utmost caution when seeking ways to handle your money. Do not bend to the promises of charlatans who only want your money for themselves. DO NOT invest in getting rich quickly schemes or in securities (stocks, etc.) that you cannot afford to lose, and at this time you cannot afford to lose any money. It would be best to keep your money in a sock or under the mattress, or better yet a simple bank savings account until you find the right place to place your money.

6.   Secure your future

Once you overcome poverty in the present by having the ability to pay your basic expenses of life, you have taken the most important step in saying goodbye to poverty and then you will be able to enhance your chances at staving off poverty. Now you will be able to take one or more of the following steps.

a. Insurance

DO NOT become insurance poor by giving in to the seductive words of insurance brokers, agents, and TV ads where of course your best interests are heartfelt by those who will profit by your mistakes. Research your opportunities for the following types of insurance.

Term life insurance is cheaper now and is cheaper when you are young and healthy than at any other time. It is possible to shop for insurance and to obtain a quarter million or more dollars of life insurance for less than $20 per month! If you have a family, this is paramount. In addition, if you develop a devastating illness that is terminal, you may often be able to cash in your policy for a portion of the payout that your heirs would receive at your death. NOTE: Currently life insurance payments to beneficiaries are not taxed on the money they receive!

Health insurance for you and any family you may have is also mandatory. If your employer offers group health insurance, it is a better option usually than an individual policy you may purchase. If you are in an extremely low pay grade, you may qualify for state-funded health insurance such as Medicaid. NEVER go to the emergency room for medical care except for a serious medical emergency, such as a life-threatening injury or a coronary attack. Most locations in this country have a basic emergency health facility commonly called a Doc-in-a-Box. These facilities offer basic care and may be staffed by physician's assistants and nurse practitioners, who are competent in providing most routine care at a much lower rate than the hospital ER. If insurance is not available for use during a serious or prolonged illness, even those with substantial amounts of money may be devastated. In addition, it should always be remembered that health insurance NEVER or ALMOST NEVER pays 100 percent of the medical bill. There are co-pays associated with EACH treatment or prescription to be filled, with almost all health insurance policies. The current Affordable Care Act's Bronze plan, a federally subsidized health insurance program, requires a $7300 deductible in some cases before the insurance "kicks in" and pays 80 percent of the medical bill. So one would need to keep this in mind when seeking health care and health care insurance.

b. Education and/or Training

What is the difference between education and training? Basically, training is based on how-to skills, while education provides a theoretical background that allows the practitioner of a skill to understand the 'why' of the processes, and the ability to troubleshoot processes required in the performance of a job. Most jobs currently require at least some training as the technological procedures performed in most industries are quite complex. So most job positions that provide a fairly generous wage require training and sometimes education beyond having a high school diploma.

One of the complaints by prospective employers is that those with a high school diploma today lack the basic skills that were required even decades ago. Learning advanced skills formally through technical colleges and schools, and to an extent in colleges, will provide more rewarding jobs than those that require little or no job preparation prior to entering the labor force. Job markets change frequently and you must be able to change with emerging technology and to research the industrial fields where growth is occurring.

Evidence shows that there is a marked difference between the salaries in positions that require a prescribed course of study than those that don't. So an education is invaluable to increasing your income and overcoming a history of poverty forever. Education provides the opportunities to enter into a chosen profession and to progress to higher levels of employment in even other fields than the one currently occupied, as many of the skills are transferable. The doors of opportunity swing wide for positions that would previously have been unavailable to you. Moreover, education better equips one to seek information that may lead to better health and investing, through a rather complex network of government aid programs and money management strategies. All of this should contribute to your ability to put poverty behind you and keep you perpetually out of poverty and perpetually in wealth.

c. Savings Account

A savings account for emergencies is a must. Such an account will enable one to cover repairs and emergency purchases when an appliance breaks down or a costly car repair is needed. Anytime you ask someone for advice when beginning a personal financial plan, often the first thing you will hear is that you need a savings account. But why is it so important to have a savings account? This section will explore the benefits and disadvantages of savings accounts.

It is quite simple to establish a savings account at a bank. Perhaps an even better option can be found at a credit union if one is available to you. Many of these are established for those who meet certain criteria, such as employment with given employers, but some are open to almost any applicant. In general, the credit unions pay a slightly higher interest rate on savings accounts and offer other services as well. If you are saving for the purchase of a vehicle, or even a home, a credit union may be able to help you in securing a loan if you have a good credit rating and if you have an account with the credit union. I hope that you are now aware of the reason for establishing a savings account for the peace of mind is immeasurable that comes from knowing you can pay unscheduled bills when they occur without assuming additional debt.

Safe Place to Store Money - Savings accounts are one of the safest place to save money. There are at least three levels of safety and protection that savings accounts allow.

1. First, savings accounts protect the saver from casualty losses. If you are in the habit of storing money in your house, you are at risk of being robbed or of having the money pilfered by friends and relatives. Money may be lost with no opportunity of recovery in the event of a fire or flooding. A bank has several layers of protection for your money, and it is most likely only a paper transaction anyway, as your stash of cash is not placed in a box on a shelf. And computer records are duplicated in case of a technical failure. Even if you lock up your money in a safe, there are news accounts all too frequently where an individual is forced to open a safe at gunpoint, or the safe is stolen and opened by force. I am personally acquainted with one man who had saved $1500 for a down payment on a much-needed vehicle. His wife obtained the code for opening the safe and spent the entire amount of money and had nothing to show for it a short time later. Shortly after this incident, they were divorced!

2. It is not easy to grab a handful of cash from a bank without thinking at least a little and to spend the money foolishly. So it is more problematic when you are required to travel to the bank and make arrangements to withdraw money. Before withdrawing any of the savings, the individual may have second thoughts about what he or she is doing.

3. In the event of a bank failure, which is more unlikely today due to a requirement for FDIC Insurance. Since the 1930s, FDIC insurance has made banks a safer investment to protect the deposits from loss. In situations where a bank mismanages your money, FDIC insurance since 2014 will protect the account up to $250,000.

4. Interest payments in small amounts are paid to depositors, although the percentage of interest paid is extremely low today. At least your money is making a little on your

investment, but if you keep your money at home, you will earn nothing more from it. And in addition a savings account will pay daily compounded interest which adds up over the years if you are able to avoid withdrawals.

d. Credit Cards and Quick Loans

When you apply for a cash advance loan, it is necessary to be careful about interest rates. Always read the entire contract and if necessary, ask someone you trust and who has the knowledge to understand the fine print (mouse type) in the contract before you sign the document. Interest is the price that you pay for borrowing money. Most interest rates that are charged by a cash advance lender vary. High interest loans usually come from credit cards and payday loans, which are risky for the lenders as they are not sure if you will pay back the loan. It is best to avoid any loan from these types of businesses. In addition, the quick loan shops where exorbitant interest payments are required, or those which hold the title to your car and will not release it until the entire bill can be paid. It is best to avoid *loan sharks* at all costs!

Credit cards may provide a great and convenient way for buying items without carrying large amounts of cash if used properly. But there is a serious risk, as many have sadly learned, when a card is stolen and used by another or when one's personal records are 'hacked' and illicit purchases are made. But if this occurs, you MUST contact the credit company immediately, both by phone and with a follow up letter to the company extending the credit card. The liabilities you will incur are quite limited if you follow this as RULE #1 if your card is stolen or your credit is hacked.

RULE #2 for credit card use is almost as or perhaps more important than rule #1. Many people look at credit cards as a cash cow and even carry several cards that are often used for routine purchases. Debt can be deferred for only a short time, and then it becomes impossible to make the payments on even a single credit card. Having a card or cards in your wallet makes it easy to buy anything you wish, but it is a surprise after a few months when perhaps several thousand dollars of debt have accumulated. Don't succumb to offers of interest free credit cards for a year or more, as it is tempting to get items you could do without on a whim.

There is some exception to this situation, however. Assume you have a large medical or dental bill, or one for an air conditioning unit or other large purchase. Obtaining a new credit card that is interest free for a year makes sense if you don't use it for anything else. Schedule payments so that you can pay the card off before interest starts to be added to the debt. But you must be structured to handle credit card debt. There are special cards that can be obtained for medical and dental expenses and applications may be available in the medical or dental office where you are being treated. Nothing but that particular medical or dental bill can be placed on the card. Then you can pay a monthly charge without interest and pay off the account within the allotted time. Never accumulate a large amount of credit card debt. If you use a credit card, use it as I do for convenience, when on a trip or when you have a number of small purchases. If at all possible, pay off the balance EACH MONTH for any credit cards you use on a regular basis.

There are many persons who are unaware of the rules for interest charges on credit cards and they vary widely between the companies. In some cases, when payments are in arrears, interest charges revert to sometimes larger balances that were financed. In addition, there are late charges and if the full balance is not paid, there are some creative charges by the credit card companies that may be applied to your account. So you should educate yourself as to the potentially huge amounts that will eventually have to be paid unless bankruptcy is sought. Some credit card balances are so large that when paying the minimum payment each month, it could take up to 20 or 30 years to pay off the balance! There was an old saying from decades ago that hold true today. Regarding the use of credit for simple purchases, the saying was "Finance a blouse and lose your house!" This statement sounds ludicrous, but think how much you might pay for a simple item if you bought it on sale, but had to pay interest each month on the item. It would no longer look like a great bargain! This statement was originally more appropriate, I would think, before blouses were made cheaply in China and houses became much more expensive.

e. Maintaining Good Credit

Remember Proverbs 22:1-3 (TLB), where a good name is to be desired before all other things. I would like to think this is also applicable where we are not considered deadbeats by creditors and potential creditors. Everyone has a credit rating or credit score, and the better it is, the better rates we obtain on loans and the ability to purchase big ticket items such as appliances, houses and vehicles. Equifax, TransUnion and Experian are credit reporting agencies who monitor the credit ratings for everyone, and even government agencies, insurance companies and financial institutions, to name a few receive ratings by agencies other than the three listed here.

In the verses previously cited, we are exhorted to choose a good name and to foresee difficulties ahead. I believe this would also apply to potential financial troubles. Verse 3 is most important in avoiding problems that could be averted.

1. If you must choose, take a good name rather than great riches; for to be held in loving esteem is better than silver and gold.
2. The rich and poor are alike before the Lord, who made them all.
3. A prudent man foresees the difficulties ahead and prepares for them; the simpleton goes blindly on and suffers the consequences.

f. Investments

Speak with a financial adviser about investment vehicles that you can use to increase even a small amount of money over the years into a larger one. It is prudent to find ways to make your money work for you, and it may be taxed at a lower rate than ordinary income but this type of advantage is apparently going away. When choosing a financial adviser, you should consult an expert in managing your assets who is not also in the business of selling stocks and bonds or other financial instruments to you. There are fee paid advisers who can instruct you on ways to research the stock markets and to spread your risks over several sectors of the economy. So if one or more sectors is in decline, the others may make money. It is not wise to buy only one type of stock as all stocks go up and down on a cyclical basis. This way you can make your money work for you as you seek to reach your goal of permanently overcoming poverty.

Retirement

If you have a job with benefits, invest in employer retirement programs. Even the smallest monthly investment will add up over the long run, especially if your employer offers company matching funds for the establishment of and contributions to a retirement program. It is never too early to start, and the sooner the fund is started, the more quickly the wealth accumulates as a substantial cash reserve. But in this day of fiscal restraint and the cautionary stance of many businesses, many of the retirement plans that were prevalent in your father's and your grandfather's day are growing more scarce.

But if you are studious enough to have chosen to work for a company that does offer a pension plan where you do not have to entrust the company with your own money, you are blessed. But you should not be secure in believing that you will have adequate income to cover living expenses when you reach retirement age. I know of two relatives and I'm sure there were others who worked for many years (in one case more than 40) at businesses with a "pension plan." They never investigated to determine the amount they would receive at retirement, expecting that the management of their respective businesses would 'do the right thing' and provide for a comfortable income. Imagine their surprise when they each received less than $300 per month in retirement. Even coupled with Social Security retirement, they did not have enough to do more than just exist. We know that monthly utility payments for telephone (and many have both cell phones and land lines) along with electricity, gas and cable bills will greatly exceed a low level of retirement income.

You should also be aware that companies fail and they are absorbed by companies with differing retirement plans. And sometimes unions are in charge of the retirement accounts for large industries. Historically, in some instances, retirement funds have been raided, leaving little to divide among retirees. Sometimes there is little recourse for retired persons and they must either continue working at least part-time to live somewhat comfortably, which is not uncommon for those who do not have adequate retirement income. So it is wise for everyone to set up a personal retirement account so there is sufficient money to enjoy the golden years of retirement. Then you can spend time with grandchildren that desire your attention and in addition, medical expenses usually grow during the later years of life.

There are many resources for setting up individual retirement accounts, and they are too numerous to describe fully in this text. Investments may be made in a variety of securities, so expert advice should be sought where you would set forth your expectations for your retirement account. Two pieces of advice should be part of your strategy when you initiate a retirement account. You should NEVER purchase only company stocks where you work for your retirement account. The chances of failure occurs where the stock goes down and you have no other stocks that may have increased to balance out the losses. Inspect the management rate for the account(s) that you set up. Some have extremely high rates of annual commissions and the annuity funds are perhaps those with the highest fees charged to you each year. They may seem small at only a fraction of a percentage point per year, but these fees add up to considerable amounts over a number of years.

I know of a real life experience where a young man with a family began to invest in an individual retirement plan shortly after entering into his third major full-time job. He did not make a large salary, but began to contribute a small amount of money from each monthly paycheck. It appeared to be difficult, but the money was taken as pretax contributions, so the income taxes for both state and federal governments were deferred until he began receiving retirement benefits. For example, he began with a contribution of $10 per month.

With a 16 percent federal tax on income and a 6 percent state tax, he was in reality only paying $7.80 per month for a ten dollar investment. As his salary increased, he began to place more money into the account, again at the pretax levels. Upon retirement, he had accumulated a balance of more than $170,000, which enabled him to withdraw more than $800 per month during retirement. All of this happened during 34 years of employment and he hardly realized the deduction from his paycheck, as he never saw the money anyway.

The investments were still accumulating returns on his investment, so he might receive the $800 or more per month and still have a sizable amount in the account for his heirs.

PART VII:
The United States and the Global Economy

No one can escape the realities of working within a global economy and some countries will flourish while others wane in influence in the global economy. Even from early in the history of our country, the federal government was formed in part to implement a tariff system to protect the industries within the United States and to regulate the monetary system. World trade has always existed, but did not have the impact that the large economies of entire countries depend upon today by working with other countries to provide for markets based on the availability of raw materials.

Governmental Intrusions into Private Business

There is practically no institution, company or entity operating in the United States that has not felt the heavy hand of our elected and appointed officials in various offices. There is little we can do except vote the miscreant out of office, and in the case of appointed officials, elect a new governing party. One of our founding fathers, Thomas Jefferson, felt quite strongly about the intrusion of the federal government that would leave the individual states with little authority, and these conditions are all too familiar today. Some of Thomas Jefferson's thoughts from around 1802 are as follows:

No free man shall ever be debarred the use of arms. The strongest reason for the people to retain the right to keep and bear arms is, as a last resort, to protect themselves against tyranny in government. The tree of liberty must be refreshed from time to time with the blood of patriots and tyrants.

You may interpret his thoughts as you wish, and we can sincerely hope that the last thought listed here never comes to pass. Apparently Thomas Jefferson had a strong aversion to a forceful central form of government, and worked to prevent the federal agencies from feeling superior to the state governing bodies and to impose its will on the states and the people residing within.

Other Thoughts of Thomas Jefferson Regarding Economic Systems

These statements were also attributed to Thomas Jefferson in the year 1802 and are appropriate for us to keep in mind as we take control of our finances on a personal level. I believe that the sentiments expressed by the following statements are at least familiar to most of you. It was certainly prescient of the great man to realize that some issues he considered problems areas and that we rail against today are coming true more than 200 years after he penned these words.

To compel a man to subsidize with his taxes the propagation of ideas which he disbelieves and abhors is sinful and tyrannical.

I believe that banking institutions are more dangerous to our liberties than standing armies.

If the American people ever allow private banks to control the issue of their currency, first by inflation, then by deflation, the banks and corporations that will grow up around the banks will deprive the people of all property - until their children wake-up homeless on the continent their fathers conquered.

When we get piled upon one another in large cities, as in Europe, we shall become as corrupt as Europe. Author's Note: I might not categorize Europe as corrupt, but other problems beset Europe, such as the attempts to deal with issues of unity in the European Union and with the influx of virulent Islamists into the cities of many of the European countries.

The democracy will cease to exist when you take away from those who are willing to work and give to those who would not.

It is incumbent on every generation to pay its own debts as it goes. A principle which if acted on would save one-half the wars of the world.

I predict future happiness for Americans if they can prevent the government from wasting the labors of the people under the pretense of taking care of them.

My reading of history convinces me that most bad government results from too much government.

State of the Economy

The economy appears on the surface to be getting somewhat better in 2014, but the rate of poverty has continued to rise, and has now practically reached a level that existed during the 1960's when President Lyndon B. Johnson declared his famous War on Poverty. Corporate profits that exist as cash on hand are today at stratospheric levels not seen in the history of this country, but this increase has been matched by a rise in the number of Americans that are receiving food stamps. It is also estimated by a variety of sources that more than 1 million school children in the United States are homeless, and this occurs in many disparate areas of the country.

The only area where a substantial increase in value has possibly occurred is in the housing market, but the increases in these assessed values resulting in higher sales figures are found only in the wealthier areas of the country. And stock prices are climbing sporadically, but much of the rise in stock prices has been attributed to Ben Bernanke. As Chairman of the Federal Reserve from 2006 to 2014, his strategy of printing more money kept stock prices afloat at levels beyond what they are really worth. So what would be the best way to measure financial success in the United States? Rather than the false picture portrayed by the stock market, which is soon bound for a major correction according to many experts, what is happening to the poor and to the middle class?

Over the past decade or more the level of economic decline and belt-tightening by the middle class in this country continues to go up significantly, but it appears that the reverses we are seeing haven't yet reached the next major wave of the economic collapse. There are dire warnings that the stock market is ripe for a major correction in which the stock prices reach a level more closely in tune with their actual value. When that occurs, the large stock holders will suffer losses of an estimated 30, 40 or even 50 percent of value of their stock holdings, and the level of economic distress in the United States will move into uncharted waters.

But if we look at how the average middle class American or family unit is doing these days, there does not seem to be any financial news to cheer about. At one time, the unique level of middle class citizens in the United States who contributed labor and had tremendous purchasing power was at the root of the success of the country. As poverty continues to experience dramatic growth in numbers in this country, the poor are not the only category of people who are experiencing difficulties.

It is indeed unfortunate that financial matters are not getting better for all of the Americans who are seeking to improve their lot. The top 1 percent who already possessed wealth are sitting on their wealth because of the political and economic climate and their net worth is rising (until the crash). In truth the 'lucky' 1 percent may not actually have a real increase in wealth, but increasing stock portfolios are only a result of perhaps the rise in stock prices even though they are being bolstered by infusions of cash from new money that is printed.

What Does the Money Supply Has to do With the Economy?

Should each of us as individuals or as a family be concerned with the supply of money in circulation in the country? Yes, we should, and for obvious reasons. As stated earlier in this text, when the supply of money in circulation increases, the prices after a short lag period will take up the slack and will increase at a commensurate rate. Why is an increase in the supply not a good thing so everybody will have more income? The explanation is a simple one. The money supply increases and after a short time the price of all goods and services increase (this is an economic fact). As the prices increase, the wage earner still has only as much purchasing power as he or she did before the income increase that most would experience. So no one profits from this scenario.

Of course, most people do not know the sequence of events that places money into circulation. A simple explanation of the manner in which money is printed and distributed is as follows. The United States Bureau of Engraving and Printing (BEP) is an office contained within the Department of the Treasury. For those who wish to learn more about this process, the Department provides a website filled with trivia and facts about dollar bills, and is quite entertaining. The Bureau of Engraving and Printing has more than 2000 employees located in Washington, DC, and interestingly has an office in Fort Worth, Texas. The printed bills, called notes, are printed exclusively by the BEP. Coins are stamped by the United States Mint, which has offices in six different sites in the country, and is also controlled by the United States Department of the Treasury. Both newly minted and printed coins and paper notes are then distributed by the Federal Reserve.

Have you wondered why the prices of goods and services seem to have increased greatly during the past several years? There is a good reason. The Blog of Huffington Post reported that by March 20, 2013, the former Federal Reserve Chairman Ben Bernanke has added $2.101 trillion dollars to the base of the U.S. money supply since September 2008 when the financial crisis first exploded. That is a 240 percent increase. The Bernanke Fed, that had sole control over the nation's monetary base (currency, coin and private bank reserves), is continuing its money explosion by adding $85 billion a month. Bernnke is no longer the Chairman of the Federal Reserve Bank, but will his successor continue on the path he has blazed? A time bomb amounting to 54 percent of the monetary base, $1.616 trillion, sits idle in the nation's private banks. These are excess reserves that the banks are not required to hold.

You might remember that earlier in this text we explored the division of all circulating money between every citizen of the United States, and each might only receive something just under or slightly in excess of $4000. So it could easily be seen that if this cash reserve were unleashed on an unaware populace, the prices would escalate wildly and there would be less money to pay for essential goods and services since the costs would rise exponentially.

The following are 21 statistics about the explosive growth of poverty in America that everyone should know. Michael Snyder, from a blog, Theeconomiccollapse.com report on April 4th, 2013, the following statements related to the declining economic state of America. Poverty can somewhat be ascertained by the applicability of one or more of the statements listed below. Please bear in mind that the following statements may have become even more dire during the past year and a fraction.

1. According to the U.S. Census Bureau, approximately one out of every six Americans is now living in poverty. The number of Americans living in poverty is now at a level not seen since the 1960s.

2. With the addition of the number of low income Americans it is even more sobering. According to the U.S. Census Bureau, more than 146 million Americans are either "poor" or "low income".

3. Today (April 14, 2013) approximately 20 percent of all children in the United States is living in poverty. Incredibly, a higher percentage of children is living in poverty in America today than was the case back in 1975.

4. It may be hard to believe, but approximately 57 percent of all children in the United States are currently living in homes that are either considered to be "low income" or impoverished.

5. Poverty is the worst in our inner cities. At this point, 29.2 percent of all African-American households with children are dealing with food insecurity.

6. According to a recently released report, 60 percent of all children in the city of Detroit, Michigan, are living in poverty.

7. The number of children living on $2.00 a day or less in the United States has grown to 2.8 million. That number reflects an increase of 130 percent since 1996.

8. For the first time in the history of the United States, more than a million public school students in the United States are homeless That number has risen by 57 percent since the 2006-2007 school year.

9.   Family homelessness in the Washington, D.C. region (one of the wealthiest regions in the entire country) has risen 23 percent since the last recession began.

10.   One university study estimates that child poverty costs the U.S. Economy 500 billion dollars each year.

11.   At this point, approximately one out of every three children in the U.S. live in a home without a father.

12.   Families that have a head of household under the age of 30 have a poverty rate of 37 percent.

13.   Today, there are approximately 20.2 million families that spend more than half of their income on housing in 2012. That represents a 46 percent increase from 2001.

14.   About 40 percent of all unemployed workers in America have been out of work for at least half a year.

15.   At this point, one out of every four American workers has a job that pays $10 an hour or less.

16.   There has been an explosion in the number of "working poor" Americans in recent years. Today, about one out of every four workers in the United States brings home wages that are at or below the poverty level.

17.   Right now, more than 100 million Americans are enrolled in at least one welfare program run by   the federal government (this is more than 31 percent of the population in the United States). And these figures do not even include Social Security or Medicare.

18.   An all-time record 47.79 million Americans are now on food stamps. Back in 2008 when the Obama administration came into power, that number was only sitting at about 32 million.

19. The number of Americans on food stamps now exceeds the entire population of the country of Spain.

20. According to one calculation, the number of Americans on food stamps now exceeds the combined populations of the states of "Alaska, Arkansas, Connecticut, Delaware, District of Columbia, Hawaii, Idaho, Iowa, Kansas, Maine, Mississippi, Montana, Nebraska, Nevada, New Hampshire, New Mexico, North Dakota, Oklahoma, Oregon, Rhode Island, South Dakota, Utah, Vermont, West Virginia, and Wyoming."

21. Back in the 1970s, approximately one out of every fifty Americans were receiving food stamps. Today, close to one out of every six Americans is on food stamps. Even more shocking is the fact that more than one out of every four children in the United States is enrolled in the food stamp program.

Perception of Workers Regarding the Economy of the US

Over the past decade, middle class incomes have been stagnating or declining, and the share of America's income pie going to the middle class has been dropping, according to the Center for American Progress. At the same time, the cost of many goods and services that middle-class Americans rely on has been going up. This fact has been borne out as evidenced by the decline of the median income of the middle class by more than five thousand dollars.

The recent loss represented a lost financial decade for the middle class during which its income fell for the first time since World War II, affecting savings and ability to invest more, according to a recent report from the Pew Research Center. And many middle-class Americans are feeling the pain; of those who say they're worse off since the recession, 51 percent say they think it will take them at least five years to recover.

The decline of the middle class has become a focal point of this year's presidential election. Each candidate claims his plan would put an end to the middle-income slide that accelerated during the Great Recession and still shows no signs of abating. But lost in the rhetoric about the decline of the middle class is the reality of the decline. Nearly everyone is aware that the middle class is struggling, but few understand how the struggle plays out in everyday life. Those mired in a lower level of income class see that those in the middle class who still have jobs appear to be doing well in comparison with their own lifestyles.

Facts Related to Income in the United States

The following statements that do not give credit to individuals are to the best of my knowledge common statements made by many, but perhaps in different wording. More of the citizens of the United States are now forced to observe what is going on in other countries. They should observe how policies adopted in this country must contain provisions for competition with industries in other countries if this country is to maintain any sort of competitive edge in being a forerunner in the economic context.

"Americans tend to think of their middle class as being the richest in the world, but it turns out, in terms of wealth, they rank fairly low among major industrialized countries," said Edward Wolff, a New York University economics professor who studies net worth.

The U.S. middle class was damaged greatly by the housing collapse that began in 2008. The median wealth (not just income) of families was $77,300 in 2010, a nearly 40 percent drop from 2007, according to Federal Reserve statistics.

Americans are also slipping behind in building wealth because wages have stagnated for more than a decade, CNNMoney noted. Median household income was $51,017 in 2012, down from $56,080 in 1999, according to the Census Bureau.

Kenneth Thomas, a political science professor at the University of Missouri, St. Louis, said other reasons why the U.S. middle class is faltering is the decline of unions, the off shoring of the jobs in the United States to other countries and the increased use of technology in the workplace. Some of Thomas' observations are as follows:

Although the United States has fallen to the middle of the pack when it comes to median income, the Credit Suisse Global Wealth report showed it is home to the highest global share of the super-rich.

"Compared to the rest of the world, the USA has a high proportion of the population with wealth above $100,000, and the percentage becomes even more disproportionate at higher wealth levels. The United States of America has by far the greatest number of members of the top 1 percent global wealth group, and accounts for 42 percent of the world's millionaires," the report stated.

"The number of UHNW [ultra-high net worth] individuals with wealth above $50 million is nearly eight times that of the next country, China."

In a column for **Yahoo**, author Rick Newman suggested the extraordinary wealth of the ultra-rich in the United States might be skewing some economic numbers higher than they actually are. "This may help explain why the economy seems to be gaining strength — on paper — yet millions of ordinary people feel like they're falling behind," Newman said. He noted that although Americans' total net worth recently hit a record high of $81.8 trillion, consumer spending is lukewarm, home buying has hit a new trough and an "alarming portion" of adults are no longer looking for jobs.

Very few people have ever been hired by a poor person at some kind of reasonable salary that would provide for financial security

Legislation cannot be done to the extent that the wealthy are phased out of prosperity and the poor will become better off Governmental benefits paid to a person or family requires sacrificial giving of taxes in many instances by others who are working

No one is given anything, including money and services unless it is first taken from someone else

Wealth is not created by anyone, even those attempting to climb the financial ladder, when a large portion of the money is taken and given to another

Wealth cannot be multiplied when one's wealth is divided and then shared with another

When half of the people become dependent on others and does not work, those sharing their rewards of working with others, decide they should no longer work and also become dependent on those that work

Myths About the Economy of the United States

1. Rich people don't pay any taxes! I have heard this phrase from countless persons who no doubt heard it from others and believed it. Joseph Barro in Business Insider, Dec. 13, 2013, states that it is true that rich people pay *most* federal personal income taxes and many poor people pay no personal income taxes and have negative federal income tax bills. A CNN article goes on to present data regarding the *federal personal income tax*, which is indeed paid almost entirely by people with high incomes. People with low incomes pay negative federal personal income taxes (that is, the government sends them checks) because of the earned income tax credit.

2. Social Security pensions are an entitlement program because the federal government says it is. Social Security, pensions are not entitlements, as they were paid for by those who were working and paying payroll taxes. Our government is currently considering paying Social Security to persons perhaps illegally from other countries who did not pay into the system, at least to any extent. And a worker who pays Social Security for only 10 years or 40 quarters is eligible for the same benefits that one who worked 40 years, or 160 quarters, will receive upon retirement. If a worker had the option of only conservatively investing an equivalent amount paid by a worker and his employer's matching contributions during thirty or more years of working, the retiree could live handsomely from the money earned by the investments in stock instead of in Social Security.

3. We are still a superpower who holds the edge in manufacturing and our citizens enjoy the highest level of living of any country. This has been found to be faulty reasoning.

But in an article from 2005 by Kenneth A Buchdahl entitled "Can the United States Compete in a Global Economy," the author offered the following observations. His first statement is quite disturbing and he states that with new economic trends, the United States is losing the global trade war and businesses, government and even families are retreating. We know that these trends have increased over the past decade. Nine years later, Thomas Heffner in "Economic Problems Facing the U.S.," December 15, 2014, gave an even more ominous prediction for the United States. He states that we are facing economic disaster to a greater extent than practically any other country has faced. Due to a lack of understanding, most of our citizens are unaware of the impending crisis, even though the signs are there. We continue to think as a superpower, but have quietly slipped into the mode of a second-class country in many respects.

There are a few reasons for this, and chief among the reasons lies in the fact that we do not produce nearly enough to sustain our own country so are forced to import most of what we need. We are selling valuable assets to others and assuming large debts in order to maintain a semblance of prosperity. At the rate and direction we are continuing, we will lose our status as a superpower sooner rather than later. Our international competitors will not cease in trying to make us completely dependent on foreign production while losing our slot as the most innovative country and borrowing massive amounts of money accompanied by huge interest payments.

We don't acknowledge that predatory foreign trade benefits our competitors and undermines our domestic industry. As an example, China manipulates its currency so that it is more advantageous for us to buy cheaper foreign products rather than domestic ones and this practice has cost perhaps millions of jobs. We encourage United States manufacturers to design, engineer, and produce in third world markets, particularly in Mexico and China.

What can we do to reverse this trend? We must develop a means for cutting production costs in this country in order to compete and to control our massive trade deficits. Improving technology to control costs unfortunately results in the need for fewer workers, which will exacerbate our pool of potential workers who are not working now. Regulations aimed at manufacturers in this country make it difficult to compete with countries which have few if any regulations governing their practice. Note that some products from China and other countries who don't have the safeguards the United States does, at times pose a health threat to our citizens. A number of harmful chemicals have been found that taint products imported from China. For instance toothpaste laced with the ingredients found in antifreeze and children's toys from China have been found that contain lead-based paint.

While regulatory systems and an increasing tax burden have resulted in raising domestic business costs, the fundamental problem is a result of three decades of documented U.S. trade and globalization policies that are detrimental to business. Burdened by these policies, American manufacturers cannot compete with workers who make much less than four dollars per hour. Even benefits paid to American workers may often exceed four dollars per hour for each worker. All of this has led to a trade deficit in the United States of more than 10 trillion dollars over the past twenty years. It has been estimated that for each billion dollars of trade deficits the country loses almost 10,000 jobs. Our current trade deficit for 2014 is 483 billion dollars, and an estimated deficit is projected for 2015 of 583 billion dollars, or more than a trillion dollars in two years. So the math for lost jobs is astronomical.

We should be careful in managing access to the markets in the United States, holding the other countries to standards developed to protect the environment and the health and safety of the workers. These standards dramatically affect the cost of production and goods produced in all countries that have the same attached costs of these protective measures. Any country that does not abide by these standards has an unfair competitive advantage. Child labor is still prevalent in some parts of the world and China does not have to abide by the pollution controls now in effect in the United States until 2030! As a graphic example, China's power production is slated to double by 2030 and their pollution in cities is at 75 micrograms per cubic meter, or three times the acceptable level set by the World Health Organization. All of these issues lead to lower costs of production, so there is not a level playing field for all countries in these matters.

Several free trade agreements exist such as the North American Free Trade Agreement between the United States, Canada and Mexico. This trade agreement was to eventually reduce the collection of tariffs between the three countries, but one unexpected result is that it has cost the United States a significant number of jobs. This is a matter that was supposed to be solved by creating standards affecting production costs between the signatory countries. Our policies should carefully protect our wealth and resources rather than simply provide the lowest consumer cost regardless of the impact on our industries and our workers. It would be possible to implement a border consumption tax, which would be an answer to the VAT (value added tax) that is present in 150 countries, but the United States has no comparable tax.

And in a complex set of procedures, exporters in the United States are taxed on goods produced here and again when they reach their destination in other countries. Domestic goods are also taxed during production, and they must compete with foreign goods that were not taxed essentially at all upon arrival in this country. Industries in the United States have become so broken down that they lack the capacity and investment capital to sustain a profitable production line. Investment in a new infrastructure and new technologies are necessary to enable America to compete with other countries. This should also be of importance. Some countries do not respect our patent and copyright laws, producing goods based on innovations developed in the United States! We must insist that this practice be halted immediately.

PART VIII:
Tale of Three Countries

It is sometimes easier to learn about a topic when given differing facts and opinions in order to determine the best course of action. Economic capabilities and actions of two countries, India and China, are provided for comparison with the economy of the United States. Remember, we are a global economy now, and the actions of one country can affect the financial well-being of another country in a drastic fashion. Since a great deal of our economic competition is now with China, and China has taken a narrow edge as the largest economy in the world, it would be prudent for us to be aware of the capabilities of China.

Efforts by Countries to Raise the Standard of Living for Their Citizens

First of all, countries may make policies and programs available to their citizens that might serve to improve the economic lot of the people. Improving life for its citizens is and should be of importance for every country. But in the end it is an individual effort and initiative that will produce lasting positive changes in the lives of individuals and families. Secondly, we cannot separate the economies into segments of the world or a single country, so a discussion of the global economy must be presented with comparisons between countries to present a more complete picture. Two countries that have tested changes in governmental policies to improve the financial status of their citizenry are India and China. These countries will be compared with the United States to contrast differences between the three countries and the different approaches toward alleviating poverty. They have done so with varying degrees of success as will be shown here.

Comparison of Economic Principles of Three Countries

A comparison of the conditions in three countries will help to develop an understanding for the reader of differing conditions, demographics and demographic changes, and governmental efforts to eliminate poverty and to improve the lot of the poor. The three countries, the United States, China and India will be outlined to help the reader understand the challenges facing the people as well as the governing bodies as to steps that could be taken to perhaps aid people in their quest for individual success. Remember, there will always be some that are poor for varying reasons, and some that are rich and/or wealthy due also to situations in the lives of each category of individual or family. There are some things the respective governments can do to ease the transition from poverty to at least a comfortable living. But it should be realized after earlier sections of this work that the governing officials cannot legislate wealth for a substantial number of its citizenry.

Ethnic, cultural and religious practices and beliefs always either help or hinder the shaping of the economy of a country. The world is a diverse place, and even with widespread travel and the spread of new ideas, there still exists tremendous differences between countries. However, these countries must compete with trading goods that they are more adept at producing, perhaps owing to climate and natural resources, to the parts of the world which are more suited to the production of other goods and services.

The World Economy

We would be unable to describe a world with its complex economic interrelationships between countries without noting how it affects the individual, since many jobs depend on production of goods or raw materials that are traded throughout the world. The world economy has forged relationships between countries that were previously averse to dealing with each other on any matter. But it is an inescapable fact that countries must compete on a global basis in order to become more successful economically. They must also transfer this wealth to their citizens so they may reach their goals of good physical and economic health along with happiness. Although world trade began perhaps several thousand years before Christ's birth, it probably never occurred to these seafaring traders that they were setting the stage for global trading. They almost assuredly never visualized that this widespread pattern of trade would be mandatory for the countries of today's complex world without access to scarce resources found only in certain parts of the world.

What amounts to global trade has been with humans for thousands of years, as it included mostly the known world. But there were inroads apparently into areas of the New World and other areas of the world of which the United States is a part. The Phoenicians are credited with initiating trade, including the spread of writing and perhaps correctly so throughout the Mediterranean basin. Shipbuilding is still a craft practiced in this area where skilled workmen still earn their living constructing such vessels. It had been postulated that travel throughout the world occurred thousands of years ago, and exciting evidence exists to show this was possible and perhaps probable.

On May 17, 1970, Norwegian ethnologist Thor Heyerdahl began a trip from Morocco across the Atlantic in a papyrus boat called *Ra II (Ra I* developed problems and that venture was scuttled) across 4,000 miles of ocean to Barbados in 57 days. In 1889 a clay doll, about 1 1/2" in length, was brought up by a well drill from a depth of 300 feet in Nampa, Idaho. The figurine was found under varying types of strata, including fifteen feet of lava basalt dated at about 2 million years old. Many small clay balls were found in the area and the presence of iron on the figure's surface indicated the object was indeed ancient. Perhaps it was transported during the great flood. Web sites regarding ancient contacts in America have cited findings of coins from Sumeria and other city-states and countries, including coins found in Phenix City, Alabama, from several hundred years BC, and to a finding in Oklahoma.

The world or global economy is no longer differentiated as to whether it is global or not as the extent to which trade occurs is generally accepted as global when we refer to *the* economy. So generally references to the economy is understood as being a global matter and is based on economies of all of the countries of the world and their respective national economies. Economies of local cities and regions of states can be seen as a system of national economies making up the global one. Most workers even in rural areas of the country know that at least a portion of their creations is being sent around the world. For instance, some cars that are assembled in the United States may be comprised of parts and components that are manufactured in up to a dozen other countries.

Market valuations in a local currency are typically translated to a consistent monetary unit based on the idea of purchasing power. The dollar or increasingly the euro is used as a standard of measurement and much of the world's economic activity is reflected in these valuations for standardization. Theories that utilize purchasing power comparability assume that it would cost exactly the same number of for instance United States dollars to buy euros over a long period of time. The exchange rate for differing currencies would also need to be comparable to the two countries buying goods from each other. A further discussion of purchasing power parity is somewhat beyond the scope of our discussion here.

In 2013, the largest economies in the world with more than $2 trillion or 1.25 trillion euros of GDP were the United States, China, Japan, Germany, France, Great Britain, Brazil, Russia and Italy. The world economy is linked to human economic activity and the economy is based on monetary terms, and the establishing of values for services and such things as black market goods. Items such as illegal drugs and corruption that exacts a toll on the economies of some countries are actually part of the world economy. But there might be no accounting as to human economic activity where there is no legal market of any kind in certain aspects of the world economy such as illegal activities. I have mentioned these exceptions here since the country where the activity occurs will collect no taxes on the activity. The money added to the economy for individual use would be in addition to the traditional flow of money in a country's economy.

What Factors Shape the Economy of a Country?

Each country has its own unique mix of culture, resources, belief systems and a multitude of other variables that are capable of assisting economic growth or hindering it. A country's economy is the result of a set of characteristics and processes that would include non-monetary factors. These include the country's culture, educational systems, intrinsic values of its citizens, history, social systems, political framework, and legal structure along with geographic features and resources. Think of countries with valuable resources such as the Middle East and its oil supplies as well as proximity to waterways with harbors for shipping the product. All of these factors put in place the parameters on which an economy is based. An economy, also called an economic system, includes production, distribution, trade and even local consumption of goods and services produced or available in given areas of the world. Entities which affect these activities relate to individuals, families, industries, organizations and government agencies.

Prior to the gradual arrival of the modern concept of a world or global economy, economic transactions were thought to be restricted to only a few areas. Some of these are distance, geographic barriers, presence of natural resources, adaptable and versatile educated labor force, and sufficient capital for research and development for each individual country. But such a view of the global marketplace would negate the value of technological advances such as automation, reducing the costs associated with production, and innovation by the citizens of various countries. And especially the value of intellectual property is a valuable resource that can stimulate the economy. Of course, the United States has been the most prolific innovator of technology, but thefts of this property by countries that use it to compete with the United States is a definite problem.

Two basic types of markets may be found in the world, and would differ between the various countries. These two are called the market-based variety and a command-based variety. In the market-based economic system, both services and goods are produced without interference from governmental authorities. Goods and services are produced according to market requirements called demand and supply. These products are distributed through an exchange of money which may be represented by credit or debit, and by barter where non-monetary exchanges are effected. The market-based style would transparently advertise the costs for the most part of the production of a product and is said to represent 'true' prices.

The command-based economy would be controlled by a central political authority or agency that would arbitrarily determine what and how many of a given product would be produced,. Pricing of the good or service and how and to whom it is distributed would also be controlled by the central political representative. The central weakness of a command-based economy lies in that it has no mechanism to manage the information (prices) about the system's natural supply and demand dynamics. A central planning committee would provide the decision for the particulars as to production, pricing and distribution of the good or service.

In the following section, the economies of three separate countries are presented. It is sometimes difficult to determine the system that is being used in the production scheme, and sometimes a hybrid occurs where a country uses the market-based approach for one commodity and the command-based approach for other products. You should be able to see that there are differences between the systems employed by the countries of the United States, China and India, and make your decision on what system should work best in a Biblically - oriented society.

View of the Economy in the United States

The common sentiment of the average citizen of the United States is that the state of the economy is not good and will almost surely get worse. Most Americans do not understand the basics of economics, and that is one of the purposes of this book. Some disturbing factors emerge that will surprise many. Today, the United States consumes far more wealth than is produced on a monthly basis. You might ask, "What does this mean for me and my family?" Basically, we are continually getting poorer as our country's national debt is growing by leaps and bounds, exceeding the GDP growth by far. To put it simply, if your assets, including money, were going down each month and your debt was rising to maintain your current standard of living, you would understand the phrase, "I'm going broke!" Some politicians and much of the media will say, "Things are just fine!" But please don't believe it for a second.

Attempts by the federal government to infuse the economy with new energy by artificial means of reviving the economy are only stopgap fixes. The releasing of oil from the strategic oil reserve and 'stimulating the economy' by bailing out failing companies will only temporarily delay the suffering by the average citizen. And it does not matter what the two major political parties in the United States do, the long-term trends require powerful medicine to reverse them. It does matter what the individual does as he or she attempts to live a frugal and self-sufficient life without government aid. The current economic disaster will continue to destroy middle class America if nothing changes in the way we approach life.

Globalization of the economy presents us with a spectacular problem. Labor costs in one part of the world may be only 10 percent of what it is on the other side of the world. So jobs leave in order for the departing company to take advantage of low labor costs. This trend may shift, and as you will see shortly, is changing to an extent, but when good manufacturing jobs leave a country, all that is left are jobs that cannot be outsourced. This would include sales jobs of foreign-produced goods in brick and mortar buildings, but even this is changing and a growing number of products are purchased online. But we should never consider putting all our economic policies and procedures under one leader for the entire world. Why? Competitive positions would be lost and a despot would eventually rule the world if he or she held the purse strings of the global business enterprise.

So we have seen a mass exodus of jobs to other countries and the jobs that remain are those that typically pay low wages. And there are insufficient numbers of jobs for all Americans to have a position where a paycheck is earned. In fact, it has been reported in the media that fewer people are working in the United States today than were employed in 1978, although the population has expanded significantly.

In addition, recent college grads are finding it difficult to obtain adequate jobs. Rutgers University conducted a recent study that revealed that over 30 percent of those that graduated from college in all major areas of study between 2006 and 2010 were not able to get a job within six months of graduation. Another unverified piece of information being disseminated estimates that almost 30 percent of those between the early twenties and thirty years of age have moved into their parents' homes for at least a short period of time to weather the economic storm. But unemployment is only a portion of the problems facing society in the United States today. There are untold millions of Americans that are "underemployed" today and some of these have stopped seeking employment, so they are not included in the ranks of the unemployed.

Chief Factor Affecting the Economy of the United States

Although a number of conditions or issues may affect the economy of a country, there will be an overriding factor that will affect the entire economy of a country. This factor may be the result of a number of other pressures on the economy of a country.

Recent Decline of the Middle Classes

Over the past decade, middle class incomes have been stagnating or declining, and the share of America's income pie going to the middle class has been dropping, according to the Center for American Progress. During this same time period the costs for many goods and services that middle-class Americans have learned to rely on have been going up. Rick Newman of MoneyNews reports that "Polls show widespread pessimism out of sync with an economy supposedly heading into its fifth year of expansion," adding the qualification that the statement is applicable for a period since the Great Recession of 2007-2009." This point of view presented by Newman may be found in his book entitled *"Rebounders: How Winners Pivot From Setback to Success."*

Historical Context

The United States was founded by an independent group of rugged individualists who believed they could accomplish much by the sweat of their brow. They spread out and conquered a vast continent rich with natural resources and expected little from the government in the way of helping them to succeed.; In fact, they preferred to operate with as little government as possible, believing that the less government interference they endured, the better they would do financially. Working their way through several wars, the country's financial fortunes were greatly diminished by the Great Depression of 1929 to the early 1940's when World War II broke out, bringing many defense related jobs into the economy.

The United States is a collection of fifty separate states which were actually small countries within themselves and which originally banded together as the Thirteen Colonies. These colonies, or states, banded together for a common defense, language, monetary system, and tariff protection from undue foreign competition. The country is governed by the Constitution of the

United States, and the federal government holds only the powers delegated to it and those that the states did not keep for themselves. One of the main goals was an effort to provide citizens of the United States with the freedom and the climate for succeeding in whatever venture they chose for forging a life on the new continent.

Effects of the Current Economic Conditions

New Census Bureau data released and compiled from the 2010 survey serve to graphically highlight the economic challenges faced by the middle class of this decade. There is an obvious decline in middle class households in the United States, and showing a further decline since the last census was taken in 2010. The dwindling numbers of families that can be categorized as middle class continue to watch their slice of the symbolic national economic pie disappear to record-low levels. From outward appearances, the top economic group is disproportionately claiming the majority of the small amount of the income growth that has occurred since the end of the Great Recession.

But is this a fair statement since the highest income levels hold most of their wealth in securities. As was pointed out earlier, these stock prices are greatly inflated due in part to the increase in cash that is placed in circulation on a regular basis. So what may seem to be obvious might not be the complete reality as seen in statistical tables, but may in part be true. In previous decades, during the 50's, 60's and 70's, particularly, the middle class increased and were able to make measurable financial gains where they held a more equitable portion of the economic wealth.

The projected future of the economy of the United States is fragmented and there is much contradiction as to what will be in store for the country in the future. According to some experts, the economic decline seen in the last five or more years seems to be fundamentally reshaping the economy of the United States. The Great Recession has affected the way the middle class feels about higher education, government, and in particular the future of individuals and their families. Even the overall physical health of some has suffered as a result of the decline. We know that the stress resulting from a feeling of powerlessness in the ability of an individual and the control of his destiny increases the level of a hormone called cortisol which tends to cause weight gain. "Their [middle class families] economic future isn't very bright," says Timothy Smeeding, director of the Institute for Research on Poverty at the University of Wisconsin - Madison. "Wages and income are flat and have even declined in the majority of cases. Transportation, childcare costs, and healthcare costs are going up, and the income isn't."

Smeeding calls the current state of the middle class "the squeeze." Even people who have jobs are being forced to squeeze more and more out of their income, despite the fact that incomes aren't growing. "These people live on the earnings. They're working on not great wages and their jobs are threatened," he says. "They don't see any hope in the future of things getting better." Middle-class households endured deep cuts in their income for the most part during the Great Recession of 2008-2009. The Great Recession is a term often reserved for the general economic decline that has affected the entire scope of the world markets.

Many were still reeling from the dot.com "bubble" or "burst" from 1997-2003 before the recent economic woes arose. What was the dot.com bubble for those who did not experience the wild ride on the world market? The dot-com bubble was also referred variously as the dot-com boom, the internet bubble or the information technology bubble. Midway between the six-year period, the NASDAQ peaked on March 10, 2000. The industrialized nations saw their equity value rise rapidly from growth in the technology field which included the internet sector and other similar fields. Investors were encouraged to wildly speculate on any stocks related to technological development. Companies used a psychological strategy to cause their stock prices to increase by simply adding an "e-prefix" or a ".com" suffix to indicate that the investment was a valuable and savvy opportunity to cash in on the internet growth that was occurring.

The combination of sometimes wildly increasing stock prices coupled with glowing stock market expectations that profits would undoubtedly occur in the near future steadily pushed up the prices of sometimes worthless companies overnight. But the drop in the values of some was as dizzying as the rise had been. The tried and true practice of paying attention to the P/E ratio (price to earnings ratio) resulted in an environment where investors were willing to overlook the traditional P/E ratio metrics due to overconfidence in the hype about technological advancements.

Examples abound in companies where investors were wealthy one day and destitute the next, with their life savings invested in ventures such as the corporate scandals of Enron, Tyco, Global Crossing, Pets.com and WorldCom, to name just a few. There are a few companies who lost a large portion of their market capital, but remained stable and whose stock later rebounded. Two of these well-known companies who weathered the storm are Cisco, whose stock declined by 86 percent and Amazon, whose stock went from $107 per share to $7, then ten years later reached $400. Whether we are in line for another 'bust,' is anybody's guess but is anticipated.

Underlying trends that have left many more and more excluded from the nation's economic growth date back much further than the Great Recession of 2007. The typical American household's annual income peaked in 1999 but has declined since then by 9 percent. More than one half of the nation's total earned income went to the middle class individuals and families in 1968, when most families were a two-parent unit and one head of household was able to earn a living wage. The small amount of economic growth that has occurred in recent years has been distributed more and more unequally, with the wealthiest households claiming most of the income gains seen in the past three years and the middle class has fallen further behind.

And things aren't going very well for the middle class in the United States even as we speak. In Money News, 12 June, 2014, John Morgan reports in his article "The Fall From Grace of the American Middle Class, by the Numbers" that the middle class, once the envy of the world, has fallen dramatically to the nineteenth spot in the world, and is even below that of Japan, Australia and most of the European countries. If this is difficult for you to digest after you were raised to think that the middle class of the United States was the single most important factor in the economic success of the country, you should look at the facts that are readily available on many internet sites.

America's middle class has now fallen to levels unheard of or even thought of just a few decades ago. The reported median income in this article for the United States places our country at a dismal 19th place in the world now on the list for adjusted gross income, taking into account the differences in the adjustment of differing currencies as well as other factors. Our wage earners are in ranges below that of Japan, Australia and most of Western Europe. CNN Money reports that the average Spaniard or Italian, other than the middle class citizens of the 17 other countries ahead of the United States, has more financial resources credited to his or her name than does the average citizen of the United States.

When numbers are derived from accurate compilation of data, hard numbers paint a stark picture of the middle-class decline. According to an August 2012 Pew Research Center report, only half of American households are middle-income, down from 61 percent in the 1970s. In addition, median middle-class income decreased by 5 percent in the last decade, while total wealth dropped 28 percent. According to the Economic Policy Institute, households in the wealthiest 1 percent of the U.S. population now have 288 times the amount of wealth of the average middle-class American family. The income decline has caused many people to accumulate high levels of debt. And as the cost of college increases, more people are saddled with tens of thousands of dollars in student loans after they graduate.

Only 23 percent of people were confident they had enough money to get them through retirement, according to the Pew report. It also found that fewer people believe hard work will get them ahead in life. These are the kind of statistics used by politicians to sell policies, but they tell little about the realities behind the numbers - or how the decline of the middle class plays out in people's everyday lives. More and more middle-income families are turning to government programs such as food stamps, Medicaid, and unemployment insurance. According to a recent Senate Budget Committee Report, "Among the major means tested welfare programs, since 2000 Medicaid has increased from 34 million people to 54 million in 2011 and the Supplemental Nutrition Assistance Program (SNAP, or food stamps) from 17 million to 45 million in 2011. Spending on food stamps alone is projected to reach

$800 billion over the next decade."

People are also saving less, particularly in the United States. Wage increases have not kept up with increases in the cost of living, forcing people to dig deeper into their savings to make ends meet. Meanwhile, many middle-class workers who lost their jobs during the recession remain unemployed. "The most pressing worry is the diminished economic security of middle-class families. The long-term unemployed have completely drained their savings," says Kristen Lewis, co-director of Measure of America, a project of the Social Science Research Council that explores the distribution of opportunity and well-being in the United States. "Those who are working have jobs without healthcare or sick leave. They have no retirement savings plan. There's no end in sight to that."

What Has Been Initiated to Help Alleviate Poverty
Governmental efforts to improve lives of citizens in the United States began soon after the foundations of the country were laid. The United States government has a system that is the envy of the world, although it has received much criticism recently. A first-class health care system where citizens are able to take advantage of private health insurance as well as some government aid programs such as Medicare and Medicaid, are funded in part by the states for those who have no insurance. A recent law, the Affordable Health Care Act, was designed to provide coverage for those with no insurance or who lost their insurance, but a number of flaws have come to light in the program.

Education and to some extent job training has long been a strong point in the United States. Education for everyone and not just the privileged few were dreams of our forefathers, and much of the country now has an opportunity to seek education, some of it free (at least to the one seeking an education). Although this service was not available to everyone throughout the history of the country, some forms of education have been available to practically everyone from the early history of the country. But in the short term, or more accurately in the past few years, the opportunities for education and training have been amplified in the face of a deteriorating economy.

Manipulating the interest rates have been used by the Federal

Reserve Bank (Fed) over many years in attempts to create stability in the nation's economy. Low interest rates were instituted during the Great Recession to bolster a sagging if not almost non-existent housing market. Subprime (making loans to people who may have difficulty maintaining the repayment schedule) lending rates and lowering of interest rates to spur lending, investment, and consumer spending have been attempted with spotty success. And when the economy is growing, the Federal Reserve Bank raises short term interest rates in order to cool down the rate of inflation. In the past, however, as recently as the beginning of this century, former Fed chairman Alan Greenspan attempted to spur the economy through low interest rates (after the dot-com crash of 2000). His efforts appear to have succeeded on the surface as evidenced by the housing boom (2002-2007).

What has Been Detrimental to Alleviate Poverty

The maintaining of the highest corporate tax rates in the world has led to the moving of companies to other countries in order for them to compete globally. The movement of the companies is not just an act of greed, of the corporate executives, but a move to stave off business failure. This loss of manufacturing and other types of firms has led to a growing problem with fewer people employed to pay taxes to finance 'entitlement' programs such as Social Security and a crumbling city infrastructure. Inversely, when the economy goes bust, they lower the interest rates to spur lending, investment, and consumer spending. And our latest and most dramatic recession is forging new challenges for the Fed.

One such adverse effect of this global economic crisis stems from frozen credit. This means that the fiscal liabilities of banks are so congested that the banks are unwilling to lend money to each other in the customary manner. To this end, the former Federal Reserve chairman Ben Bernanke instituted a recent low set of interest rates that have actually failed to encourage banks to lend to other banks and to businesses and the average consumer. With the serious economic atmosphere, there is little or no certainty that a repayment of the loan will occur. The housing boom that occurred from the lending of money to those individuals who previously could not obtain a loan was at the center of the financial crisis and the credit freeze we're now experiencing. Low interest rates didn't work this time!

The Community Redevelopment Act was put in place by President Carter in an effort to encourage minority home ownership. Again, the details are murky, but the Clinton administration, seemingly obsessed with multiculturalism, is given credit for dictating where mortgage lenders could lend. This originally helped to create a market for high-risk loans (sub-prime) that have negatively influenced the balance sheets of many of Wall Street's largest and best known financial institutions. These tough new regulations forced formerly unwilling lenders into high-risk areas. They had no choice except to lower their lending standards and make risky loans that sound business practices would guard against making or they would face stiff government penalties for failure to do so. Unfortunately, the lending institutions that were forced to make loans that would almost surely result in foreclosure of properties bought with these loans labeled the lenders as being greedy and as predators!

Another problem with the housing market is that of home values declining as a glut of foreclosed and abandoned homes became epidemic, especially but not exclusively restricted to the larger cities. And in many areas of the country people who previously owned homes have had the experience of owning a home that they owe more money for than the property is worth. They were forced into solutions that would not be a choice they would accept in better economic times. Short sales, in which the homes were sold for less than the amount owed on the loan became almost a rule rather than an exception in some areas. So a well-meaning regulation turned into a nightmare for those who could least afford to suffer the indignity of losing a home. Many dreams have been shattered by this loss of the largest investment most people will ever have.

View of the Economy in China

It has been reported widely during the past few months that China is the largest trading partner with many countries. China now holds the edge over the United States, which had held the position for many years. But 2014 was the last year in which the United

States could claim to be the world's largest economic power and China at the beginning of 2015 holds the top position. China will probably remain atop the heap for the foreseeable future, and even beyond.

This is familiar territory for the country, as for most of the history of mankind, China was the largest trader in the world.

Chief Factor Affecting the Economy of China

As in the United States, there are many issues related to the changing of the economic patterns of China. For centuries, China's economy was agrarian-based, and only recently have massive numbers of people from the countryside moved into the large cities and found jobs in the production of goods to be shipped overseas. Some of these people are finding their voices and there is a great deal of ferment between the classes found in China. Bringing together a diverse group of ethnic peoples has been and is still a social problem that is difficult to solve.

China as an Emerging World-class Economy

As you can see from the previous report, China is one of the strongest and fastest growing economies of the world, and has managed to overcome the United States just recently. We will discuss the changes that have and are occurring in China. As we all know if we can read a label regarding where a product is manufactured, China is an emerging economic giant and the middle class there has one of the highest and still raising rates of income growth in the world. A Communist country which for centuries had closely controlled its citizens is now dominant on the word economic stage.

The formal administrative branches and departments of the government are headed for the most part by the Communist Party of China, a group of four to nine older men, and the military enforces all decisions by this governing body. The legal power of the Communist Party is guaranteed by the constitution of the People's Republic of China with supreme political authority and control over the state, military, and media. According to a prominent government spokesman, a Western style of government will never be realized where various parties vie for election to major offices within the government.

Historical Context

The country of China was a closed and xenophobic entity that built a wall around the country and did not appreciate interlopers that tried to enter. In short, this was true and a more detailed explanation follows. Generally, pessimism with cultural diversity is inversely correlated with the openness of a society. North Korea and Saudi Arabia are two of the most "closed societies," and they are extremely pessimistic about sociocultural, namely political (though this could also include economic or ideological), diversity. While not as closed socially as North Korea and Saudi Arabia, China should be considered a closed society due to discrimination against the Buddhists in Tibet, and Christians in the large cities and Muslims in Sinkiang Autonomous Region.

But China began to open up to capitalism more than three decades ago, although the Communist Party maintains a tight rein on governmental affairs currently and show little sign of doing otherwise. Administrative issues to this day allow for little or no dissent. The Tienanmen Square Massacre, which many Chinese have been led to believe never occurred, was an overt demonstration against a society that sought more open dialogue and participation in the government but Beijing is not closed to the extent that Pyongyang and Riyadh are. The widely published document, "The Nine Commentaries on the Chinese Communist Party" shows that the government operates on the premise of fear, and will distort the truth to its advantage as needed. It is estimated that more than 40 million people have been brutally murdered by the country, including many religious groups and any that speak against the words of Mao. "Imperialistic Propaganda" is the buzzword for any information the Party feels should not be heard or believed.

Current Economic Conditions

Why should we be concerned with rising economic unrest in China? The Chinese government heads the leading global economic power in the world, but wants all of the political power to rest in the hands of the four to nine party 'bosses' Almost certain incidents of unrest will continue as China progresses towards becoming a full-fledged advanced economy. A fast growing economy such as that found in China will foment distrust of the government policies when there is little opportunity for individual efforts to start businesses and to gain personal wealth. A natural sentiment of the citizens as their per capita income increases is a demand for increased respect as humans, a moral provision of fairness and a desire for a more democratic form of government is inevitable.

The government needs to deal with minorities who rightly want a voice. And citizens will undoubtedly want to experience openness and accountability by the governing officials and to have a voice in decisions made perhaps through the ballot box. All countries of the world have experienced their own unique situations as they have sought forms of government that needs to change over time. Processes that allow individual decisions affecting each person and his or her family would appear to make for a more vibrant and effective economy. But it can be a nuisance for the central government or potentially disruptive. But it is thought by a number of economists that no immediate threats are posed to China's economic development (Miles, The Economist).

As in many advanced countries, China might do well to allow movement from rural areas to the cities, at the risk of upsetting those who are prospering in the cities. These prosperous groups, a growing middle class, may be unsettled by the influx of cheaper labor and more poor people with little education or transferable work skills. Services and a good lifestyle might become diluted with a larger population in the cities. But the government will also impose higher property taxes to pay for government services for the influx of rural persons, leading to even more open demonstrations of protest against the sociological changes.

What Has Been Initiated to Help Alleviate Poverty

Governmental efforts to improve the lives of Chinese citizens have been the efforts of governmental offices to focus on the poverty rate in rural areas, which is much greater than that found in the cities. Economic reforms in 1978 introduced market principles that were carried out in two separate phases. The first phase that began in 1978 and extended into the early 1980s, involved the release of the government's stranglehold on agricultural land, opening the doors to foreign investors. Permission was also granted to allow more entrepreneurship in the agricultural sector of the economy has helped. Farmers are now able to acquire the human labor and other resources such as seed, fertilizers, farm equipment, etc., and accept full responsibility for success or failure in the ventures.

But most industrial enterprises remained in the hands of the governing body until the second phase of reform began in the time span ranging from the late 1980's and into the 1990's. The government began to privatize much of the industry previously 'owned' by the state. Price controls were removed along with protectionist policies and obstructive regulations. But the banking institutions and the oil and petroleum-based products remained under government control, which still prevents China from being an entirely market-based economy but operates as a hybrid.

What has Been Detrimental to Alleviate Poverty?

Various areas of protest even with expanding economic opportunity for its citizens have resulted in increasing unrest. The country's one-party government is more concerned than ever about social and economic instability as the middle class increases in wealth. Since protests are illegal in China, the Chinese do not enjoy constitutionally ordained rights and freedoms such as being able to engage in free speech without fear of reprisal.

The single governing party places restrictions on many things we in America take for advantage, including expression of feelings and beliefs, association, assembly and freedom of religion. Independent labor unions, not sanctioned by the ruling Communist Party are controlled in all areas of China, says the Human Rights Watch's 2014 World Report. Even ethnic groups with certain cultural beliefs and practices may be forced to abandon some of their practices. It is reported by World Report in 2014 that there are an estimated three hundred to five hundred protests staged each day in China.

Protests have occurred ranging over a variety of causes and issues. At least some of the average Chinese citizens may be undergoing a cultural shift where they feel that the government policies that have been in place for years may not always be best for the individual. These protests include farmers contesting land grabs by the government. James Miles, China editor of The Economist, reports that most of the 'land grab' protests occur when farmers are pushed off their land which is then converted to government use. And those who are being forced from their houses where they may have lived for decades to make way for urban development that provides larger economic benefits for the government. Environmental protests have been organized by a middle class against rampant pollution, declining air quality in the cities and parts of the country, and careless disposal of environmental toxins from factories that are poisoning the land for the average citizen.

Another major concern of the Chines is the treatment of ethnic minorities. The Tibetans suffered death at the hand of government forces in Lhasa in 2008. Chinese forces are practically in an occupational role in some areas of the country where protests are being limited to prevent their spreading more widely. In The Tiananmen Square Massacre that was participated in by thousands of protesters, many of the students, Chinese forces reportedly killed between 400 to 800 civilians who were demonstrating in official reports. But *Globe and Mail* correspondent Jan Wong placed the death toll at approximately 3,000 to 7,000 individual demonstrators.

In Xinjiang, Chinese soldiers continue to kill Urghurs indiscriminately. The fear is that this reaction by the central government could pose a threat for the growing quest for power by the middle classes. Many are speaking out but there are still acts of violence against anyone who dares speak out. But with social media and the ability for news to spread rapidly, it should put a damper on violence or clamping down by the government as they attempt to quell dissent. Examples of the protests are many and are widely documented on various sites on the world wide web. It is the poor who are doing most of the protesting with information begin spread among the demonstrators and to the world.

Another factor that might slow the economic growth in China is the re-institution by the current Hu-Wen Administration in 2005 of more heavy regulation and control of the country.

Manufacturing is where China has found much of its financial growth but which has weakened in recent months as reported in Electronics Weekly). But even with the dramatic growth in recent years, decreasing, China is still seen as the best choice for low-cost manufacturing.

Rising wages have been widely reported as a factor in some job relocation, and a shrinking demand for manufactured goods is causing some companies to rethink plans for increased investment. Other Asian countries, particularly those in South East Asia, are getting a second look as sites for future growth of industries. Government intervention has not remedied the situation and the competitive edge where China had been identified as a cheap source of labor is losing its impetus. Some major companies are considering relocation to other countries and processes involved in the textile industries have actually been moved outside of China. This would definitely be detrimental to alleviating poverty among the poorer classes.

What has Helped Alleviate Poverty

Unprecedented economic growth occurred during the span from 2005 to 2013, increasing by an enviable 9.5 percent per year during this time. In 2010, China became the Asian Continent's largest economy, surpassing that of Japan, and four years later has surpassed the United States in economic might. China was predicted to attain the status of the largest economy in the world by the year 2025 but has done so much quicker, achieving this milestone eleven years before the target date

The widespread success and implementation of economic policies has resulted in some significant changes in Chinese society. Some large-scale government-enacted programs use effective planning that occur along with market advances, serving to reduce poverty through growth of the labor force in a number of non-agricultural businesses. Income levels have increased and divisions of assets in a more equitable fashion have reduced the numbers of the poor.

The New Left is critical of capitalism. Some aspects of the Chinese economic reforms bringing financial gains to the country are favored by some, but a number of government officials would like to see a return a Maoist socialism. Central planning by the state is accompanied by a renewal of attitudes supporting industrial enterprises that are state-owned and operating under the guise of collectivism, also known as Communism.

Reforms beginning in the late 1970's has resulted in a significant increase in per capita income and a resultant decline in the poverty rate from 85 percent in the early 1980's to a remarkable 13 percent rate in 2008. But there is still discontent even with the astounding success of the improvement of the lives of many millions. But income disparities are growing and are prevalent in the differences in living standards between rural and urban areas. A shift in government policy to encourage migration from areas with little opportunity to areas where jobs are available has led to crowding of urban areas but a rise in income for many. Increased funding for education and health care for the poorer areas and for poor families should reduce disparities between social services received by the wealthy and the poor. The future for China appears to be rosy pending the solution of several major problem areas.

View of the Economy in India

Even though a large portion of India is underdeveloped and heavily rural, growth in technology has led a surge in the economy of India. The country is rich with human resources with a huge, well-educated population that is under 35 years of age. They have embraced a global economy and enjoy a growth rate of more than 8 percent. Foreign companies have invested heavily in call centers and jobs that are easy, "out-sourced" at a lower wage coupled with an English-speaking population that resides in India. Extremely high levels of education in math and science are prevalent where other developed countries are failing in this area.

What is the Chief Factor Affecting the Economy of India?

India is an extremely diverse country and is still emerging from a colonial style of government. Rapid growth of the population of the country has made it difficult to provide the social programs needed to address all of the citizens of the country. Even in the cities, the old caste system still prevails, but is also a strong factor in the rural regions as well. The caste system in India is a system of the sometimes self-imposed segregation somewhat based on the six major religions of India which separated communities into hereditary groups. Although blamed on the Hindu way of life, some argue that the British colonials constructed the system where administrative jobs and governmental appointments went to the upper castes.

Discrimination against lower castes was outlawed by Article 15 of its constitution, and laws and initiatives have been established to prevent discrimination. Affirmative action programs are in place to aid in insuring all groups have opportunities in India. But a lesser reason for discrimination in India may lie in the number of languages spoken. There are 22 scheduled languages sanctioned by the Indian Constitution but there are 438 separate languages that exist, some spoken by only a few, as reported by the Economist.

Heavy Population Density and Growth

India is one of the most populous countries in the world, with a population of approximately 1.2 billion, or roughly one-seventh of the world's population. The country currently has an enviable Gross Domestic Product (GDP) of approximately 9 percent growth. The GDP is updated each month by the Bureau of Economic Analysis (BEA) and indicates how fast the economy has grown during the previous quarter. Ideally the growth should be between 2 and 3 percent for an increase in jobs to meet a growing labor force. The GDP is adjusted monthly for current rates of inflation but growth that occurs too quickly will result in uncontrollable inflation. India's growth rate ranks as one of the highest in the world. In contrast, the United States in 2014 showed only a 0.1 percent growth rate for the first quarter but rebounded to 2.4 percent during the second quarter, according to The Capital Spectator.

But in spite of being one of the world's fastest growing economies and amazing advances, poverty in India continues to increase and especially in rural areas where the majority of the Indian population live. A healthy GDP rate has not translated to a more equitable dispersion of economic riches across the population of the rural areas. This problem of poorly performed distribution is likely due in part to a lack of access to services and opportunities that leads to the inability for upward financial mobility outside the cities.

Historical Context

India is an ancient country with continuous civilization in the Indus River since 2500 B.C. Both urban and agricultural sectors of the population, each sustained by the other, led to significant change. Remember, Columbus called the native North Americans 'Indians' because he was trying to discover a new route to India for trade and at first thought he had succeeded. Two thousand years before Christ, Aryan tribes migrated from Europe and adapted to the culture found there along the Ganges River. Many kingdoms with flexible boundaries flourished in the 4th and 5th centuries A.D., and northern India, unified under Gupta Dynasty, adopted the Hindu culture and political administration stabilized.

Turks and Afghans invaded India a 500 year period bringing Islam which blended with the majority Hindu religion. This hybrid created cultural differences equally on both religions. In 1619, the British established an outpost at Surat on the northwestern coast and began a significant period of British influence. The East India Company opened permanent trading stations in the late 1600's at Madras, Bombay, and Calcutta, each under the protection of native rulers. British influence expanded and by 1850 controlled the majority of present-day India, Pakistan, and Bangladesh. In 1857, rebellious Indian soldiers in north India caused the British Parliament to transfer political power from the East India Company to the British Crown, administering most of India directly and controlling the remainder through treaties established with local rulers.

Late in the 1800s, self-government began with Indian councilors employed to advise the British viceroy and provincial Indian councils. And in 1920, Indian leader Mohandas K. Gandhi transformed the Indian National Congress political party into a body opposed to British colonial rule. Independence was achieved through nonviolent resistance and noncooperation and on August 15, 1947, India became a dominion within the Commonwealth of Great Britain. Serious breaches between Hindus and Muslims led to the partition of British India, forming East and West Pakistan with

Muslim majorities. India became a republic within the Commonwealth after establishing its Constitution in 1950.

Current Economic Conditions

Only a meager 1 percent of Indian GDP is spent on health, to include preventive medicine, while China, Brazil, Russia and other developing countries spend 3 to 4 percent of their respective GDP's. Illness takes a toll on the initiative and energy level of citizens of a country, where many may be unable to avail themselves of opportunities to grow economically. So in comparison, public expenditures as a percentage of the GDP of India for health issues is only about one-fourth that of a number of other countries. So after 60 years of fighting poverty in India since independence, the government should be well aware that insufficient money is being spent on its citizens for public health-related needs. This is a tremendous detriment to both the physical and economic well-being of the entire country and must be addressed for the nation to become fully developed.

Characteristics of poverty in India focus mostly on the lack of food, housing, health care and educational opportunities for the poor. At least half of those living in India lack adequate shelter, and almost three-fourths don't have access to toilets other than the use of fields and streams for voiding and bowel movements. One-third of houses do not have a nearby source for any type of water, even non-potable sources. More than a third of the villages do not have properly constructed roads connecting them to larger cities and more than 80 percent do not have secondary schools. In addition, the lower-caste members or untouchables are not included in the poverty statistics along with women and minority ethnic tribes. The exclusion of these groups may lead to massive social problems and will continue to exacerbate existing and growing tensions.

What Has Been Initiated to Help Alleviate Poverty?

A wide range of anti-poverty policies have been introduced since the 1950s and most of these took more than 20 years before being fully implemented. A decline in the country's poverty rate from 60 percent to 35 percent occurred between the 1970's and the early 1990's. But economic globalization of the economy and other policy changes resulted in a repeat trend of an increasing poverty rate. Although joining the competitive global marketplace was expected to create growth, this in fact did not occur. So why was India's experience at odds with those that occurred throughout the world? (**http://www.poverties.org/poverty-in-india.html#sthash**)?

As is the goal of most countries, the question remains as to what the government authorities can do to reduce poverty. Availability of nutritious and sanitary food would is a good start toward providing a healthy population to seek advancement. Sanitary facilities that are constructed perhaps near groups of houses, especially in the crowded cities, are a step in improving methods of disposing of human wastes. And construction of substantive homes that would not be destroyed in a strong wind or storm and a consistent educational system for everyone would eventually change both the physical and the emotional climate among the massive numbers of poor in India. And because there is a simple and straightforward link between rural poverty and agricultural productivity, the end goal is to raise the crop productivity per person in order to aid in alleviating poverty. As a consequence policies should focus on spurring investment leading to technological progress.

Developing agriculture as an attempt to alleviate poverty in India has managed to yield a few successes. When certain anti-poverty programs accomplished what was expected of them, they have had a great influence on the social structure and have helped people in moving up the social ladder. The problem is mostly that reforms have been conservative and incomplete while something more direct and readily visible and understandable would be better and sustainable. After the 1991 economic reforms were established, subsidies actually went down because of a looming fiscal deficit for the country's government and as a result poverty again began to increase to previous levels.

These safety nets started to disappear concurrently with the reduction in subsidies designed to help the farmers become more productive. Reforms were adversely affected by a continuation of a social structure based on religion and other factors in rural India. Even certain corrupt members of the citizenry began to exploit the rural populace and resisted land reform and the logic of entrepreneurship.

A program of micro-finance or micro-loans is an example of something that has helped with the housing shortage. These loans are designed to help individuals repair or build a home or to start a small business. The program has to an extent reduced uncertainty for those with initiative to want a better home or a business. But it is not extensive enough to completely solve the problems of poverty. There has been government action to reduce the prejudice toward the inter-class (or caste, such as the untouchables) that were left on the fringes of society, and who faced overt discrimination.

What has Been Detrimental to Alleviate Poverty?

Limited reforms seem to have been a complete waste of effort due to the size of the problems faced. Of the post-independence reforms, land reform is the most effective in accomplishing positive results. By reducing the numbers and power of intermediaries and simplifying and standardizing the system of tenancy, production relations became more efficient, and as a result the rural wages went up. But land should have been redistributed equitably rather than in a system similar to an ancient European feudal system. Incentives and subsidies are handed out to the biggest of the landowners, and is perhaps the major cause of poverty in India. Personal incentive for those who received land would have caused the recipients to feel empowered to improve their living conditions and their financial lot.

The manufacturing sector is starting to boom so now is the best time to improve agricultural productivity and employ the jobless or underemployed migrating to the cities. While drought is prevalent in many places on earth, a number of Indian regions have plenty of water. People resources to exploit opportunities on the land need to be included rather than being excluded.

Child labor in India is also a serious problem, with no hope of advancing above dangerous and dirty work with poor pay which is rampant in India. And as with other developing countries around the globe, urban poverty in India is a direct effect of rural migrations of those fleeing areas of poverty. This creates a massive unemployment and underemployment issue in the target cities and and large urban areas to which the immigrants travel. It also results in disproportionate housing problems with a shortage of acceptable housing. With inadequate housing to protect the thousands of new arrivals, houses are built of scraps of substandard materials and in a natural calamity, even these rude shelters are completely destroyed. Since there are so many people working in agriculture and living in rural areas, the agricultural sector has (and should have) an unrivaled priority in policies aimed at poverty in India. Tremendous obstacles to the reforming of agriculture and its associated processes still exist.

The presence of sprawling slums paint an extremely harsh picture of poverty where there is little in the way of sanitary facilities such as toilets and access to potable water. The spectacular growth of the major cities in India has made poverty in India incomparably more visible through its famous slums in which news stories abound with graphic depictions of the sites. If there are proportionally fewer urban poor nowadays, their sheer number has been increasing as they emigrate to the cities with few skills to find a better lifestyle. They spend about 80 percent of their income on food and the waning level of public services creates new unbearable costs that in the end will lead to extreme situations where Indians are denied basic services they once were able to access easily.

Do the cities create a source of instability? Becoming accustomed to performing degrading work for a few rupees is demoralizing with the loss of dignity, since a little money is better than none. But the choice of living on the edge constantly is another factor to be considered. By seeing one segment of the population in the cities reaping the benefits of formidable growth at the expense of the laborers who perform dangerous and dirty work is one of the most dangerous and persistent features of poverty in India, creating envy and the potential for violence.

It would appear that globalization would have had a positive effect on poverty in India when India embraced the concept in 1991. But the global economy has not benefited India as much as some other countries. With market liberalization in combination with privatization and deregulation, it would appear that India would have been able to manage this transition as well as did China, but this has not been the case.

There is at least some resistance among some people toward privatization, even though it is not in itself to blame for economic inequality. India is a land of great complexities, with the merging of several significant cultures. Historically we know that ruling colonial powers such as Great Britain and Rome have never been able to change such a diverse set of cultural beliefs and values into a homogenous and peaceful society. So at least some of the failures listed here may be traced to the history of the country beginning thousands of years earlier.

Tensions between social groups make reasonable dialogue and negotiations leading to concessions by both sides of an issue an impossibility. The opening of Indian markets to the world did contribute to reducing poverty in India by raising the income of a large number of people and opening access to education to many. A more effective system would be helpful a India grows in strength and numbers of persons so employed. This will provide financing for policies to be devised and steps taken to increase the efficiency and effectiveness of programs to aid the poor in escaping poverty.

Recently, the decentralization of the administration was an attempt to improve such efficiency. However, as local governments were left with more power of oversight, the anti-poverty programs had in fact worse results than before and this needs to be remedied where local administrators are held accountable for the progress made in reducing poverty. These officials have little incentive to help the poor and those living in poverty do not have enough power to denounce these representatives of the government to any higher ranking official. But it is all a learning process, and perhaps the barriers will be removed over a period of time.

Conclusion

The purpose of providing a study of three countries was intended to show that the more freedom the populace has, most often more production is achieved and the financial status of individuals and families is improved. In the United States, we see that too much regulation and loss of our competitive market position has hampered the economy, creating higher poverty rates and loss of the middle class. For China, much wealth has been created among the formerly poor persons, after emerging from Communism to an extent. But there is now a movement seeking a return to more state-controlled enterprises, which is collectivism, a term for Communism. In India, after trying a number of strategies where land became more available for the former lower castes, those of the higher caste are again obtaining more rural land and hiring the poor workers at lower wages.

PART IX:
What Can I Do to Avoid Being Poor or to Escape Poverty

As a country, and our review of the economies of China and India, we can see what works and what has not worked for those two countries. Perhaps we could study the reasons for their financial successes and adapt them for our own use as a country. But no one system with equal parameters will work in all countries, so modified systems must be created to allow for diverse peoples and diverse conditions. When these areas have been addressed, such as disparities between groups within our borders, individual responsibility can be taken in making an effort to better ourselves and members of our family. By doing so, we become a human resource and contribute to the overall economic climate in our country.

The following topic areas are most essential in avoiding poverty or of just plain being poor for the individual or family. These topics will be discussed at some length as we move through the text. Therefore, to avoid poverty seven steps are important:

- Keep track of your earnings and expenditures
- Spend less than you earn
- Start saving as early in life as possible
- Invest a portion of your savings (always)
- Choose investments that balance safety of capital with maximum return
- Invest in your education to improve your professional standing
- Constantly seek to upgrade your job position and therefore your income

Then, first of all, a modest amount of work will be required in order to effectively set out on a pathway to success. Remember also that the reason to seek security and financial peace is not a singular goal to get rich or even wealthy. But it could happen that after a sufficient time, perhaps years, by being consistent in sticking to a plan, you experience an unexpected surprise. You and your family may suddenly realize that all of you are in better financial shape than you had ever dreamed. Please let me provide one more story which includes three people. A well-known talk show host had three women on her program some years ago. They had all achieved a fairly substantial level of financial success, as all three were now worth more than one million dollars. One common characteristic between the three was that none of them had ever made an extremely high salary. One was a school teacher, and if memory serves me correctly, one was a waitress and the other a motel maid.

None of the three had a formal plan except to save a bit of money on a regular basis. One of the show's participants said that for some days she was able only to save literally a few pennies, but she persisted for years. Apparently most of their money was placed into the safety of interest bearing savings accounts, perhaps in a credit union where higher rates of interest may be received. I know that at least one of them placed money in a retirement account but if any money was invested otherwise in stocks it was not clear. And they might have achieved even higher financial rewards if they had purchased risky stocks rather than with the safe investment of a simple bank saving account that earned only a small amount of interest.

But the consistency of putting away at least something on a regular basis, and then perhaps when a tax refund arrived, a portion of this was added to the savings and the accounts grew at a steady pace. Eventually all three women more than likely surprised their families when they revealed, if they did (which might not have been a good idea), that they were now millionaires. I might add the warning that sometimes it might not be wise to reveal your financial success with family members for obvious reasons.

Again, remember that failure to heed essential advice that bears repeating from an earlier section of this work, such as that dispensed by Rick Santorum in a recent presidential campaign, will almost surely relegate one to a life of poverty. A study done in 2009 determined that if Americans do three things, they can avoid poverty. Three steps to follow that should be undertaken early in life and these principles should be taught to young people at home, in school, church, and any variety of social organizations where youngsters congregate. First of all, work is essential, even if it only provides enough money for school lunches, books, some clothing, etc., Second of all, graduate from high school and absorb all of the knowledge and skills available. Third, one should be married before having or fathering children.

Young men are not meeting the standard for real men if they father a child or children and leave the rearing and nurture of the child or children to the single mother, her family or for the taxpayers to financially support. Of course, the government can not nurture the child adequately, as a child needs both parents, and the child will be placed in a childcare facility or preschool nursery. If these three things steps had been taken on a national basis for at least the past few years, the poverty rate would statistically only be 2 percent of what it is today.

The Obama administration now has a program targeting at-risk youth, but these programs are not allowed to promote marriage and abstinence to young girls as a way of avoiding poverty and bad choices. Why? Because to do so would be a value judgment, and shame on those who would judge others in this way! Governmental programs focus on disease prevention and preventing pregnancy, and as Dr. Phil says, "How is that working for you?"

Sadly, schools can no longer even teach sex education with the physical and psychological ramifications of random and wanton sex. They have to be neutral with respect to how people live and behave. But they do perhaps erroneously in the absence of parenting take on the role of teaching birth control and prevention of certain diseases. The problem is that being neutral in teaching values and personal responsibility results in relegating many to lifelong poverty and ignorance. This government-enforced neutrality on the subject results in individuals who make the wrong choices that hurt themselves and other people's lives.

It is a cop out when the agencies of the government support organizations that say they will help young women and men to make good choices but do not elucidate what constitutes a good choice. The best choice would be one that will have no adverse consequences on society, on an individual, and his or her family.

This is absolutely unconscionable and is prejudicial to those who need to be taught morals, values and responsibility to one's self and to society. Sadly it is the child born into a less-than-ideal environment that will suffer, perhaps for a lifetime due to choices made by the parents.

Regardless of what we are led to believe, the majority of people in our society are poor and the rich are very few in number. And for the most part, the rich earned what they have. The main reason leading to poverty is the same reason our federal government is in dire straits. And taking from those who have and giving to those who don't have is only a temporary fix and will do nothing to alleviate the burden of poverty in this country and the world. Most of us (and the government) spend more than we earn, if you can call the government's revenues earned income (it was earned by someone, once upon a time). If we save only a penny every day, and remember what Ben Franklin said about this practice of a penny saved is a penny earned, we will be richer today than we were yesterday.

Approach of Massive Transfer of Wealth
In this book, the value of work has been emphasized. Also the fact is that those who work have a healthier attitude as well as body. Then we find out that those who achieve wealth without working, such as those who inherit a business and allow it to fail, almost never maintain the wealth throughout three generations. Recent news focused on the following sequence of events that are soon to happen. As the world's richest individuals called "Baby Boomers," who for the most part worked hard and earned financial success but are now either retired or approaching retirement, the wealth will be passed to primarily offspring who have not worked for what they have to a great extent.

Over the next three decades there will be trillions of dollars falling into the hands of the children of Boomers or younger family members. We will observe the biggest wealth transfer in history from one generation to another according to a number of official and unofficial reports. According to the Wealth-X and NFP Family Wealth Transfers Report recently published, as much as sixteen trillion dollars will be passed along to offspring and others. This wealth of those termed ultra-high net worth individuals (UHNW's, those holding more than thirty million in assets) will change hands, producing large number of multimillionaires.

"As self-made UHNW baby boomers start passing on their wealth to their children, the importance of entrepreneurship and hard work will be put to the test," the previously cited report stated. It is estimated that the number of ultra-wealthy persons grew to more than 211 thousand during a recent year, with a total combined wealth of $29.7 trillion, with 6 trillion changing hands in the US over the next 30 years. It is somewhat unnerving to think that we may suffer an even further decline of individuals who possess a work ethic and who are willing to work to increase personal wealth. And will those who were not recipients of this largess become even more dependent upon the individuals who now hold such vast wealth?

Evaluate Your Income

It will be important to have a system to evaluate your income and the payment of expenses, so more will be discussed later on this topic. It is very important to determine just how much revenue an individual or family is receiving each month. It is essential that this be done, and unbelievably a substantial number of persons in this country and no doubt the world would be unable to even come close to accurately estimating their monthly income. Why should we use a monthly basis to evaluate income? The main reason is that most of our routine bills arrive on a monthly basis. And if you are paid biweekly, the two-week paycheck is multiplied by twenty-six rather than twelve, and then divided by twelve to determine the *net income per month. It is important that you understand this calculation. There are fifty-two weeks in a year, and divided into two-week increments, there would be twenty-six paychecks. Then this money would be a calculation of an accurate accounting of a month's income. Use the following calculation when pay is received every two weeks, with an assumed net pay of $1500:

**$1500 X 26 = $39000 /12 = $3250/month
(Adjusted Net Monthly Income)**

Net income is the amount of money remaining after payroll deductions for taxes. If health care insurance, retirement fund payments and perhaps some discretionary payments for miscellaneous expenses are deducted, this will make the calculations easier. One must remember not to again deduct the items already deducted from your paycheck on the income and expense statement you prepare. To make it simple, expenses deducted from your paycheck will not appear on your worksheet where you are determining your monthly income There will be further explanations regarding this later.

Most people do not keep an account of income and expenses so planning can be done accurately for the future. This is wrong. Keeping account of money coming in and money going out is a good habit and is to be commended. It has a dual benefit in that we know how much we have spent and also for what item in order to determine where savings might be realized. It may take a year of records before estimates of what will be spent each month are accurate. This is because there are seasonal variations in utilities, maintenance, transportation, and many other costs during a year.

Note that heating bills will be higher in the winter and air conditioning bills will be higher in the summer. Remember that taxes, insurance and certain requests for certain other payments such as taxes and insurance arrive once per year in most cases, so allowances must be made for these payments. In addition to knowing both our income and expenditures, we should also make it a point to keep a positive cash balance or to make it simple, that <u>we spend less than we earn</u>. It may seem impossible at first, but please bear with me on this.

Decide Where You Are in the Economic Class System

Why is it important to know where you stand financially in relation to others? I knew one couple in which both wife and husband worked and they had a combined annual income well in excess of $100,000. But he insisted in my presence that they had very little money and perhaps none at the end of some months! Please recall from earlier discussions in this work that some are poor, but actually make more than several times the poverty level, while some families find ways to exist comfortably on less money than do others. Where you live and what you already own or have access to will dictate where you fall on the scale of financial security.

"You (now) have far less disposable income and increasing levels of debt," says David Madland, director of the American Worker Project at the Center for American Progress, regarding today's economy. "You have this fundamental squeeze on most members of the middle class. It's impacting their quality of life and their outlook for the future." But regardless of these sentiments, it is possible to improve your lifestyle beyond what you would first believe. And for simplicity, you must know how much your income is, and how much you MUST spend.

How Much do You Spend?

It is fundamentally important to know the items for which your money is spent. Certain items are not essential and may be beyond your means during a given month. Many do not look at the wisdom of their expenditures and in fact give little thought to them. Of course, a certain amount of money is needed for essential costs of daily living. But we should reduce any excessive expenditures for food, shelter, transportation, and clothing as much as possible.

What are Some Simple Ways to Lower Costs of Living?

The recurring expenses common to running a household must be carefully examined to lower the costs associated with daily living. Those items consuming the largest portion of the monthly income should gain the most attention in cutting household expenses.

Expensive Foods

We should avoid expensive luxury foods which often aren't as nutritious as cheaper foods, but they are attractive and tasty, often because of the additives. Instead, use a wide variety of local foods so the family will obtain all of the essential nutrients and minerals we need in the diet at a lower cost. Buy fruits and vegetables only in season and watch for advertising specials where fruits and vegetables in season are often cheaper than at other times of the year. Shop at farmer's markets rather than at the big supermarkets when possible, and even plant a few vegetables such as tomatoes which can be done even in limited space.

Processed Foods
Processed foods such as ready-to-eat meals and microwaveable dishes are convenient to prepare, but often have many additives for color and preservation that might affect one's health and are quite expensive. Take your lunch and perhaps a thermos of coffee to work instead of buying it at least part of the time. Eating at home may be roughly one tenth the cost instead of restaurant meals. Avoid or at least minimize habits such as smoking and drinking alcohol, which are not only a financial drain but may exact a toll on good health.

Housing
For adequate shelter, we can reduce our cost of living by selecting a modest accommodation. When single, it is simpler than with a family to share a living space with a friend. Both house payments or rent and utility costs can then be shared.

Utilities
Utility expenses include electricity, water, garbage pick-up, sewer charges, gas for heating, telephones and cooking. The cost of utilities can be reduced by turning off lights and other electrical items when not in use. Thermostats should be lowered when we are absent from our home and at night. Avoid extra conveniences on telephone bills for services such as call waiting and call messaging. Land lines may be avoided if one is able to rely on reliable cell phone service or by using one of the new and cheaper phones that operate through use of the internet service or by TV cable.

Transportation
For transportation when one lives and works in a city, use public transit, walk or ride a bike. More and more cities are providing bike lanes for those in cities who may find it easy and offers an opportunity for needed exercise by biking or by walking to work. One strategy to save money on transportation is, when possible, to live near one's work place.

Buying a Vehicle
The purchase of a vehicle is of such importance that it requires a section separate from transportation costs. It is possible to buy a good and fairly new vehicle from a private owner and avoid the payment of sales taxes which is significant in most states. In addition, they are generally cheaper from a private sale than when purchased

from a dealer. Always obtain a Carfax report to determine if the car or other vehicle has been seriously damaged and then repaired. Have a reputable mechanic examine the vehicle at a modest cost before making the purchase. One well-known economic adviser with TV and radio exposure says that one's accumulated wealth can be measured by the number of vehicles purchased (the more cars bought, the less wealth one has). Some feel it is necessary to purchase a new vehicle every two or three years and in a lifetime, the financial loss for this practice will range into several hundred thousand dollars depreciation and finance charges. In addition, in most states, newer, more expensive cars cost more for ad valorem taxes and insurance. And surprisingly, studies show the average age of a vehicle on highways today in the United States is eleven years!

Vehicle Repairs
Always shop for good prices when auto repairs are needed. But as in medical procedures, always get a second opinion. I have been the victim of unnecessary repairs, and have avoided unnecessary repairs with a few short remedial actions. Perhaps I can avoid the brickbats thrown at me, but repairs performed at the dealer tend to be much more expensive. But there may be more protections at a dealer's shop on any existing warranty, etc.

As an example, which might be of value when explaining myself, occurred when I had a failure of the motor that rolled up the window of a pickup truck. The vehicle was not old, so I went to the dealer to determine if the repair would be covered under warranty or as a recall problem. Neither of these options was available to me, and I was given a repair price of almost a thousand dollars! I was told the part was almost $800 in cost. I went to a nearby auto collision repair shop and the problem was fixed for $300. I asked where he purchased the new part. He had purchased it at the dealer who quoted a price of almost $800 just for the part! I have several other personal experiences that I could relate, but won't do so in this manuscript.

Clothing
For clothing, always wait for sales. Also, buy off season clothing and save it for the next year. For instance, summer clothing goes on sale in the fall, and only six months later will be adequate for the

warm weather of spring. Consignment shops often have bargains for clothing that may be or appear to be practically new at a fraction of the cost of new clothing in retail stores.

Household Items

Look for bargains at 'dollar' stores or thrift stores. Sometimes the difference between for instance the same brand of toothpaste at a dollar store versus a chain pharmacy or grocery store may be as much as 100 percent. Buy toiletry items at a dollar store and shop for bargains for toilet paper and buy in bulk. For elective and non-essential items, postpone the purchase until you can pay cash. Buy off-brand items or for appliances, scratch and dent items may be available at greatly reduced prices with no reduction in useful service.

Insurance

Do not be 'insurance poor' but insure you have adequate health insurance to cover catastrophic illnesses and injury. Another important area is that of life insurance. One who has children and is relatively young should carry enough coverage to insure the continued care of spouse and children in the case of death. A relatively young person (women have even cheaper rates) can have one-half to a million dollars of **term** life insurance for less than $30 per month for most who are healthy (but buy when you are young). I emphasize term insurance as whole life and modified plans are more expensive. These may be better plans for the wealthy, where the value of the policy goes up over the years, but term insurance rates are locked in for a period of time.

Saving and Investing

The reasons for saving are manifold. Savings accounts may be used as a reservoir of cash to pay for large repair bills such as a new transmission or for a new appliance or the purchase of a car. The ability to pay cash for an item may provide you with a discount. I bought two sofas for which I paid cash and was given a 10 percent discount and was not charged sales tax on the items at one outlet store! This manner of purchasing saved me almost $200! In addition to monitoring and reducing daily expenses, we should try to save and invest at least a nominal amount. When we start investing money, the investment and the income it produces may be small. But gradually our investment will become larger and larger. Then we can look for opportunities to invest in more profitable ways. At this stage, safety of investment should have priority over income earned from the investments. Fifty percent of the investments must be in the safety category. Then comes the investment for income where minimum risk taking is acceptable.

When we start looking at more profitable investments, many doors open, revealing the possibility of a better return. Every dollar that comes into our hands should earn at least a few pennies before it leaves us for good. If this idea is firmly impressed into our mind, we will automatically look for ways to invest with good returns. The most important point to remember is that we should protect our capital. It is a good time to remember the parable of the talents (money) found in Matthew 25:14-30.

The simple story by Jesus involved a wealthy man who left differing amounts of money with three of his servants before departing to far lands for a considerable period of time. The man distributed wealth among the servants, and two of them invested and earned even more money, which they returned to their master when he arrived from his travel. The third servant merely hid his portion and earned nothing. The master rebuked the third servant for being evil and lazy, and commanded that he be thrown into the outer darkness, where there was weeping and gnashing of teeth. And we do not want to be judged as was the third servant!

It is said that there is a sucker born every minute, and you must avoid being one by becoming aware of the pitfalls of investing and educating yourself to make prudent decisions for investing your hard-earned cash. The world is full of people with deceitful habits who promise to give us a large income to induce us to invest with them so that they can cheat us out of our capital. These are the people who may be difficult to recognize because they often give the appearance of a clean cut, knowledgeable and earnest person desiring to do nothing more than to help you achieve wealth. We should be most concerned about these types and to make certain we do not deal with them. But most of them are so clever that we will not be able to detect them until we get bitten.

How do we know if a person approaching us with a deal that is too good to be true would stand up under scrutiny? You can rest assured that if a deal is failure-proof, that it is too good to be true. Why would someone try to help you rather than take full advantage of the opportunity himself, or to sell only to friends and family? Therefore, a judicious inquiry about the sales weasel from people who had previous dealings with him (or her) will be very useful.

Usually, the principle is that the lesser the income to be gained, the safer the investment. But this will not always be true. Our principle should be to produce the maximum income from our investments with total safety of the capital. This should be the outlook throughout all our dealings with securities agents. Don't be afraid to ask about previous business enterprises that were offered by the agent and when and how many participated and how they fared. But remember that you yourself will be one of the best investments available to you. Avail yourself in education and training and in the development of new skills that will gain a good job for you and will advance your job and career.

Surround Yourself With Optimistic and Ambitious People
This is an often overlooked strategy to become more successful and happier as a consequence. It's a simple thought, but is sometimes difficult to do especially if we have hung with persons who will surely not be successful in the way we want to be. Ask yourself the following questions and then from your answers, determine who would best fit the mold of those who would stimulate you and perhaps lead you to your goals. You mustn't be afraid to lose some of this support group, even support from your family, if any of them would potentially affect your drive to succeed.

1. In a 24-hour period who are the people I associate with most? Some of your contacts will most often be family members, but you will need a list of at least five people.

2. Once you have a list of people with whom you are surrounded on a regular basis, you should determine why you seek companionship with them. Are you amazed at what they have done with their lives to this point, or that they are constantly working to improve themselves?

3. What kind of ambitions do these people possess, and have they been successful up to now?

4. Do these people exhibit an infectious atmosphere of happiness and optimism and show enthusiasm about the things they care for the most?

5. Do these acquaintances pick you up when you are down, or offer alternative actions when things go wrong?

6. Which members of the group will you keep for moral support when you need it most?

Perception of the Income Divide Between Classes

We hear a great deal about income inequality in this country and in 2014, President Obama gave a speech about the topic. But what is income inequality and is there income inequality? Yes, there is income inequality and in some cases it may be a result of wrong-thinking persons who are in charge of companies. But the majority of income inequality stems from the examinations of those earning wages at the lower end of the wage scale, and then comparing them with those vilified persons who are self-employed business owners, CEO's, white collar workers, and even blue collar workers with a set of skills that enable the individual to earn a salary much greater than minimum wage.

What is the solution to 'income inequality?' Would it be wise to take by force more money from those who pay the majority of income taxes in this country and 'give' it to the poor? Actually, the best solution would be to prepare students in high school to be functioning members of society. They should be required to have a basic knowledge of the foundations of this country and with the academic skills necessary to obtain further education and training in order to earn a living wage. What do I mean by 'required?' No documentation of having learned and retained certain values, understanding and knowledge would result in not receiving a high school diploma. It is a fact that in some schools a diploma is considered a meaningless document that is not evidence that any knowledge was gained.

Another surprising finding (for me and perhaps for you) was a study cited in a Time magazine study that showed the results of a pre-test administered to high school graduates prior to attending college. A post-test following completion of college showed no cognitive advances in roughly 30 or greater percent of the college graduates. A recent research project following thousands of college students from 2005 through 2009 concludes that students are not learning the basic cognitive skills required for functioning properly in life, namely critical thinking, complex reasoning, and communication skills.

Seeds of Discord Between Classes of Citizens

Classes of citizens, ie., low, middle, and upper class relate primarily to annual income. Then each of these three classes are subdivided again into low, middle and upper. For example, there is a classification for a low low, a low middle and a low high grouping. It sometimes grows confusing, and who sets these figures to define income levels anyway? Depending on other conditions, the income levels may be meaningless anyway, where a lower salary in some geographic regions may enable a person who is somewhat self-sufficient to live quite well.

There is discontent when an individual works forty or more hours per week and has a hefty amount of taxes removed from his pay, but sees others that don't work at all, for whatever reason, and that pay no taxes, but perhaps receive a tax refund. It seems to the worker that some citizens may vote for a living while he or she works for a living. In early January 2014, Bob Lonsberry, a Rochester talk radio personality on WHAM 1180 AM, said this in response to the president's "income inequality speech." He agreed there are two Americas, the America that works and the America that doesn't, the America that contributes and the America that doesn't.

It's not the haves and the have nots, it's the do's and the don'ts. The Great Divide in America is not the Grand Canyon or the Mississippi River. It is based on civic responsibility, where some believe it is a duty as a citizen of the United States to support themselves and their families, to obey the law and to maintain order. It does not have to be about political parties and the blame cast at each other as to which party has a corner on justice and the right way to do things. Some politicians even say that it is not just for some citizens to make less than others regardless of the occupation or position held.

Why would someone work while going to school, maintain a clean legal record, and seek a better-paying job? Where is the reward if a job would pay no more than the pay for a person who didn't complete high school or barely did? Should this person with no credentials make as much money as one who worked hard to achieve his status in life? Equality is not achieved by taking from the successful and rewarding the unsuccessful. The best approach would be to try to prepare the unsuccessful to become more successful in vocational areas that would provide a better living.

In most cases the wide variations in income levels in the United States is due to consequences, where poor choices or in many cases, no choices are made as to what kind of work to pursue or where to live or even if one chooses to work or not. Those who prepare themselves for the future by taking advantage of educational and training opportunities by choosing wisely and responsibly, face a far greater likelihood of success. On the other hand, those who choose foolishly and behave irresponsibly are almost certainly doomed to a life of failure. And unless you are an idealist who thinks everyone should be able to live a utopian life without effort through government largesse, you are in the minority. Many in this country accept the fact that increases in family and individual income should be the rewards for diligently performing one's job.

Each person has a choice of whether to drop out of high school or decide to not attend college or other technical training and education. This choice will greatly affect one's life and the income that will be earned. Those who choose to avoid education and training will assuredly have a different outcome than an individual who completes high school and perhaps college that leads to a meaningful career. I know that this is repetitious, but it bears repeating. Not completing high school and birthing or fathering a child out of wedlock before seeking a career will result in a recipe for a life of poverty. And there are few who live with these burdens who have the will power to escape the shackles of poverty and ignorance. Having children without two parents not only affects the parent with the responsibility to rear the child, but it affects the life of the child.

Kay Hymowitz reported in December of 2012 in The Atlantic, in an article entitled "The Real, Complex Connection Between Single-Parent Families and Crime," that the majority of prison inmates grew up in fatherless homes. A number of complexities brought out in this article report that a crime rate drop occurred in the 1990's and early 2000's but was not a proven fact. It was believed by some that it was potentially due to overcrowding of prisons, resulting in fewer persons being remanded to custody.

A 1987 "Survey of Youth in Custody" reported that *70 percent of inmates did not grow up with both parents*, and a 1994 Wisconsin study of juvenile delinquents revealed that only 13 percent grew up with both their married parents. But of course an individual has no choice as to whether his parents marry or stay together. But to sum it up, in any case, if children are born to a single parent, their lives are likely to take one course, but if born where there is a mother and a father in their lives on a regular basis will likely result in an entirely different course.

Most often in life the destination at which we arrive is determined by the course upon which we embarked early in life. Again, summarizing what Bob Lonsberry, a Rochester talk radio personality referred to earlier, said about President Obama's income inequality speech, he gave the following example justifying a difference in income. "My doctor, for example, makes far more than I do. There is significant income inequality between us. Our lives have had an inequality of outcome, but, our lives also have had an inequality of effort. While my doctor went to college and then devoted his young adulthood to medical school and residency, I got a job in a restaurant. He made a choice, and I made a choice, and our choices led us to different outcomes. His outcome pays a lot better than mine. Does that mean he cheated and Barack Obama needs to take away his wealth? No, it means we are both free men in a free society where free choices lead to different outcomes."

The Biblical scripture called the Law of the Harvest simply states in Galatians 6:7, (KJV), "Be not deceived; God is not mocked: for whatsoever a man soweth, that shall he also reap." This verse is sometimes applied as, "The harder you work, the more you get." Our fear should be that entitlements will replace effort and initiative as the key to upward mobility in American society, as this seems to be the sentiment of many people and politicians alike.

A true story of not willing to work in order to be prepared for a good paying position goes as follows. I was leading a group of high school students through a technical college. One young man was enthralled by the equipment used to design machine components. He asked the machine tool technology instructor how much he could make if he became a machine tool technician, and was told he could start at perhaps $50,000 per year. His next question related to how he could obtain such a job for performing the duties of a machine tool designer. He was told he needed a good background in math, with emphasis in trigonometry. He quickly lost his interest in that career field, saying, "No, man, that stuff is too hard! I can't do that!" He wanted the money, but did not want to expend the effort.

What to do When Steps Taken Result in Failure

First of all, you must persevere and not give up. What if someone says, "I have followed all of the advice given me by those who know how to succeed and have read this book and followed its suggestions fully, yet I am no better off than I was before. I can see no light at the end of the proverbial tunnel." What then? The urge would be to abandon the effort and return to the former life with no goals in sight, but that is the wrong thing to do. First of all, reexamine your figures from your list of income and expenses, and determine if there is a cut or cuts you could make in your expenses after giving some thought to the process. Then determine if more income is possible through asking for a raise and/or to revisit the possibility of taking on a part-time job. This is a step which may be difficult in certain circumstances, such as for those having one or more small children. But remember the caution given earlier about having children without being prepared.

For a single person, it is quite easy in most instances to move. A move to another location where jobs pay higher salaries and housing is cheaper may help. In addition, a single person may advertise in the local newspaper or other media to determine if someone needs a roommate (but this also calls for a healthy dose of caution). Sometimes the rent will include utilities and other expenses, making life simpler and it becomes easier to start saving and investing for the future. Also, a good geographic location requiring easy transportation to the workplace will be one of the characteristics to consider when looking for a more economical lifestyle.

For the single parent with children, or the two-parent family, perhaps with children, the situation requires more careful thought and then planning. It may be possible to advertise for someone wanting a job and who might be retired or widowed. This person may be able to spend the day economically with the individual or family which has one or more small children, while either or both spouses work. An added bonus of an evening meal may be prepared by the hired homemaker when those working arrive at home. Many of these economic misfortunes are tied to the change in lifestyles for everyone, even those who are dragged kicking and screaming into the daily rat race called life. Some of the reasons we have arrived at such a junction in everyday existence could be:

1) **Everything is about the economics of the world.** For the last half of the 20th century, an American household with one decent job could afford a decent home. But when most households evolved into a two-income family unit, the price of everything increased. Remember that earlier we found out that *the price of all goods and services are based on the amount of circulating money*? So now two incomes are required except for the highest wage earners, and a much larger portion of the household income is now required to buy a home. And large down payments are required as surety against default on a home loan. That's one reason why many families never seem to have enough money for daily expenses.

2) **Most people live a life that is out of balance.** The majority of individuals and families live on the brink of financial destruction.

Many of the people of the United States and indeed the world is said to be only one or two paychecks away from poverty. In a family, if one of the spouses loses his or her job, and the family budget is set for two incomes, this will in most families result in financial chaos. Fear can be a motivator that makes many work harder, but this results in much nervous tension where proper sleep may be impossible. It should be noted that those who work two jobs and who work at night are more likely to be obese and to suffer from a variety of both physical and mental ills.

3) **The effects of technology results in a loss of privacy and rest.** Computers, smart phones and high tech cameras that keep watch over our workplace, home and other areas we find ourselves have resulted in our being at work or at others' beck and call 24 hours per day. And many people live to obtain the next higher tech item before acquaintances can possess one. This feeling of constantly waiting for a connection to work, family and other institutions demanding our attention is also detrimental to our physical and mental health.

And then there's the story of hacking as an additional source of stress. We must be careful with spending, investing wisely and placing sensitive personal information on line sites. There are always lurking hackers ready to burst up the middle or to do an end run around the firewalls and virus software protections to take our money without working for it and with no remorse. And behaviorists have tracked our spending habits, our leisure habits and everything that we do that is not of a habitual nature. We are at the mercy of those who can access our data at will. I hated to throw this in but it is a fact of life today.

4) **The Original United States government offered a social contract with Americans**. The original settlers formed a government that provided for financial and personal security and privacy that was not present in their countries of origin. These written contracts are the United States Constitution and the Bill of Rights. But this social contract has eroded over the years, and the free exercise of one's rights to freedom and happiness is somewhat a myth today. Governmental bureaucracy, both federal and state,

have established burdensome processes in order to freely take advantage of a capitalistic society. The early settlers worked to complete their dreams with little interference from government And now we must pay as we go since our entire economy is propped up by a credit system that in some cases resembles a pyramid scheme. This is to the disadvantage of those who work hard to reach their desired goals.

5) **We are watching the eventual extinction of the middle class.** In the not too distant past a good middle class job enabled many people to comfortably own a modest home. But with the expansion of the credit system and of the money supply, there are very few 'regular' jobs that make it possible to buy a home, unless both spouses are working. Prior to about 1970, only the income from the principal worker in a family was included in the earnings part of a loan application. In most cases the wife, even if working, but not the sole earner or the primary wage earner, did not have her income included. When both incomes began to be included when calculating the amount one could pay for a monthly mortgage, the prices of houses began climbing upward.

6) **Costs of living are reflected in the local job market based on high paying jobs.** In areas where high-paying jobs are available, such as in Silicon Valley, a modest home will cost more than a million dollars. The same home in other areas will sell for less than half that amount. So if you do not have a high-paying job, it is best to steer clear of areas where most of the jobs are high paying, such as high tech industries. In the past, a diverse group of jobs would be found in most neighborhoods, but with today's disparities in living costs, many areas of the country would be closed to most common jobs that don't pay high wages. Only high-paying jobs will allow the worker to live in certain areas of the country and will further segregate the economic classes. Economic measures implemented after the Great Recession have done little or nothing to improve the lot of the middle class.

7) **Then where should we live?** Unemployment has shrunk slightly, but only in certain geographic areas of the country. Some

areas still seem to have more people out of work that are working, if one observes the numbers of people out and about in the neighborhoods and stores during the day. But many of the jobs included in the numbers of employed work less than 40 hours per week, so the statistic is completely misleading. Most jobs that were added as the recovery ensued are low-wage jobs that would not enable a comfortable lifestyle. So if you have the luxury of being able to pull up stakes and move to an area with a better set of opportunities for you, it will take some research. And not everyone can move because of family ties and issues that tie one to a particular locale. It seems that all of America lives as if in a state of looking for an emerging neighborhood where it might be possible to afford a dreamy 3-bedroom apartment or home in a safe area. The country is filled with seekers who are searching to find a place to live and work where the wages are at least relatively high and the cost of housing, utilities and transportation are low.

The Solutions to Financial Problems Should be Simple

In today's internet environment, even if one has no computer, the libraries and perhaps other venues will allow access to surfing the web. Help may be found in solving many of your financial problems, but you must be savvy and should not believe everything you are told. A significant number of the 'debt counselors' who perhaps advertise their services online or on TV and radio are charlatans wanting only to help themselves. So as a part of your education, learn to ask the appropriate questions and to figure out the actual costs for yourself as you might understand after reading the next paragraph. Look for scams that are posted on the internet and even talk with those who are trained in such matters or to those who may have been taken advantage of previously.

Help With Credit Card Debt, Taxes and Student Loan Debt

All of these types of debts are onerous burdens for many, if not most Americans. Problems with these types of debts are so important in the financial health of individuals and families that separate treatment of each of these will be found in the next few paragraphs. The best defensive strategy against financial problems is not to make these debts in the first place, but as human beings, we usually learn most from experience and not formal education. But in many instances, if we wait a day or two before making a purchase and look for better bargains, and there always are better bargains, we often would abandon our 'need' for certain items. Ask yourself if, first of all, you *need* it, secondly, is there an alternative product for less money that would serve the purpose for which you wanted a product in the first place, and is there a possibility of borrowing or renting a product that might not be used frequently. But what if you already owe sizable amounts for such loans?

But everyone must remain vigilant and carefully research any advertisement that promises to 'fix' the consumer debts of individuals and families. Most of these are for-profit companies who have their own financial health at interest than an honest attempt to improve the lot of those who most need it. There are those who would claim to help you, but are actually seeking ways to enrich themselves under the guise of assisting you in getting out of debt and to set up a plan to help you overcome your financial struggles. Unlike many years ago, there are a number of ways that one may become financially strapped. Some of these are as follows:

1. **Credit card debt**

The average credit card debt for those saddled with this kind of debt was $15,611 in December of 2014. Credit card debt occurs subtly for many without any realization of the magnitude of the debt. Often a debt-ridden person will seek another credit card with a period of time where no interest gathers to pay off a debt-riddled card. But the process does not end here for many. The original card, paid off by the new card carrying no balance, will again be put to use. The interest-free time limit at which no interest is charged on the second card is rapidly exhausted, so now, two cards are carrying a balance. This sometimes escalates to obtaining a third card, then perhaps a fourth or fifth card! Eventually, the only remedy is bankruptcy.

The median household income for a family is roughly $50,600 in 2013, based on salary surveys conducted by a number of governmental and private groups. Remember that the median salary refers to a figure where 50 percent of the responders reported a salary of less than $50,600 and 50 percent reported a salary greater than this amount. The average salary is somewhat higher, and includes those earning more than $200,000 (more than 4 percent earn this amount or more). One can readily see that the average credit card debt is approximately one-third of the annual salary of most wage earners. If only the required minimum amount is paid on each card held and use of the card continues, the debt becomes astronomical. Even if minimum payments are made on time and on a monthly basis, the debtor will never eliminate the credit card debt.

Credit counselors (but beware of whom you trust) will employ a number of strategies to eliminate the accrued debt. First of all, do not use the cards. Do not carry them with you as a temptation, but store the cards in a hard to reach area, or best of all, destroy them. It might be wise to keep only one card for emergency use, such as for an automobile repair, but when a lump sum such as a tax refund is received, pay off the card you were forced to use. And, for example, if you have five cards with a balance, pay the minimum on four of them and pay off the card with the *smallest* balance first. Then progress to the next card with the smallest balance.

A dirty fact that many of the users of credit cards are unaware of is as follows. Credit card issuers are constantly barraging individuals by phone, internet and television ads to obtain a card, even if one has no particularly good credit rating. It is common for a company to offer a card with interest free periods of 1 year to 18 months in order to 'pay off' other cards. Although it is best for the company if the individual continues to pay the minimum payment per month for years, there is also another advantage for the issuer of the card(s). The issuer finds it a favorable to allow the interest rate to rise on accrued balances, sometimes to 30 percent or more, until even the minimum monthly payments become an impossible burden. If one defaults or goes into bankruptcy, the credit card issuer more than likely has already collected a large portion of the original debt through minimum payments made. In addition, the credit company has charged the merchant a fee as a percentage of the purchase up front.

So the debt then accumulates even when a minimum payment is made on time until the original principal has been increased by multiples. These debts are called accounts receivable by the card companies and therefore become assets, or something of value. Companies offering credit cards can write off these debts as non-collectable and can then sell the accounts for a fraction of what is owed to debt collectors. These collectors may use intimidating and sometimes illegal methods in attempts to collect the debt.

You should be aware that the bill collectors can only attempt to collect the debt for up to 7 years in most states. But they will continue to try to collect the original debt, and often resell those accounts which they had no success in collecting to a second or even a third company. You may IN WRITING submit a request to the collection company to not contact you again regarding these bills. In most states where the debts that have been sold were made more than 7 years before, they may be uncollectable. But you should also be aware that some token payment or communication (telephone, written, etc.) regarding an attempt to pay during this 7 year period will start the clock all over again in many instances.

If you are highly disciplined, you might obtain a card that provides a year or more of interest-free debt, and pay off as many of the cards as possible. But you must then make a schedule taking into account the number of months you have to pay off the card before interest begins to accrue, It is important to pay the amount required to satisfy the debt in a particular length of time on a monthly basis so you do not fall victim to the scenarios just described. Those cards which you were unable to consolidate must be addressed with disciplined effort to also pay them off. In fact, it would be unethical as well as immoral to accumulate debt on a credit card with the intention of not paying the debt and allowing 7 years to elapse.

Many consumers do not shop for the best type of credit card. Many credit card companies offer low interest rates, and points may be earned for air fare and for hotels, motels and car rental. Most Americans don't shop their plastic (credit cards), and as a result, pay too much in interest or fail to optimize their rewards. But credit cards should be sought with the same care as when buying a consumer product and trying to get a good deal on the purchase.

2.   Home Mortgages

The average mortgage held in the United States in 2014 was approximately $155,000. There are a multitude of loan programs available for low-income individuals and families offered by federal and state, and in some cases, private plans. At the time of this writing, mortgage rates are at the lowest level in modern history, and have remained at this level for a number of years. They are less than half the rate offered in the late 1980's and the early 1990's. Much prayerful consideration should be taken before deciding to buy a house or to rent a home until the finances of the individual or family change.

Some cities offer houses at a very low cost that require rehabilitation, and if one is able or has friends and relatives to help, may turn a bargain into a wonderful home at little cost. Buying a house has both advantages and disadvantages. You are able to deduct the interest paid on a mortgage from your income, resulting in a tax saving. When paying rent, you do not enjoy a tax break of this sort. But one advantage of renting a house lies in the fact that the repairs are generally performed by the landlord, whereas in buying a house, you are responsible for repairs and maintenance.

Many who buy a house do not factor the cost of property insurance which is required. There is also a required insurance called PMI insurance for those who are unable to make a 20 percent down payment except in special circumstances. Property taxes, which are growing larger in many location, are based on the value of the house as assessed by tax assessors who work in conjunction with appraisers who set the tax rate.

In most cases, the taxes, insurance and principal (amount owed on the property) can be packaged into the monthly payment for the house. Help in finding cheaper interest rates for homes, which, if used for refinancing to a lower rate, might allow one to two months of no house payments. And the closing costs may be refinanced into the loan itself, resulting in payments that may still be lower due to lower interest rates. But in my opinion, this is not a good idea.

If you can wangle a better interest rate with no closing costs, and this is sometimes possible, you will be ahead of the game. But in a scenario where you may have paid for instance, four years on a 30-year mortgage and you refinance for a lower interest rate, caution should be exercised. If you pay closing costs that are financed into the purchase and you add 4 or more years to your mortgage, you might not be getting a bargain and your monthly payment may even increase! The additional charges plus four more years of payments will cost you thousands of dollars than you would have had paid with your old mortgage. But if you plan to keep the house for only a few years, and you can obtain a lower monthly payment by refinancing, such an option would make sense.

The ultimate goal of searching for a good mortgage is to find an even better one than the first one you examined. Many lending firms advertise certain rates but require a larger percentage rate of interest based on credit scores, above the advertised rate. Lower interest rates are awarded to those with excellent credit ratings. If you borrow $250,000 with a 30-year at a 4 percent fixed-rate mortgage you'll pay $179,674 in interest over the life of the loan. But if the rate increases to 6 percent, then you'll end up paying the much larger amount of $289,595 in interest over the life of the loan! Under the latter scenario, the difference in cash outlay over the life of the loan is almost $110,000. This would be enough to enable one to retire at an earlier age, and might even be enough to start a small business.

For those with children who wish to attend college or advanced training, the money that is saved with a lower interest rate could go for improving one's skills or assisting children in attending college. And remember that not everyone should invest the time and money to attend college. The potential student should have the attributes necessary to complete a college education (many don't and the money spent is virtually wasted). Any money saved by a favorable interest rate on a mortgage may also enable you and/or your spouse to be able to perform enjoyable work while earning significant amounts of money. This would also be invaluable in helping grandchildren by establishing a college fund for each of them.

When you begin shopping for a mortgage for the purchase of a home or to refinance the one you might already have, there are many avenues of help on the internet that will enable you to get the best deal possible. First time home buyers are often able to get special rates and military veterans are eligible in most instances for a 100 percent loan to buy a home. Don't forget to join a credit union through your work, but there are also credit unions that do not require that you work in a particular area or for a particular company. These rates may even be better than those offered by a community bank, which is also a good option to explore for a loan at low rates.

3. Student Loan Debt

The average student loan debt in 2014 stands at more than $32,000. The reporting year for the college Class of 2014 begins with an overall average starting salary of $45,473. By June of 2010, for the first time the total student loan amounts exceeded that of credit card debt. More than 40 million students and past students owe loans used to pay for educational costs. There is some fraud here where loans were used for other purposes but for the most part is related to legitimate debt incurred for educational expenses.

It is virtually impossible for students to seek relief of debt for education by filing bankruptcy. Some institutions such as Sallie Mae continue to use the increases in student loans that are unpaid to their advantage. These loans may follow the student or former student to the grave, and can perhaps be charged against the estate of the deceased person. Perhaps 7 million Americans have had their credit scores ruined when they are unable to pay back the loans. And unfortunately, some of those owing loans were unable to complete their education or to earn enough to pay the loans along with living expenses. Income tax refunds may be involuntarily transferred to lending institutions where debts are owed. In addition, those owing student loans are ineligible for federal jobs and in some cases, even state jobs. In addition, they cannot apply for educational grants or scholarships or even be accepted to an institution of higher learning if they owe outstanding debts to other educational facilities.

How can one combat these problems? First of all, it is easier to avoid student debt than to pay off the loans later with promises of high-paying positions. College and other training programs paint a rosy picture of the opportunities that will arise, and will provide a story or two of those who have succeeded beyond their wildest dreams. So choosing the college or program to attend is paramount. Community colleges and technical colleges offer affordable college credit classes that can later be transferred to a university if one wishes. Some states award grants and scholarships to disadvantaged persons who have the ability to pursue higher education or training. Be realistic and survey the job market to determine the best programs to enter and the best-suited college or other institution to enter.

4. **Taxes**

If you have access to a professional who can advise you on tax matters, it is wise to seek help rather than attempting to navigate the complexities of the tax system on your own. Any time one can avoid paying valid taxes, it is to the consumer's advantage. It may take study of this book and other sources in order to determine how to save on tax bills. It is not an accident when some people seem to be better poised to take advantage of tax breaks and in the end, seem to accumulate more wealth than others. It is hard work to find opportunities to save on consumer goods as well as taxes, and to make prudent choices in wisely shopping for necessities. In this book a number of practices that result in saving money are available but must be sought.

There are bargains every day, but they must be evaluated to determine if they will be advantageous to you. For example, you might pay more for a product that you will use on a continuous basis, or for a long period. If this is not the case, a cheaper version that will be used only occasionally or for a short time will be advisable.

Some that earn or receive low wages or other sources of income seek to keep their income low to avoid taxes. That is not a good practice. Remember, you are never taxed at 100 percent of your income. So you would not want to keep your income below $40,000 per year just to avoid taxes. A 15 percent tax rate is assumed for the income earned here, but would not include state income taxes. If you could earn $60,000 you might pay perhaps $3,000 more in taxes in return for earning $20,000 more in income which would be a great deal! But also remember that regardless of your circumstances, you will still have at least some deductions which will lower the 15 percent to sometimes much less when a higher level of income is offset by deductions.

An important point to remember is to ALWAYS pay your taxes on any income that is taxable at the time you receive it. If you work for a weekly schedule or any other arrangement, or if you are self-employed, taxes are withheld at the time the income is received or on a quarterly schedule, in the case of those who own a business. Many people have become enmeshed in problems with the Internal Revenue Service because they are unable to pay taxes on their income. Your future wages can be garnished (withheld from a paycheck), your credit may be damaged, and you may receive hefty fines and late penalties. There are a number of people sitting in prisons in this country for income tax evasion, so it is important to report all income. Most income can be verified and for any payments such as stock dividends, lottery winnings and any number of other categories of income.

5. **Importance of a Good Credit History and Credit Score**

These two entities used in determining credit worthiness of the individual and perhaps the family is intertwined but are not exactly the same. A credit history report shows how you've managed your credit so for at least the past several years. Every time you pay your bills or apply for credit, you are building credit history and that information is noted by the national credit reporting agencies. When you make mistakes on any credit processes, those mistakes show up in your credit history information, too. The importance of your credit history cannot be overrated and must be kept up to date constantly. Information contained in a credit history will be of interest to many areas of your life, related to the need for credit.

All of your transactions from rent payment, timely utility payments, car payments, credit card payments, medical bills, etc., are all used in developing a credit history. A bad credit history will almost assuredly increase your monthly mortgage payments by causing you to receive a higher interest rate on a loan. Credit history also affects car payments and other large ticket items that are financed. Insurance premiums will be higher and it may be harder to receive phone or TV cable service. Landlords and some potential employers can and will also look at your credit history report before they rent to you. With a poor score the required deposit may be higher and the rent may be raised to cover any potential early termination of the lease.

We don't have a Year of Jubilee in this country or anywhere in the world to my knowledge as the people were described as having in the book of Leviticus, in the Old Testament. At this celebration, all wrongs were forgiven in the celebration of the seventh year, as described in Deuteronomy 15:1-11, and all debts were likewise forgiven. The intention of encouraging the building of a good credit score was of course not mentioned in the Scriptures. But in Proverbs 22:1, the advice given is that a good name is more desirable than substantial riches and is to be esteemed above the possession of silver and gold. It is not the same thing, for sure, but is similar to what is expected of us when we seek credit.

Your credit history determines your credit score, which is an overall rating of your "riskiness" to lenders and other businesses. Three basic institutions, Experian, Equifax and Transunion constantly monitor your credit score and the scores by each of them may vary slightly. A high score, 700 or higher, is good, but not excellent. It should be noted that each time a new credit card is applied for, the credit score will go down for at least a few months and canceling a credit card will likewise negatively affect your credit score. A low score, less than 600, is not so good and will definitely be reflected in the interest rates you will pay and perhaps will increase some other costs too, if you succeed in completing a credit transaction.

Now the FICO (Fair Isaac Company) score is chiefly used to determine the credit worthiness of an individual. Data from the 3 credit agencies is compiled to provide this score and the score is becoming increasingly more important in determining if the loans will be allowed or new charges will be accepted. The FICO score consists of the following weighted components:

Percentage of Weighted Components of FICO Score

Component	Percentage
Payment History	35.00%
Amount(s) Owed	30.00%
Length of Credit History	15.00%
New Credit	10.00%
Types of Credit	10.00%

There are costs, as mentioned previously, when the credit history is not managed well. Credit history may lag behind your real-time credit decisions made in the past few days. Scores are quickly obtained by businesses today and the effects of bad credit history will linger for years. Serious problems on your credit history that show a record of bankruptcy, collection liens, foreclosures, and other financial problems such as tax liens for unpaid property taxes can affect your ability to get a more affordable mortgage. It will also affect your opportunity to rent a house or apartment, or even stymie your efforts to get a good job. Landlords take your credit history seriously when determining if you are likely to pay your rent on time. Phone companies and cable service providers may even refuse service to you if your credit history isn't at least adequate. But beware of those who want to charge a fee to fix your credit. There are many scam outfits out there, and one of their methods to be avoided is to seek credit using a 'new' Social Security number. This is a serious crime that may result in incarceration if you are convicted, even if someone else performed the application for you!

6. **Cut the Cost of Insurance**

Health insurance is a must and has already been discussed as a need for everyone. The topic was also discussed at length in the earlier section regarding the basics of setting a budget by which to live. Savings in the area of health insurance should be based on the risks of your family members, such as age, physical condition, etc. Modest savings can be realized by shopping the various insurance brokers.

But there are significant differences in the premiums for car and home insurance. Even if you do not own a car or a home, it is wise to have renter's insurance, which for the most part is quite reasonable to cover cataclysmic losses. Also remember that flood insurance is not included in home or renter's insurance and must be purchased separately through a program subsidized by the US government. It is sometimes advantageous to go to an insurance broker and discuss what coverage you need or can afford. A higher deductible, which means you are responsible for the first five hundred or a thousand dollars or even more before the insurance pays anything costs considerably less than one with no deductible.

Also, it is important to remember that you should not submit a large number of small claims. Doing so will affect the cost of your premiums in the future and could even lead to cancellation of your policy. It is more difficult and more costly in the long run to be forced to find another insurer if a record of a number of claims have been filed. How can you solve the problem of not using insurance for various small claims? It is advantageous to set aside perhaps a thousand dollars and to not disturb the money for reasons other than covering minor damages to the home or to the car. You may add to this money periodically and it will eventually become a tidy sum that could be used to replace an appliance for instance when it becomes necessary.

7. **Auto Purchase**

Since the United States is laid out over broad expanses of land, except in the larger inner cities, a vehicle is necessary for most individuals and families. This country is not known for having mass transit that is affordable and convenient so the majority of citizens find it almost mandatory to have some sort of vehicle. It is more expensive to purchase a new vehicle, but with the availability of more dependable automobiles, a used vehicle purchase become more prudent. Just driving a new car off the sales lot causes a downward spiral in the value of the vehicle even before the first oil change becomes due. Vehicles last longer than they did a decade or more ago. It is not unusual to be able to obtain three hundred thousand miles or more from a car that is properly maintained. The availability of zero cost of financing will lure many of the new car sales firms, but remember that you are paying much more for a new car than for a used one.

Finding a better car loan is important and financing should be obtained BEFORE selecting a vehicle for purchase. Remember that credit unions tend to have the lowest rates when financing an automobile. And low rates for a used vehicle will trump the advantages of the higher price for a new car with zero financing charges every time. A great deal of information is available online to aid you in choosing a vehicle suitable for your needs. How many miles do you drive per month? A small and cheap car may not be appropriate for long trips where comfort is desirable. But a small economical car for shorts trips may be a factor in your selection. Do you have children that will require safe child seats that would require more room in the vehicle as this will be a factor? Safety records are available for almost all vehicles, so if safety is a priority for you, you should determine the classes of vehicles that afford the greatest safety for its occupants. So decide on what you need in a vehicle and obtain a credit line BEFORE springing for the purchase. DO YOUR RESEARCH!

A search of local classified ads and the well-known sources for autos that are for sale, such as Craig's List, eBay, and others may help you find just what you want after completing the research as to your particular needs. It is a great advantage to the purchaser who finds a private owner who is selling a vehicle since a purchase from a private owner. These sales are termed 'casual sales' and are not subject to sales tax as required in sale by a retail auto dealer. Many states charge a 7 percent tax and sometimes more in some states (a few states have no sales tax). This can amount to several hundred dollar savings in most instances. And private owners may sell a vehicle for the amount they would receive if they used the vehicle for a trade in, which is lower than both the wholesale and the retail prices. So all of these factors should be taken into consideration.

Budgeting Tools

The goal of this book is to provide you with some helpful hints for keeping your finances on track to enable you to brighten your economic outlook. This information should help you to lower your stress and that of your family as well. But the road to success is not paved with rose petals and requires a great deal of actual work, both mental and physical, to set out on a course to conquer those nagging debts and to achieve your goals of education and wealth.

Take control of your future as it is your responsibility alone and not that of the state or federal government, or of your extended family to provide for you and your family. If you prefer to use the internet for setting up a template for success for the future, there are many sites that you may surf until you find one or more that meet your needs. One such site is called "Power Wallet" and this allows you to consolidate your bank account information, to set some goals and to track the ways in which you spend your money. And this site is totally free for your use. But you will be provided some simple worksheets at the end of this publication that will also enable you to examine what you income and expenses so you can plan for the future.

What to Do if You Obtain a Sudden Infusion of Cash

What is proposed by most people when presented with this question is most often completely wrong. The typical individual would immediately say, "I will pay off my credit cards." The answer for most should be dependent upon how much money is received. And a bolus of millions of dollars skews the playing field, but the approach should be the same. First of all, you are responsible for yourself and your immediate family. Unless it is a well-known fact and beyond your control, you should tell no one. A common refrain of lottery winners is that they discover they have new friends and long lost relatives immediately if not sooner. So, what is the answer?

The approach is the same for large or small amounts. First of all, if possible, keep it quiet and don't shout out the news from the rooftop. Secure the money in a protected account, and if the amount exceeds the amount that can be insured by the bank, a financial planner (from a distant city preferably) should be consulted. Find out if the money you received is taxable, but in most cases lottery winnings are taxed before you obtain your payout. If taxable, determine roughly how much you will owe and place it in a safe place so you will not be burdened with a large tax bill at the end of the year.

If you said you would pay off your credit card(s) that is absolutely the wrong answer. These debts should be the last to be paid! I will explain. You must pay your rent, house payment, or car payments first including any payments in arrears. Your car and house can be repossessed as well as your car and you might have no home and no way of traveling to work. Then you would be in danger of losing any type of tangible property for which you owed. If your credit card is canceled, so what! Get another one, but only if necessary!

First of all, you must use what you have wisely and use it for improving your future. A tithe should come first, as this helps you learn to be faithful to those things that count the most. Of course immediate needs (not wants) include shelter, then food, followed by attention to utilities. If these are already adequate, but you have transportation problems and it is important that you be able to work, you should explore getting better transportation unless the vehicle you now own is still serviceable. But RESIST the urge to hustle to the nearest auto dealer and pay a large portion of your new found wealth on a new car! Then you should establish a savings account for immediate emergency expenses.

Also RESIST getting a new large screen TV at exorbitant prices or a new smart phone for everyone in the family that will cost hundreds of dollars. Now you should concentrate on your debts if any money is left after insuring your future. If you owe money on a number of credit cards, this is again dependent upon how much you receive. You should take the card with the *smallest* balance, and pay it off. If you have several with roughly equal amounts owed, select the one with the highest interest rate and pay it off.

Do not cancel a card when it is paid, as this will adversely affect your credit score. Place it in an inaccessible area and forget it is there. It might be helpful, if you don't possess a large measure of will power, to cut the card in strips. But keep the strips to remind you of your past problems with debts. Then work backwards, eliminating as many cards as possible, providing you have sufficient money available. This is the time, if you have several small balances, to obtain an interest-free card and pay off as many of the small balances as possible with it. Set up a payment plan for the new card, making monthly payments that will pay off the card before interest begins to accrue.

If a considerable amount of cash is received, a retirement account should be initiated. If you work, you should explore the possibility of your employer adding matching deposits in a retirement account. A number of firms do this, usually at a rate of fifty cents for each dollar invested by the employee. But this is equal to an immediate 50 percent return on your investment! And future growth will occur for the employer contribution as well as your own, multiplying the amount you will accumulate. In extreme circumstances which should be avoided if possible, you may borrow against your retirement account for emergency expenses. But do NOT draw money from the account! There are federal rules which exact a penalty for early withdrawals as well a tax bill that will be due at the time of the withdrawal.

What should I do after initiating the previous steps just outlined? If you were able to place money in a retirement account such as a 401k or a 403b, you should establish a savings account separate from the emergency fund set up earlier. Even if you are only able to save a few dollars per month you should maintain this account for buying items later, paying cash rather than using a loan that charges interest. Remember the woman, a hotel maid, who was on the Oprah Winfrey show a number of years ago. She placed her tips in a savings account, and some days she only had literally a few cents. When she reached retirement age, she had accumulated more than a million dollars, although she had never made a large amount of money. After more than thirty years of work in this area, she literally had saved more than a million dollars when she retired.

You should strive to eventually accumulate a minimum of six months' salary if you work. If you don't work, you should determine what the expenses are for six months at your current lifestyle. Start earlier than later, even if you can only put a few dollars per month into the account. If you lost your job, or if you encountered unusual but necessary expenses, the purpose of this fund is to cover those areas.

If you are able to increase your job skills through education or training, which would lead to a higher salary, you should investigate these possibilities as soon as possible. Again, beware of so-called training programs that promise a good job after only a few months, that will ONLY cost you a few thousand dollars. These programs are designed to enrich the administrators of the programs and not the students who attended. Investigate the job market to see what positions are available, how much they pay, and what you will need in the area of education or training to obtain a position. Technical colleges and community colleges provide economical paths toward achieving meaningful education and skills.

Summary

This author must seem hardhearted at times, but I am merely inserting a dose of reality. The governmental agencies that are supposedly addressing the difficulties facing those in our country who are not able to live comfortably are actually addressing the problems in a manner that increases dependence upon the government (the taxpayers, as nothing is free). Governor Scott Walker at a 2015 conservative summit in Iowa seemed to stress that the success of government should be best assessed by the number of persons who are delivered from dependence upon government programs. As water does, many people will take the path of least resistance when it comes to taking a leap of faith and making a plan to use their abilities and talents to make a better life for themselves and their families.

Does this mean we should not help those in need, except for those who suffer from disabilities and infirmities that prevent their living a fuller life? No, to the contrary. We should help in a way that lifts those people up, and not to give them a life of hopelessness from which it is extremely difficult to escape. None of us should be so uncaring as to fail to feed and provide shelter to those in need. And often the existence of a multitude of social or medical problems prevents any upward mobility. It would be wonderful if churches and those that have the means could develop ways to aid those in need without making them dependent upon the government. The numbers are growing for those who are in dire financial straits and lack of action by Christians will only exacerbate the problems.

We should not be judgmental as that would destroy any rapport we might achieve with the downtrodden. Regardless of their actions or inactions that placed them in the position they are in, they still need help and are God's children. In Deuteronomy 15:5-11 (KJV), we are instructed as follows:

> *5 Only if thou carefully hearken unto the voice of the LORD thy God, to observe to do all these commandments which I command thee this day. 6 For the LORD thy God blesseth thee, as he promised thee:* ***and thou shalt lend unto many nations, but thou shalt not borrow; and thou shalt reign over***

many nations, but they shall not reign over thee. 7 If there be among you a poor man of one of thy brethren within any of thy gates in thy land which the LORD thy God giveth thee, thou shalt not harden thine heart, nor shut thine hand from thy poor brother: 8 But thou shalt open thine hand wide unto him, and shalt surely lend him sufficient for his need, in that which he wanteth. 9 Beware that there be not a thought in thy wicked heart, saying, The seventh year, the year of release, is at hand; and thine eye be evil against thy poor brother, and thou givest him nought; and he cry unto the LORD against thee, and it be sin unto thee. 10 Thou shalt surely give him, and thine heart shall not be grieved when thou givest unto him: because that for this thing the LORD thy God shall bless thee in all thy works, and in all that thou puttest thine hand unto. 11 For the poor shall never cease out of the land: therefore I command thee, saying, Thou shalt open thine hand wide unto thy brother, to thy poor, and to thy needy, in thy land.

So there we have it. If we obey God's commands and listen, we should stop borrowing from other nations so that they will not reign over us as a nation. Then we are specifically commanded to help our brother in need. Note that we should give to him to meet his needs and in verse 8 his wants would be equated to his needs, and not a desire to obtain pricey baubles for his entertainment. Our country should carefully determine what an individual or family needs in order to rise up financially. This is more preferable than to place a individual or family on a course where outlays of money are required for a lifetime and even into future generations.

PART X:
How to Document Income and Expenses

PREPARING A BUDGET

There are several areas that should be included in the planning for a budget that are not directly related to how much you do spend and how much you plan to spend in the future. The goal for maintaining a healthy budget is to spend less than you make each month. This sounds easy, doesn't it? Needless to say, if you already have financial challenges, accomplishing this goal can be a really difficult proposition. It is tempting to use credit and savings, if you have any, but efforts should be made to avoid this temptation.

There are several basic benefits of establishing a budget. It provides a clear picture of where you are currently from a financial standpoint. A budget provides a framework in which you are able to improve the financial condition for yourself and any family for which you are responsible. A budget helps you track income and expenses and to avoid expensive overdraft fees and late charges, unnecessary fees which plague many in a low-income condition. It is also possible to budget a small discretionary amount to spend for fun, without feeling guilty or by taking money away from another area where the expenses are incurred.

Income and expenses should be monitored on an ongoing basis, at least every month, but twice per month monitoring may help you to avoid problems before they occur, and to remedy the situation in time to avoid needless expenses. David Bach, writer of "The Automatic Millionaire" and force behind FinishRich.com, describes as the "latte factor." Bach revealed that he was surprised to find out how much he spent on lattes each month, and when multiplied for an entire year, the total amount was staggering. Any time you can avoid buying items that you do not need, or can suffice by buying a cheaper version, the amount of money saved over time will amaze you.

I have for years been in a position to work directly with and to counsel persons with whom I worked or that I supervised. One young man, who earned a relatively good salary, but who was required to pay child support, a constant drain on his finances, came to me and asked for a raise. I knew that the possibility of receiving a raise except during the evaluation period that occurred only once per year was impossible. So I sat with him on more than one occasion and delved into his financial situation. Of course he had no budget and could not even list all of the areas where he spent the money.

After a couple of sessions, I helped him realize that he was buying alcohol and cigarettes in amounts that added up to several hundred dollars per month! The increase that he claimed he needed was almost exactly the amount he was spending unnecessarily. At first, he was belligerent and insisted he 'needed' his tobacco and alcohol to help him cope with life. But a few months later, he became involved in Alcoholics Anonymous and became more aware of the reality that he needed to refocus his life and develop more healthful habits.

Knowing generalities about your finances is wise, but it is still necessary to develop a chronological (time-based) budget to avoid dings to credit scores and paying excess charges due to oversights. Late fees on utilities and other recurring expenses such as rent or house payments will exact a toll on your finances over time. You should also remain aware of the fees that are erroneously charged to you. I have a personal example of this, as I will now describe. I was a busy college student with a family who worked more that 50 hours per week on a regular basis, therefore I had little time to pay attention to small details. When I purchased my first house, I was careful to make my payments on time. Eventually I became aware that I was receiving additional charges to my account for "late charges" but I did not notice this entry on my receipts for at least several years.

I called the mortgage company and was told that I was always late with my payments. I knew this was not true, as my payment was due on the first of each month, but I had until the tenth of the month before being charged a late fee. So when I received an income tax refund in February, I paid the house payment on the twentieth of the month, ten days before the payment was due! And the mortgage company was located only an hour away, so I knew that the mail was received perhaps no more than two days later. So, you guessed it! I received a late charge again. The late charges of more than twelve dollars at that time (early seventies) was quite a sum and accumulated over a several year period. Interest also accrued on this late fee! Added to my mortgage principal, it actually added almost a year to the end of the loan period. This company still refused to admit that they had been wrong, even in the face of evidence of canceled checks, etc. But soon afterward the mortgage was sold to another company. I never received another notice that my payments had been late! So, pay attention to details!

The major purpose of a budget is to help in planning a family's future and is helpful for higher income as well as for low-income families. An unexpected expense of fifty to one-hundred dollars can wreak havoc on the budget for a low income family. So having a fund that is constantly supplemented by a few dollars per month can help to avoid these devastating occurrences. A family who has a substantial income or one who has this supplemental fund to tap into for unexpected expenses will soon see that the security from such a practice is paying dividends. Comfortable families can weather financial surprises but families on the financial ropes can suffer serious hardship from even a $100 surprise. An effective family budget not only tracks what has been spent but predicts and cushions against upcoming expenses.

Budgeting for an individual or family requires a tracking system by initially gathering financial information. This includes all income that is on a regular basis and that can be counted upon. Other types of income should NOT be spent, such as income tax refunds, sales of unneeded items, interest payments to you, and any sporadic or unexpected sources of income. These funds could handily be placed into your emergency fund when all recurring bills are accounted for. All utility bills, loan payments, such as for a home and rent payments should be placed on the worksheet you will create.

If you are able to use a computer, a spreadsheet can be used to quickly account for income and to delete payments for bills for your convenience. But a printed worksheet, a calculator and a pencil will do fine for creating and maintaining a budget. These documents paint a picture of a family's monthly cash flow. Creating the first budget can be extremely overwhelming, but reveals over a year's time the expenses that fluctuate each month Bills such as those for heating and cooling can be averaged by the utility companies who will send a bill for approximately the same amount each month but you must tell the company you wish this to be done! It is commonly reported that only about 40 percent of families in the United States have taken the time to create a budget. This is not something that can be overlooked if you plan to build some sort of wealth with the goal of becoming completely debt-free.

Most people know approximately how much money they earn each month, but have no idea how their expenses can be broken down to provide the possibility of perhaps starting to save money on some areas of the expenses. Some find that they are spending money on things they want and that they probably can't afford rather than what they truthfully need. Regardless of how much or how little you earn, a budget will allow you to do more of the things you need to do in providing for your family and for giving to others who may need help from you. Of course, you could say that those people should create a budget too, and you are correct in assuming this.

Assets

Most budget processes do not include an assessment of the assets in possession of the individual or family composing the document. It is the opinion of this author that one should assess assets available as entities that can be used to better the finances of a family, particularly in the long run. There are two types of assets, called tangible and intangible. Tangible assets are monetary resources as well as physical property that may be turned into cash if needed. There might be some items in your home that you do not need and that you could sell and receive money to place in your account. Remember, it is necessary to practice flexibility in one's finances in order to change with what is happening at the time. Intangible assets are those characteristics that may strengthen the fiscal position of the individual and the family when properly used. You will be asked to list your tangible and intangible assets when you begin work on your budget. Some intangible assets may be useful in earning money you might require to strengthen your financial condition. Use your imagination for this table, and you can add or delete entries as you gain a clearer picture of your worth.

The first step of budgeting is your decision to embark on this process. It is a time-consuming process at the beginning, but will pay dividends in the future. Secondly, you should know how much you have and this is your net worth. You may have savings accounts, IRA's, 401k's, a home or rental property that are paid for. These are tangible assets. Proceed to list your intangible assets such as educational degrees or diplomas, special skills and any gifts you have that may allow for additional work. Or there is the possibility that it could even be turned into full-time work, rather than what you are currently doing to earn a living.

Next, calculate how much you will bring in each month after payroll deductions have been taken out of your paycheck. Some may have irregular income, such as dividends or royalties that are paid annually, quarterly or biannually. Only include those you are sure of. Don't assume you will receive an income tax refund in the thousands, and you should not use that kind of entity in your income for the year, or your hope for a salary increase in the near future. It will be necessary to determine your annual income over a year's time, but six months often gives a fair idea of the income you can expect. To get a jump on your expected income for the year, you could look back over the previous year and add any adjustments, such as a mid-year salary increase, to gauge the amount you will be working with on your newly-minted budget. For those working strictly on commissions, it will be necessary to estimate income based on your low months of income. But after a year of recording the income, an average can be calculated for each month.

How Much do You Owe

You should determine how much you owe for all debts that are incurred as short-term debts. Long term debts such as mortgages that are amortized over a period of years are important only for the amount obligated for the year in which you are performing calculations. Car payments with more than a year remaining would be treated likewise. You should then determine your recurring monthly payments. If you make a house payment every two weeks, take the entire amount you pay in each payment, multiply it by twenty-six, or one-half the two-week periods in a year, then divide the total by twelve in order to determine how much you spend each month on a recurring basis.

Payments to be made on credit cards should be for more than the minimum payment when you owe significant sums, or you would never escape the shackles of credit card debt. NOTE: Suppose you paid the minimum payment each month of $175 on a $5,000 credit card debt accruing interest at 18% (some cards carry an interest charge of up to 29 percent). As shown in these figures, it would take thirteen years to pay off the debt if you no longer added to your debt load, and you would pay more than $2900 in interest. Now would be the time to consider taking the plunge by applying for an interest-free card that is good for 12 to 18 months. With an 18 month period, and paying equal amounts of $278 per month, you would be free of this debt in 18 months. This decision would be predicated upon two things. You are able to pay for your obligatory monthly bills and will not continue to use the card upon which you are paying.

The table provided is constructed showing the most important areas of your expenses. Remember, you should first ensure you have a home, food, then adequate utilities and transportation if transportation is necessary. Remember, in some cities, it is easy to survive by walking to nearby stores and to your place of work. The first figures you enter will be estimated, and can be recalculated after you are satisfied with a preliminary set of figures. Consult your checkbook and other means of payment in order to determine how much to allocate for each area of recurring debt. If you have the records, you may have bank statements, receipts and canceled checks to aid you in determining these figures.

Remember, if you don't have sufficient income to cover the expenses you have entered, examine your payments to see if you can cut back in any area by using the helpful hints for saving on expenses such as food, clothing, and medical care. And remember that after a year of utility expenses, many of these companies will average and provide you with a monthly amount to pay year round. This helps a great deal with budgeting, and sometimes you will actually be ahead on your payments.

Use of Budget to Track and Monitor Expenses

When you have established a realistic budget, it will be convenient to see where your hard-earned money is going, and will enable you to keep some of your expenses in check. It may take more than a year to become adept at taking care of documenting your expenses so you can gauge as to whether you are spending too much in one area. The figures given in the table that follows for tracking income and expenses is merely an example of what you could do with a little thought. The right hand column is much like your checking account balance, where you have a running total at any time. You must take care to add each payment as it occurs, since getting behind will result in potential disaster, as you might have already experienced. We will assume some expenses based on a $2200 per month income for convenience. No one knows your expenses better than you, so the tables provided are only for guidance and the figures used are similar to those the author has experienced.

The assets table as follows can be seen as a saving account, where you have the resources but you should not tap into the tangible accounts on a routine basis to cover your expenses. But initially it might be necessary until you have become familiar with what you must do to remain afloat financially. The intangible assets are those you might resort to for extra money to supplement your income as needed.

ASSETS
These are Examples Only

TANGIBLE	INTANGIBLE
Roth IRA	Ability to prepare income taxes
Saving Account	Counseling skills
Rental Property	Writing skills
Retirement Account	Editing skills
Life Insurance Policy	Gourmet cook
	Singing skills (weddings, funerals, etc.)
	Instrumental music ability
	Skilled in mechanical work or carpentry
	House and pet sitting
	Cleaning apartments, houses for landlords
	Retail clerk during holiday seasons

RECURRING EXPENSES

Tithe	Based on 10% of income	220.00
Home	Rent per month	400.00
Food	Varies by number in family (home preparation preferable	300.00
Electricity	Some homes are total electric, so gas would be deleted if this is case	150.00
Water	Water and sewer usually combined	60.00
Gas	See also entry for electricity	50.00
Saving	Start low, but don't neglect this item	25.00
Vehicle	Include payment (cheap, used vehicle)	250.00

Medical	Medicaid, Medicare (co-pays, misc.) (deductibles may apply)	350.00
Clothing	Remember consignment shops, thrift stores, and discounted sales	100.00
Misc	Miscellaneous issues arise regularly	100.00
Transport	Gas, insurance, taxes, repairs	200.00

Sample Budget Using Figures From Recurring Expenses
January, 2015

	Monthly Expenses	Other	Monthly Income of $2,200.00
Tithe	$220.00		$1,980.00
Home*	$400.00		$1,580.00
Food	$300.00		$1,280.00
Electricity	$200.00		$1,080.00
Water	$60.00		$1,020.00
Heating Gas	$50.00		$970.00
Saving	$10.00		$960.00
Transportation	$250.00		$710.00
Medical	$300.00		$410.00
Clothing	$100.00		$310.00
Miscellaneous	$100.00		$210.00
Vehicle Insurance	$100.00		$110.00
Vehicle Gas, Repairs	$100.00		$10.00
Balance end of month			$10.00

*Rent or House Payment

Calculating Net Worth

The net worth of an individual or family is elusive. Assets should include retirement accounts, equity in the property (difference between appraised value minus the balance owed), **cash value** of insurance policies, banking account balances, stocks and equities owned, property, jewelry, valuable furnishings, etc. The total owned less the liabilities owed (any debts requiring payment) equals the net worth of an individual or family.

Assets Minus Liabilities = Net Worth

Many will say that there is not enough money for 'having fun.' That is true in most households, and many go into debt to have fun, and then the fun turns into pain eventually. The fun comes after the budget is perfected, and it is true that some sacrifice is necessary at the beginning. In addition, some soul searching should take place as to where cuts could occur if any. Then consult your list of intangibles, and determine if there are any avenues open to earn extra money. In addition, it may be necessary to seek an entirely different occupational area. This too can be stressful, but there are multiple opportunities open for increased training and education at little cost through state and federal programs. Call your local community or technical college and make an appointment to determine if there are some areas you may wish to enter. Carefully choose an area and don't fall prey to schools operating for profit who will 'facilitate' your getting a loan, and then you may not get a job in the area despite the promises of the school, and if you do, you will be paying for quite some time for this 'help.'

PREPARE A PRACTICE BUDGET

You may use your own figures using those with which you are familiar by following the labels on the following blank table. Or you may make up some numbers to maintain your privacy. Remember, anything that is valuable to you is worth doing. If it were easy, and everyone did what you should do, there would not be any opportunities for many others. Just as you were told throughout this book, it is necessary for a person to start at the bottom and work one's way up the economic ladder. If everyone stared at a high income, no one would be able to buy anything since the prices paid reflect production costs of the product being sold. A Whopper Junior might cost $7.95 if everyone working in the fast food industry made $15.00 per hour. HINT: Use a pencil so you may erase some of your entries.

RECURRING EXPENSES

Tithe	Based on 10% of income	_____
Home	Rent, house payment per month	_____
Food	Varies by number in family	_____
Electricity	Some homes are total electric	_____
Water	Water and sewer combined	_____
Gas	See also entry for electricity	_____
Saving	Start low, but don't neglect this item	_____
Transp	Include payment (cheap used vehicle	_____
Medical	Medical Insurance, co-pays, etc.	_____
Clothing	Remember to buy thriftily	_____
Misc	Miscellaneous expenses	_____
Transport	Gas, insurance, taxes, repairs	_____

_____, 201_

Monthly Income $, .00	Monthly Expense	Other	Balance
Tithe			
Home*			
Food			
Electricity			
Water			
Heating Gas			
Saving			
Transportation			
Medical			
Clothing			
Miscellaneous			
Other Transp (gas, insurance, repairs)			
Balance at end of month			

*Rent or House Payment

REFERENCES

http://www.americanprogress.org/issues/labor/news/2013/09/17/74489/3-charts-showing-how-middle-class-incomes-continue-to-stagnate-while-overall-inequality-grows-2/

http://www.answerbag.com/q_view/1769268#ixzz36vhAx7jP

http://answerparty.com/question/answer/how-many-dollar-bills-would-it-take-when-each-dollar-was-lined-up-end-to-end-to-reach-the-moon-and-back

http://atlanticmedia.122.2o7.net/b/ss/atlanticcities-prod/1/H.23.6--NS/0" height="1" width="1" border="0" alt=""

http://www.bing.com/search?q=minimum+wage+of+percent241.40+in+1970&form=MSNH14&refig=9cfcca80c5e1467d96b14062d020fce7&pq=minimum+wage+of+percent241.40+in+1970&sc=0-19&sp=-1&qs=n&sk=&ghc=1&cvid=9cfcca80c5e1467d96b14062d020fce7

http://www.bing.com/search?q=21+statistics+about+the+explosive+growth+of+poverty+in+America&form=MSNH14&refig=64c57d4efaa34d03b2ebc066c55ab080&pq=21+statistics+about+the+explosive+growth+of+poverty+in+america&sc=0-22&sp=-1&qs=n&sk=&cvid=64c57d4efaa34d03b2ebc066c55ab080

http://www.bing.com/search?q=TANF+work+requirement+for+welfare+benefits+no+longer+in+force&form=MSNH14&refig=6E26CB9CF22D4C388DF2D092

9B5D721E&pq=tanf+work+requirement+for+welfare+benefits+no+longer+in+force&sc=0-21&sp=-1&qs=n&sk=&cvid=6E26CB9CF22D4C388DF2D0929B5D721E

http://www.bing.com/search?q=NCCP&form=MSNH14&x=125&y=10

http://sfsays.blogspot.com/2011/03/public-housing-revisited.html

http://www.businessweek.com/smallbiz/content/nov2009/sb20091112_157141.htm

http://www.businessinsider.com/no-the-rich-do-not-pay-all-the-taxes-2013-12#ixzz3CptU0Az1

http://www.businessinsider.com/decline-of-theus-middle-class-2013-10

http://www.capitalspectator.com/q22014-us-gdp-nowcast-2-8-5-15-2014/

http://www.celebritynetworth.com/articles/entertainment-articles/how-heiress-barbara-hutton-blew-through-a-900-million-fortune-and-died-penniless/

http://www.census.gov/hhes/www/poverty/

https://www.cia.gov/library/publications/the-world-factbook/geos/us.html

(http://www.consumerismcommentary.com/study-college-students-arent-learning/#sthash.wWMNDrOm.dpuf).
http://www.electronicsweekly.com/electro-ramblings/industry-comment/comment-is-china-losing-its-appeal-as-the-low-cost-manufacturer-of-choice-2014-01/#sthash.SzHZ3N2r.dpuf

http://frac.org/federal-foodnutrition-programs/national-school-lunch-program/
http://globaleconomicanalysis.blogspot.com/2013/08/government-

spending-as-percentage-of.html

http://economyincrisis.org/content/major-economic-problems-facing-united-states

http://money.howstuffworks.com/how-much-money-is-in-the-world.htm

http://www.huffingtonpost.com/robert-auerbach/the-bernanke-feds-printin_b_2992500.html

http://www.joshuakennon.com/1-out-of-every-25-households-millionaire-united-states/

http://www.kgbanswers.com/how-many-dollar-bills-stacked-up-would-it-take-to-reach-the-moon/4205496#1xzz350Ggwk6G

http://www.Moneynews.com/Personal-Finance/middle-class-wealth-median-income-net-worth/2014/06/11/id/576478/#ixzz3C0CRVGGS

http://www.multpl.com/us-average-income

www.naceweb.org/uploadedFiles/Content/static-assets/downloads/executive-summary/2014-april-salary-survey-executive-summary.pdf

http://nccp.org/tools/table.php?db=pol&data=text&state=&ids=&states=GA&title=50-State Data&pol=&csv=1

http://www.newyorkfed.org/aboutthefed/fedpoint/fed01.htmlhttp://nces.ed.gov/programs/digest/d10/tables/dt10_044.asp

http://www.politifact.com/truth-o-meter/statements/2012/aug/27/reince-priebus/republican-national-committee-chair-reince-priebus/

http://www.poverties.org/poverty-in-india.html#sthash.xbbn1z7C.dpuf

http://www.quotationspage.com/quotes/Ralph_Waldo_Emerson

http://www.statista.com/statistics/192361/unadjusted-monthly-number-of-full-time-employees-in-the-   us/

http://www.theatlantic.com/sexes/archive/2012/12/the-real-complex-connection-between-single-parent-families-and-crime/265860/

http://theeconomiccollapseblog.com/archives/21-statistics-about-the-explosive-growth-of-poverty-in-america-that-everyone-should-know

http://voices.yahoo.com/unpuzzling-fool-his-money-soon-parted-4104083.html

http://www.watchdog.org/43198/**ebt-fraud**-and-abuse-looking-past-your-state

http://en.wikipedia.org/wiki/Midas_Curse

Contact the Author

Dr. John W. Ridley
805 Birkdale Blvd.
Carrollton, GA 30116

jridley@hotmail.com
jwridley1@gmail.com

www.ingramcontent.com/pod-product-compliance
Lightning Source LLC
Chambersburg PA
CBHW071907290426
44110CB00013B/1304